The 5-Ps of Change

Over the last decade, there has been a growing demand for effective organizational change management strategy in the US business sector, with millions of professionals seeking guidance, especially when considering the significant investments aimed at improving and optimizing organizational systems and processes.

This book provides a comprehensive guide to successfully lead organizational change by implementing strategies focused on five foundational change management pillars—Purpose, Planning, Process, Performance, and People. This book is intended to equip executives, business leaders, technology managers, and organizational change practitioners with practical insights to make positive and lasting changes in the organizations they lead. This book distills 25+ years of IT program, project, and change management expertise into an essential guide, while demystifying the complexities of organizational transformation within commercial, government, and non-profit organizations.

Crafted from the authors' hands-on experience implementing major IT development projects within Federal, State, and commercial sectors, this book offers actionable steps to engage, inspire, and lead people along the organizational change continuum.

The 5-Ps of Change

A Strategic Roadmap to Successfully Lead Organizational Change

Donnell S. Josiah, PhD

Routledge
Taylor & Francis Group

A PRODUCTIVITY PRESS BOOK

First published 2025
by Routledge / A Productivity Press

605 Third Avenue, New York, NY 10158
and by Routledge
4 Park Square, Milton Park, Abingdon, Oxon, OX14 4RN

Routledge is an imprint of the Taylor & Francis Group, an informa business

© 2025 Donnell S. Josiah, PhD

ISBN: 9781032898469 (hbk)
ISBN: 9781032894119 (pbk)
ISBN: 9781003544883 (ebk)

DOI: 10.4324/9781003544883

Typeset in Garamond
by KnowledgeWorks Global Ltd.

Contents

About the Author

Dr. Donnell S. Josiah is a distinguished technology executive and passionate management consultant with over 30 years of experience. With profound expertise in implementing large-scale technology initiatives within frameworks like SDLC, ITIL, PMI, P3MM, and PROSCI, Dr. Josiah has successfully led high-profile projects across Federal, State, and commercial sectors. His academic credentials in Organizational Change Management, complemented by his PMP and other industry certifications, underscore his adeptness at steering complex technological transformations.

Originally from the Caribbean island of Antigua and Barbuda, Dr. Josiah exemplifies the power of persistence and faith. Despite early educational challenges, his unwavering determination saw him earn multiple degrees, including a PhD in Applied Management with a focus on Organizational Change. This journey has equipped him with a deep appreciation for excellence and the transformative power of education.

Beyond his technical acumen, Dr. Josiah is celebrated as a pioneering thought leader in organizational change management, particularly through his "5-Ps of Change" model, which has driven transformative changes in diverse sectors including Technology, Healthcare, and Education.

His managerial expertise is further highlighted by his senior oversight roles for Maryland state agencies, ensuring alignment with technology and program requirements.

Dr. Josiah's unique ability to integrate science and engineering with the arts of music production and performance sets him apart as a multi-talented virtuoso. As the founder of three business ventures—ChangeDynamix, joDah Ministries, and ARK Recording Studio—Dr. Josiah leverages his multidisciplinary background to make a substantive impact in both technology and music industries.

In his book, "Overcomers, How to Change Your Life in 31 Days," Dr. Josiah inspires readers to chase their dreams with conviction and purpose. His commitment to helping individuals unite their purpose with passion is evident in his work, which provides tools to transform everyday people into extraordinary individuals. With a heart for people and a love for God, Dr. Josiah remains dedicated to making the world a better place through innovation, collaboration, and unwavering faith.

Transitioning from personal empowerment to organizational transformation, Dr. Josiah's latest book, *The 5-Ps of Change: A Strategic Roadmap to Successfully Lead Organizational Change*, focuses on effecting change across all forms of organizations. By leveraging his extensive experience and unique "5-Ps" model, he provides actionable insights and strategies to help organizations navigate and thrive in the face of change, ensuring sustainable success and growth.

Preface

The journey to writing *The 5-Ps of Change: A Strategic Roadmap to Successfully Lead Organizational Change* is rooted deeply in my professional experience and dedication to guiding large-scale IT projects. As a senior leader responsible for overseeing Major IT Development Projects (MITDP) in Maryland, I have had the privilege of providing strategic, programmatic, and technical guidance to various state agencies. My role involves not only offering advice to IT program management teams but also ensuring the health and agility of these projects in alignment with the State's System Development Life Cycle (SDLC) and Agile methodologies.

The impetus for this book stems from a clear recognition of the need for a comprehensive change management strategy that harmonizes executive vision, mission, and mandate with practical organizational process improvements. In my interactions with various stakeholders, I have witnessed firsthand the challenges and triumphs of managing change. These experiences have underscored the necessity of a structured approach that considers the nuances of stakeholder assessment and impact, as well as the critical aspect of end-user adoption.

The "5-Ps of Change" framework presented in this book—Purpose, Planning, Process, Performance, and People—emerges as a strategic roadmap designed to navigate the complexities of organizational change. Each "P" is meticulously crafted to align with the mission of achieving sustainable transformation. Purpose defines the strategic vision and goals; Planning outlines the roadmap to reach these goals; Process emphasizes the importance of methodical execution; Performance measures the outcomes against set benchmarks; and People focuses on the human element, ensuring that those affected by the change are engaged and supported throughout the journey. To further ensure that the 5-Ps methodology was thoroughly explored, and to provide comprehensive coverage of each change pillar, OpenAI's ChatGPT 4.0 aided by providing initial brainstorming and surveying of topics congruent with the 5-Ps framework. AI content was limited to initial drafts, which were then researched, validated, and rewritten to maintain the unique spirit of the author, and in keeping with scholarly integrity, consistency, and accuracy.

The "5-Ps of Change" framework, buttressed by over 20 years of management experience, provides a call to action for leaders, project managers, and change agents to embrace a time-tested holistic organizational change management strategy. By implementing the 5-Ps of Change from the inception of project initiation through to the final stages of system or process implementation, organizations can achieve meaningful and lasting transformation. It is my hope that this book will serve as a valuable resource, providing insights and practical tools to successfully lead and manage change in today's dynamic environment.

As you embark on this journey, I encourage you to fully embrace the principles and practices outlined in this book. The path to successful change is challenging, but with a clear strategy and a commitment to its execution, successful change adoption is entirely attainable. Let *The 5-Ps of Change* be your guide in transforming your organization, and ultimately lead to the attainment of your strategic goals.

Introduction

The "Wonder of the Seas" is a modern engineering marvel that has claimed the title of the world's largest cruise ship in 2022. Weighing in at 236,857 tons, this *Royal Caribbean* floating city transports 5,734 passengers and 2,300 crew members on its 16 passenger decks and 2,867 staterooms. This ocean wonder sails in good company: including its sister vessels, the "Symphony of the Seas," "Harmony of the Seas," "Allure of the Seas," and "Oasis of the Seas"—all prior contenders for the largest vessels ever built. While new ocean wonders of larger size and grandeur are being built, including "Utopia" and the "Icon of the Seas," there is one thing that each of these luxury cruise liners have in common. No, it is not the sheer opulence of their exquisite spaces, nor the technology that is infused throughout their cabins, but it is the relatively small vertically-housed fin-like steering mechanism that sits behind the propeller that is ultimately responsible for the direction of the vessel. This steering mechanism is called the rudder. But why would a book about change management begin with an exposition on luxury ocean vessels, and more importantly, the relatively minuscule component—the rudder? That is the purpose of this book: to highlight the central fact that the smallest levers often exact the largest force on the change continuum for an organization. This book serves to introduce

DOI: 10.4324/9781003544883-1

these levers as foundational change management pillars, since they are the basis for understanding critical concepts and constructs about change management, and by extension, how change is best undertaken within today's organizations.

It has been said that the only thing constant in life is change! This is true for organizations of any size, affiliation, denomination, agency, or demographics served. There is, and will always be, the need for change. Change that requires people to do things differently. Change that requires, and often demands, the implementation of new processes and workflows. Change that deploys new systems and upgrades outdated technology infrastructures. Change that impacts human capital development. Change that seeks to achieve improvements in organizational agility, efficiency, human–social collaboration, leadership interaction, human capital development, and ultimately, the realization of new organizational cultures that produce increased returns for the organization. While there is a plethora of other reasons why change is required, and sometimes necessary, the truism is certain; the only constant in the life of an organization is change!

But what are the levers of change? Why are they important? How are they best utilized? These are all great questions, and unfortunately, many responsible for leading change within today's organizations are ill-equipped to use them. On the other hand, senior executives and leaders who are charged with the adoption of systems, methods, and tools narrowly equate change initiatives, and more broadly Organizational Change Management (OCM), to human capital development, personnel training, and other forms of professional development programs. Others also make the cardinal error in thinking that change management is reserved for the "Chiefs" within today's organizations—the Chief Executive Officer (CEO), Chief Technology Officer (CTO), Chief Administrative Officer (CAO), Chief Information Officer (CIO) Chief Operating Officer (COO), and a host of other executive leaders and managers. But even this limited view lacks merit.

Organizations, by definition, represent a collective group of people, ideas, and human interaction that coexist based on a collective set of mutually beneficial goals centered on the organization's purpose. This interaction creates a social dynamic with cascading effects and far-reaching impacts. Stated another way, an organization is a collection of people who collectively work toward a common purpose, employing a division of labor that informs the structure and hierarchy. Whether you are an executive or a line worker, a leader or a follower, your membership within this human–social construct exposes you to the continuum of change that occurs within the organization. That's why understanding the pillars of OCM is so critical for organizational success.

Organizational Change Management Pillars

Before delving into the "pillars of change" and uncovering the methods, tools, and theories around change management, let's establish a working definition of OCM. OCM is a cohesive set of principles, techniques, tools, and competencies that are aligned with human–social frameworks, within which organizational goals and imperatives are defined, managed, and implemented.

> **OCM: A systematic approach that aligns the organization's strategic vision with people.**

These goals (business, technical, infrastructural, and human–related) impact how new technology systems, tools, and business processes affect organizational efficiency, and moderate intangible changes that influence organizational culture and behavior. Competencies are a cluster of related knowledge, attitudes, and skills that affect a major part of one's job, correlate with performance, can be measured, and can be improved (Parry, 1996).

Therefore, OCM is a systematic approach that aligns the organization's strategic vision with its most important asset—its *people*.

OCM, and by extension, human–social collaboration within an organizational context, has at its foundation, people. Thus, "people" must be included in the philosophical and organizational decision-making relative to the change that is being undertaken. Stated in mathematical terms, the foundational needs of people represent the lowest common denominator for all aspects that inform OCM strategy. Why?

- The organization's vision, strategy, and operations impact people.
- The organization's services, programs, and initiatives impact people.
- The organization's projects, programs, and portfolios impact people.
- The organization's mission, processes, and strategic outcomes impact people.
- The organization's technology, systems, and collaboration platforms, impact people.
- The organization's culture, attitudes, and pervasive behaviors are shaped by people.

Each of these examples highlight the centrality of people in the OCM continuum, and establish the foundations upon which five OCM pillars are established:

Pillar #1—PURPOSE: The definition of executive vision and strategy that legitimizes the change effort and explains why it is being undertaken.

Pillar #2—PLANNING: The articulation of metrics and processes necessary for goal attainment and the steps necessary through the careful execution of project-related plans.

Pillar #3—PROCESS: The systematic assessment of organizational effectiveness that contrasts required legacy improvements against required skills, attitudes, and

THE
5-Ps
OF CHANGE

PERFORMANCE
The measurement and evaluation of progress towards change objectives.

PEOPLE
The engagement and empowerment of individuals to drive and sustain the change.

PROCESS
The implementation of structured steps to execute the change effectively.

PLANNING
The development of a strategic roadmap to guide the change process.

PURPOSE
The articulation of a clear and compelling reason for the change.

competencies needed for the execution and adoption of future processes.

Pillar #4—PERFORMANCE: The definition of metrics and optimized standards against which new systems, tools, and techniques are evaluated relative to organizational enhancement targets.

Pillar #5—PEOPLE: The central focus along the change continuum that operationalizes executive vision, adopts new processes, establishes new behaviors, and sets the stage for creating shared value systems across the organization.

These five pillars represent the 5-Ps of change (Purpose, Planning, Process, Performance, and People) and provide the framework on which this book is premised. In the chapters that follow, discussion around the 5-Ps of change will introduce OCM principles and strategies, and provide helpful insights around defining effective organizational change management processes, while challenging systems of thinking necessary for process optimization, and defining the framework that helps to clarify reasons for undertaking change within today's evolving organization.

Before unraveling each of these constructs, it's important to establish the boundaries that define the OCM discipline, and provide a brief introduction, some historical context, and a quick overview of some of theoretical models that inform change strategy.

An Introduction to Organizational Change Management

One of the defining terms upon which OCM is premised is "vision." The vision that precedes corporate growth is a direct correlate to executive leadership, sharp business wit, and the ability to lead others through difficult times of change. Corporate executives often sit in these positions of change and chart the course to what either begins the prologue to the company's success story or, on the contrary, its obituary. The reality of either outcome is predicated on the notion that the only constant entity in their world of business is the entity of change, and how executives approach this sensitive and intricate topic ultimately determine their longevity.

The history of the personal computer (i.e., the PC) tells the story of how "change" not only results from executive vision, but how it results from environmental, personal, and other ancillary factors that mandate its existence. For example, the New York Times published an article in 1962 about John W. Mauchly's presentation to the American Institute of Industrial Engineers in which he made the bold conclusion that the average boy or girl would become masters of the personal computer. At the time of his presentation, corporate pundits snuffed at his remarks, jeering that the smallest "personal" computer—that at the time required the space needed for today's average refrigerator—would become a household item. But International Business Machines (IBM) understood firsthand the implication of this prediction and what it would mean for corporate profitability. IBM, recognizing the opportunity and timing in bringing the PC to the forefront, led the revolution from mainframe technology to micro-computing technology, revolutionizing the emergence of the "personal computer." Decades later, organizational change theorists and practitioners, including Marc. H. Meyer, Mark Anzani, and George Walsh (2005) proclaimed Mauchly's vision as a reality, where now computers are the preponderate of all electronic gadgetry. Since their entrance into the personal computer arena, IBM refocused its marketing strategy that leveraged processes that assessed user needs and frustrations, and ultimately informing new products line decisions for both hardware and software products (Meyer, 2005).

The innovation that led to the adoption of the personal computer illustrates how customer-driven needs inform corporate change initiatives, and how these initiatives evolve in view of opportunity and timing. While this is just one example that represents significant technology shifts, history is replete with similar innovations that challenged the status quo and dared to challenge what was considered impossible technological feats.

Organizational change has since become a critical enabler for corporate success, and the study thereof has become a catalyst that drives executive vision and strategy. Both corporate research and academic study have resulted in theoretical models that seek to explain and predict measurable outcomes related to executive decisioning around "change." Models seek to predict outcomes based on purpose, scope boundaries, and expected outcomes; the degree to which is revealed by the strength of phase-related planning, the definition of project-related milestones, and ultimately the articulation of the precise steps needed for effective "change" adoption. Unlike discrete mathematical models that exist in "black and white," organizational change models adopt philosophical and ideological perspectives, and often arrive at unique conclusions informed by assumptions about the nature of human behavior and social organizations. This "human–social" construct influences change adoption variability, and in many cases, the moderating reason why change initiatives fail. When organizational change efforts fail, enormous resources of time, money, technology investments, and human resources are squandered. Despite multimillion-dollar acquisitions and the effort needed to ready technology platforms for use, people lose interest, and their declining commitment to the change effort results in dissatisfaction, increased stress, frustration with leadership, and the general sense of apathy surrounding the change effort.

The management of change is a tough assignment, particularly when considering the interdependency of human–social elements required for success. What often complicates the process is the lack of consensus on the factors that are most influential in ensuring successful change adoption. This reality is further compounded by the fact that people often approach change with a skewed reality of the factors necessary for a successful change effort. Their perspective is biased through personal experience of prior failed attempts, individual opinions, group-think, and perspectives shaped by misinformation. This is why effective communication is central to all change initiatives, and the reason why it never should be relegated to the training and development phases of the initiative. Rather, effective change practitioners will ensure that discussions around change are codified in the project's charter (purpose), elaborated in all planning documents (planning), infused in all process related assessments (process), benchmarked in performance metrics (performance), and infused in all areas where people are expected to interact with the outcomes of the effort (people). These are the 5-Ps of change, and the purpose for this book. Understanding each of these pillars will broaden your perspective on OCM, and when done correctly, will significantly minimize the chances of failed change initiatives. These truly are the "soft" side of change, but the "hard" facts to learn!

The study of OCM often relied on the "softer" side of change management, relying on factors such as culture, corporate leadership, human resource management, personnel motivation, and others, However, while these "soft" factors are critical OCM success enablers, exclusive management of the same with little regard for other fundamental components will ultimately prove to be inadequate for organizational change success. Notwithstanding, while it is immensely difficult, and quite a formidable task to change and/or reorient the attitudes and relationships that are engrained within the fabric of corporate systems, these "soft" factors serve as barometric indicators that measure the adoption readiness. However, if change initiatives are to be successful, an additional perspective –regarded as the "hard" side of change management –also must be considered. The term "hard factors" in change management refers to real and measurable characteristics that influence OCM effectiveness and include factors such as:

a. Strategy: A well-defined change strategy that specifies the change initiative's vision, goals, and objectives.
b. Structure: The organizational structure that delineates current and future lines of reporting, personnel roles, and clearly defined duties pre and post the OCM engagement.
c. Processes: The review, assessment, and reengineering of legacy business processes and workflows in view of future enhancements to the same in order to achieve organizational goals and efficient business operations.
d. Technology: The acquisition, development, and/or provisioning of new technology systems aimed at boosting productivity, improving communication, deepening cooperation, and fostering the adoption of new technology and systems to promote and maintain positive change.
e. Resources: The assignment of competent financial, human, and technological resources to facilitate change adoption.

While there may be additional factors not listed, a poorly defined change strategy, the lack of a supportive organizational structure, ill-defined processes pre/post the change, inadequately configured technology solutions, and the lack of competent resources will invariably lead to the collapse and repeated failures of organizational change initiatives.

To summarize, organizational change is a complex and dynamic process that requires leaders to exercise proactive management to navigate organizational challenges; demonstrate thoughtfulness in creating opportunities for optimization and growth; and possess the ability to create positive environments for efficient and effective human–social interaction. Successful organizational change is motivated by the need to adapt to "soft" and "hard" factors that affect the organization's structure, processes, and culture, and employs optimization strategies to facilitate technological advances amidst uncertain market conditions in pursuit of organizational goals. Successful organizational change initiatives therefore require a deliberative approach that focuses on performance improvement, increases efficiency, and boosts productivity, to maintain organizational competitiveness. Successful organizational change further requires leaders to architect solutions across the entire lifecycle of the project/program with clarity around the 5-pillars of change previously introduced (i.e., purpose, planning, process, performance, and people). Attentiveness to "soft" and "hard" factors requires leaders to make deliberate and planned changes to the organization's processes, structures, policies, and practices in response to changing business objectives, while facilitating individual, team, departmental, and enterprise-wide improvement initiatives with decisive vision and a clear sense of what is expected at the conclusion of the change effort. The first step in this critical process is to define the purpose of the change effort, so let's delve right into that next.

Chapter 1

Purpose

Introduction

Change occurs whether we want it to or not. The cycle of life shows how the tenderness of youth ultimately succumbs to the wrinkles of age. Legacy systems show how efficiency and productivity decline due to changing business demands and advancements in technology. These are simple but profound realities that result from organic environmental change. While change often occurs organically, organizational change should be planned strategically, pursued purposefully, and executed with intentionality.

> OCM should be planned strategically, pursued purposefully, and executed with intentionality.

But why undertake the difficult and often disruptive process associated with organizational change? On the surface, the answer appears simple, but an exploration of the various areas affected by change reveals a more complex and interdependent construct. Why?

- Change impacts people.
- Change impacts processes.

    DOI: 10.4324/9781003544883-2

- Change affects technology selection and adoption.
- Change costs time and money.
- Change disrupts the status quo with the promise of organizational improvement.
- Change challenges religious customs, social constructs, and ethnic norms.
- Change, well you get the point.

While there are countless reasons why organizational change is pursued, one thing is true: the only constant in life is—change!

In today's rapidly evolving business landscape, organizations are continually faced with the need to adapt, stay relevant, and offer value to their stakeholders. Organizations must therefore constantly evolve to maintain their competitive advantage, adapt to ever-changing business requirements, and adjust to the constant emergence of new technologies and their associated demands. Thus, organizational change, whether inspired by technological advancements, shifting customer expectations, disruptive market forces, or by the need to meet shifting stakeholder needs, the ability to effectively lead organizational change has become a critical enabler for long-term organizational success. However, amidst the complexities and uncertainties of change, the first pillar that stands as the critical enabler for success is—defining the *purpose* for the change.

Simply stated, purpose refers to the underlying reason or objective that governs a change initiative within the organization. It defines desired outcomes or goals that the organization seeks to achieve, and provides clarity and direction around expected outcomes to its stakeholders. Stated another way, a clearly defined purpose serves as the "north star" that aligns the organization's efforts with the needs and interests of stakeholders, to foster a deep sense of meaning, significance, and a sense of community for all involved in the change process.

Defining purpose therefore seeks to answer the following questions:

■ Why is change necessary?
■ What are the expected outcomes?
■ What benefits will be derived?
■ What improvements will be achieved beyond the status quo?
■ How will people respond?
■ To what degree will those impacted by the change embrace or reject it?

Gaining clarity on these questions is critical for change adoption and provides a construct that helps frame the organizational change initiative. Additionally, gaining clarity on these questions helps to:

1. Align stakeholders—by defining a shared understanding of the reason behind the change, so that all stakeholders can work toward a common goal.
2. Focus effort—helping to prioritize actions and resources, ensuring that they are directed toward the most important outcomes.
3. Provide a reference point—that focuses decision-making and allows stakeholders to assess whether their actions are aligned with the change effort.
4. Enhance commitment—that increases commitment and buy-in that ultimately leads to higher levels of stakeholder engagement, and ultimately success of the effort.

The complexity of organizational change is often characterized as both a *science* and an *art* because it involves a combination of systematic approaches and creative thinking to effectively manage and implement change within an organization. Let's delve deeper into this seemingly bifurcated construct:

Science: Organizational change is regarded as a science by virtue of the body of knowledge and empirical study around human psychology; thus, effective change management practice requires a command of the dynamics of organizational behavior, human psychology, and scientific principles and methodologies. It incorporates several disciplines, including psychology, sociology, management theory, and systems thinking. Scientific methods, data analysis, and empirical research aid in problem diagnosis, root cause identification, and the development of evidence-based interventions. Change management models and frameworks therefore provide a systematic approach to planning, implementing, and evaluating organizational change initiatives.

Art: Organizational change is regarded as an art by virtue of the soft skills necessary to moderate human–social variables that influence sustained organizational behavior. Since organizational change requires a creative and adaptable mindset, effective change management practice requires the ability to navigate the complexities of human emotions, attitudes, and cultural factors within an organization. Effective change management strategy therefore requires foresight, intuition, and the capacity to inspire and engage stakeholders. It further requires effective communication, and the ability to identify, mitigate, and manage stakeholder resistance. Finally, it creates an environment that is conducive for stakeholders to adapt to new organizational systems and processes following the change initiative. For these reasons, organizational change is regarded an as art, since human–social collaboration introduces uncertainty, and requires change leaders to make informed decisions based on the organization's specific context and dynamics.

The twofold approach that integrates science and art is central to defining an effective change management strategy, since the science of organizational change relies on foundational principles and factors that influence change, while the art of change involves the application of this knowledge in flexible and intuitive ways. Therefore, the careful balance between scientific methods and artful execution of change strategy requires both the rational and emotional aspects of the organization to be considered, and hence the reason why the first pillar in the change continuum is to define the purpose of the change, and how it will impact people—individually.

The process of defining purpose encompasses much more than just stating an organization's aims or objectives. It entails articulating a vision that motivates, directs, and compels all areas of an organization's operations. It further seeks to inspire internal and external stakeholders with a clear sense of the future: one that stakeholders are able to galvanize enthusiasm around in pursuit of a shared goal. Establishing clarity of purpose also provides a sense of organizational continuity and stability amidst turbulence, and provides a unifying force that rallies stakeholders around a common cause that provides meaning and fulfillment.

> **Purpose articulates a vision that motivates, directs, and compels action across all areas of the organization.**

Another reason why defining purpose is a critical enabler for successful organizational change is that it enables organizations to adapt and transform with agility. Agility is the ability of an organization to adjust quickly and efficiently to changes in the business environment, exemplified by the organization's ability to define, accept, and respond to the need for change, and then subsequently, demonstrate a keen willingness to adapt the organization's operations so as to seize new opportunities, improve efficiency, and inspire stakeholders to pursue a future with mutually considered benefits. The premise for mutual consideration (i.e., the organization meeting people's needs, juxtaposed with people committing to the organization's interests and goals) is central in defining shared interests, serves as a guiding principle for decision-making, and helps leaders prioritize activities aligned with the organization's strategic direction. Further, a clearly defined purpose minimizes the risk of distractions, preempts and counteracts sources of misinformation, and articulates a coherent change agenda that ultimately maximizes the effectiveness of the change initiative.

Considering the depth and breadth of organizational change strategy, it's unfortunate that many view its execution as solely a professional development exercise that is relegated to personnel training activities. To the contrary, effective organizational change management strategy must expand beyond this limiting mindset and go a step further to account for actions, activities, and interests of external constituents who consume the organization's products and services. For that reason, defining purpose is not only critical for internal alignment but also serves as a critical enabler for external engagement. This is particularly true for socially-aware organizations (i.e., organizations that are customer-focused and driven to meet their business needs) since they must constantly demonstrate priority for their customers' interests, needs, and desires over organizational profitability. In doing so, socially-aware organizations attract loyal customers, deepen relationships with committed investors, and effectively engage with all stakeholder groups, implementing programs that ultimately seek to improve the wider community.

A well-defined purpose communicates authenticity, builds trust, and fosters long-term relationships. It also attracts and retains talent, as stakeholders are increasingly motivated by more than just financial compensation—they want to be part of something meaningful and purpose-driven. This is why the first pillar in the organizational change management process—defining a clear purpose statement—is so critical; since a well-defined purpose statement provides a solid foundation for the change, aligns and inspires stakeholders, guides leadership decision-making, and inspires stakeholders toward the attainment of shared organizational goals.

The benefits for defining a clear purpose statement also provide tangible results, since a clear purpose statement sets in motion the acquisition of new skills, methods, tools, and techniques needed for effective change adoption. It also focuses attention and equips the organization to navigate organizational change challenges with clarity, resilience, and a sense of direction. Amidst ambivalence, uncertainty, and individual resistance to the "changing of the status quo," effective change leaders understand that defining a clear purpose statement serves as the driving force that propels the organization and its stakeholders toward a future that is both meaningful and sustainable.

So, who are organizational change stakeholders? What roles do they assume in the organizational change process? That's the topic of our next section.

Organizational Change Stakeholders

Organizational change management stakeholders refer to individuals or groups who have a vested interest in the outcomes and success of a change initiative, as they are either directly or indirectly impacted by its outcomes. To successfully facilitate organizational change, it is imperative to identify and involve all relevant stakeholders involved, and/or impacted by the change effort. It is equally important to take into account the interests, needs, and desired outcomes affecting each stakeholder group, being keenly aware of divergent and/or convergent points of view.

Along the change continuum, not all stakeholder groups are equally impacted. Thus, effective change leaders must assess the degree to which the organization will change, and analyze the relative downline impact to individual and/or group functioning. However, and as a precursor to discussing the various types of stakeholder groups, organizational change management categories are often stratified along the following divisions of labor.

Vision and Strategic Direction: Executives and senior leaders often provide strategic direction and champion the change effort.

Management and Implementation Oversight: Managers facilitate communication, ensure alignment, and support employees throughout the transition.

Tactical Execution and Change Adoption: Employees actively participate, adapt, and provide feedback to shape the change.

Process Facilitation: Change agents or consultants guide the change process and provide technical expertise.

Well-defined stakeholder roles and responsibilities (a) reduce ambiguity, (b) improve accountability, (c) promote collaboration and cohesion in the implementation of change, (d) prevent duplication of effort, and (e) streamline decision-making processes that may impact the following stakeholder groups:

Senior Management

Successful organizational change efforts do not occur in a vacuum; rather, commitment from top-level executives and senior management is a fundamental component for success. The term "senior management" refers to senior-level personnel who sponsor a change initiative, provide strategic direction, allocate resources, and empower change leaders with the requisite authority to make decisions in keeping with organizational change goals. Included in this group are executive leaders who provide project sponsorship, a critical enabler for creating synergy, a shared vision, and facilitating commitment across all functional teams and departments. Lack of visible executive support instills doubt, compromises leadership effectiveness, and ultimately threatens the success of the change effort.

Employees

When it comes to leading organizational change, employees are a critical stakeholder group. Organizational shifts in processes and functions will invariably affect this important group, as they serve on the frontline and often feel the effects of the change firsthand. During the fragile period of change adoption, it is this stakeholder group that must accept and adjust to new business processes, learn new technology systems, and adjust to new organizational workflows. Gaining buy-in and facilitating enthusiasm during this delicate period are crucial for change success. Effective change leaders employ strategies that catalog employee perspectives and knowledge gained throughout the change effort, as this information often provides invaluable insight for process optimization, thereby helping leaders refine the change effort, uncover hidden obstacles, and reveal solutions not previously considered. For these reasons, employees play a crucial role in the feedback process that informs executive leadership on how the change is progressing while creating an environment where fellow coworkers, teams, and external stakeholders can rally around the change. Through this interactive process, employees facilitate group learning, help to allay fears, and ultimately create a climate that is conducive to achieving the goals of the change initiative.

An important ingredient required for organizational change success is employee support and advocacy. It is during this process where change advocates articulate persuasive value-driven statements that offer assistance and foster an optimistic outlook on the transition. This is critical, as resistance to the change effort is amplified by fears associated with acquiring new skills in order to become proficient with new technology, processes, or roles. Thus, employee readiness to learn, improve, and grow is crucial, as it requires dedication and commitment to continuous improvement and personal development.

While executives set the vision, employees are the ones who carry it out! Success therefore depends on the ability of employees to adjust to new circumstances, offer suggestions and criticisms, collaborate with others, learn new information and techniques, promote the change they are helping to implement, and aid in its ongoing improvement. Their participation is essential to the attainment of organizational change goals, and lasting change across the organization.

Human Resources (HR) Department

The Human Resources Department plays a vital role in organizational change management and serves as the interface between technology and human–social interaction. HR focuses on the "people" side of change by ensuring that the organization has the necessary capabilities, skills, and competencies to navigate the change effort. To navigate the fragile aspects of change adoption, HR stakeholders provide critical support necessary to influence organizational change management outcomes. They do this by assuming various roles along the organizational change continuum. One of which includes working closely with senior leaders and change agents to develop a comprehensive change management strategy that assesses the impact of the change on employees, and developing the necessary mitigating strategies to allay risks that threaten the change effort.

HR also facilitates effective communication across the organization in order to facilitate engagement and bring about awareness of the anticipated organizational change outcomes. They broker communication across the organization, first starting with senior executives and ending with employees, so as to ensure consistent, timely, and transparent messaging throughout the change initiative. In a related role, HR also facilitates employee professional development activities by identifying and providing avenues for employees to develop new skills and competencies needed to fully respond and adapt to the outcomes of the change endeavor. By coordinating with managers, supervisors, and technology leaders, HR stakeholders are able to assess the impact of the change on the workforce, and identify potential gaps in skills, or identify the availability of resources needed to support the endeavor. The outcome of this assessment informs the development of employee training programs that focus on the development of new skills to further enable the workforce to fully adopt the change.

Facilitating the needs of people is often regarded as the "soft side" of change management, and as will be discovered later, failure to adequately anticipate, respond, or cater to their needs will ultimately undermine the success of the change initiative. For this reason, HR acts as the bridge that provides direction and support. They also enable decision makers to better manage the softer side of the organization by anticipating and managing employee resistance and providing adequate mitigation to ward off possible conflicts. HR further examines the change program through the "lens of people" by collecting input from relevant stakeholders, recommending areas for improvement, and advancing steps that can improve current and future organizational change efforts.

Project Teams

Project teams play a crucial role in the planning and execution phases of organizational change. Project teams represent groups of individuals who align organizational change goals with executive vision and carry out the necessary activities relative to planning, implementing, and monitoring the organizational change initiative. Project teams are led by project managers who are responsible for managing all aspects of the initiative and who facilitate and coordinate strategic implementation activities with subject matter experts.

Project teams support organizational change initiatives by performing the following critical functions:

Change Planning and Execution: The first and most important step begins with codifying the organizational change vision in actionable steps with measurable outcomes. This is aided by the development of the change management plan that articulates objectives, timelines, resource needs, anticipated impacts/outcomes, and the definition of scope boundaries in collaboration with all relevant stakeholders.

Cross-functional Collaboration: Effective stakeholder collaboration requires cross-functional team engagement to fully document needs, expected outcomes, impacts, and timeframes associated with the change initiative. Change leaders work with members from various departments or domains of expertise to define the boundaries of change by working with employees, managers, and subject matter experts to collect feedback, address concerns, and implement effective communication strategies. Effective communication strategies rely on providing frequent and relevant updates, soliciting feedback, and responding to concerns or oppositions to the change from all stakeholder groups. Opposition to the change, whether tacit or overt, is often a risk that must be carefully managed and mitigated to avert the collapse of employee morale, build confidence through new skills and training, and ultimately increase the chances of success for change adoption. That's why cross-functional team collaboration is critical to organizational change management efficacy, and requires change leaders to monitor progress, assess risks, and supervise the implementation of new processes, systems, tools, and techniques resulting from the implementation of the change initiative.

Risk Management: Project teams utilize risk management strategies to mitigate risks that threaten change adoption and the seamless integration of new organizational functions. Risk Management therefore entails the assessment and management of potential hazards by carefully anticipating potential obstacles and/or difficulties, and devising mitigation strategies to minimize disruptions to maximize change adoption.

Measurement and Evaluation: Project teams develop metrics and indicators to evaluate organizational change efficacy and impact. They monitor progress by defining performance metrics, acquiring performance data, and assessing outcomes against predetermined objectives. This enables the team to identify areas for improvement and recommend course-corrective measures to bring about alignment with organizational change goals.

Knowledge Transfer: Project teams serve as a data collection hub that collects, reports, and analyzes data resulting from the change initiative. These data provide a repository from which information can be gathered and disseminated throughout the change process. Information may include, but not limited to, best practices, lessons learned, stakeholder feedback, and success milestones that can be used to guide future change initiatives or assist other teams within the organization.

This 360-degree perspective is why project teams play such a crucial role in organizational change management, since they facilitate planning, execution, and monitoring of the change initiative, as well as engage stakeholders, manage risks, and evaluate results. Their expertise and coordination are essential to the successful attainment of organizational change management goals.

Customers and Clients

Customers and clients represent another critical stakeholder group, since products and services resulting from the change initiative are directly, or in some cases indirectly, affected by organizational change goals. Not only are the organization's products and services affected by organizational change, but customer experience relative to how products are consumed and services rendered are invariably affected by change. Organizational change management leaders often rely on this stakeholder group to provide valuable insight for product enhancement and service optimization recommendations. Their insights, preferences, and requirements often inform product design, service offering portfolios, and ultimately implementation and delivery recommendations. Customers/ clients provide feedback via surveys, focus groups, or via direct communications, as their input further enables organizations to comprehend how a change may affect service delivery quality.

Another area where customers and clients play a pivotal role is through their acceptance and adoption of new products, services, or processes. To increase change adoption success, customers must be informed of the benefits of the change throughout the continuum of the change initiative. This enables transparency, fosters buy-in, and enlists the group's participation in the change process. During the process, their concerns must be addressed, warnings heeded, and recommendations listened to, for the seamless adoption of change management outcomes. In certain instances, organizations involve customers and clients in the testing or piloting of new products and/or procedures. This allows them to collect valuable feedback, identify potential problems, and refine the change strategy prior to its full implementation. Additionally, participation in testing yields valuable insights that aid in the enhancement of change initiatives, and ultimately leads to wider acceptance and adoption of the change. Customers' acceptance and adoption can be facilitated by providing effective communication, enlisting support through strategic engagement, providing avenues for knowledge transfer, providing explanations and clarifications to build confidence, and providing support to instill desired outcomes and behaviors consistent with organizational change goals.

Another area where customers and clients play a pivotal role is through change advocacy; since satisfied consumers often promote the benefits to new clients, build loyalty to the organization, and through their favorable word-of-mouth, further enhance success, acceptance, and change permanence. Therefore, when customer and client's interest, needs, and desires are attended to, the result yields satisfied consumers who then advocate for the organization's products and services, and build goodwill through long-term relationships with the organization.

Suppliers

It stands to reason that before there are products and services to be consumed, there must be suppliers. Suppliers are defined as external partners or vendors who provide the organization with products, services, or in some way facilitate the delivery of the organization's service offerings. At first glance, this stakeholder group may appear insignificant; however, a closer study of their value proposition reveals their vital role when change initiatives involve procurement, supply chain management, or managing supplier relationships. For these reasons, organizational change planning must account for procedural changes, service delivery interdependencies, and other associated impacts to suppliers when considering organizational change initiatives.

Organizational change management leverages supplier relationships in a variety of ways, and is best facilitated when the following supplier roles are adopted:

Collaboration and Communication: Given contractual relationships, service delivery requirements, and other business-related requirements, suppliers must be informed of any change that may affect existing business relationships. Changes may require enhancements to existing products and services, new delivery schedules, or modified pricing structures to meet organizational change goals. The willingness of suppliers to facilitate these changes and provide support during the transition is essential. For these reasons, change leaders must engage suppliers early in the change continuum and employ effective communication strategies to ensure that the nature, timing, and prospective consequences following the change are fully understood. Through collaboration and effective communication, leaders will help to align service delivery expectations with organizational change goals, and thus ultimately facilitate seamless organizational change transitions.

Risk Mitigation: Suppliers often possess unique insights and industry-specific knowledge that can be utilized during organizational change. These insights, which include best practices, industry trends, emerging technologies, and innovative solutions, can significantly enhance the organizational change initiative and aid in mitigating associated risks. Further, suppliers may also assist in identifying potential supply chain disruptions, propose alternative solutions, or provide assistance in contingency planning. Therefore, collaboration with suppliers on organizational change management initiatives aids in mitigating risks and makes for a more robust and resilient change implementation.

Change Process: Organizational change by its very nature is grounded in continuous improvement, and this being one of the most important goals of organizational change, feedback and suggestions from this important stakeholder group are invaluable in the continuous improvement process. Suppliers often identify inefficiencies in processes, products, or services, and provide optimization recommendations. Their unique market insight invariably leads to innovative technology proposals, workflow enhancements that improve business operations, new or existing product enhancements, and new business processes and service offerings for the organization. Consistent with the motif of doing change "with" stakeholders, versus "to" them, engaging suppliers as partners will ultimately cultivate a culture of continuous organizational improvement.

Regulatory Agencies

The statement that "no man is an island; no man stands alone" is also true in organizational change. Regulatory agencies and/or organizations are government entities or industry-specific regulatory bodies that monitor and ensure compliance with regulations. Their role is pivotal as change initiatives often include impacts to business and non-business-related environments. For this reason, it's critical for stakeholders to be engaged in, and informed of, change initiatives very early in the change management process. While this is particularly true in severely regulated or compliance-regulated industries, regulatory agencies generally engage in organizational change by adopting the following roles:

Compliance Guidance: Regulatory agencies provide organizations with compliance and regulatory guidance. Compliance requires adherence to regulatory standards, performance monitoring, and often include reporting thresholds that trigger course-corrective actions. Regulatory agencies may also issue new guidelines or requirements that affect planned activities, requiring additional monitoring and reporting. Organizations must fully understand and incorporate regulatory standards into their change management planning, since initiatives often require the issuance of approvals, permits, or licenses to meet organizational change goals. In so doing, organizations will avoid untimely disruptions and avert stiff legal and/or regulatory penalties.

Audits and Inspections: Organizational change often requires verification and inspection of work products, business processes, and monitoring of produced artifacts. Regulatory agencies implement audits and inspections to ensure compliance with applicable laws and regulations by implementing unscheduled reviews and inspections that assess the degree of the organization's compliance with imposed statutes and requirements. Thus, it is essential for leaders to adhere to guidelines and address concerns raised by regulatory agencies during audit and/or inspections, as these agencies are authorized to impose sanctions and penalties for noncompliance. For the organization to avoid fines, legal actions, or in some cases avoid damaging its reputation, organizations must ensure that change initiatives comply with regulatory requirements.

Reporting and Documentation: Regulatory agencies frequently require organizations to maintain documentation pertaining to their operations, along with maintaining an accurate change roster of modifications resulting from the initiative. Organizations must therefore ensure that resources are adequately allocated to fulfill this requirement while ensuring accuracy. This is essential, as regulatory agencies require timely delivery and accurate development of all supporting organizational change-related documentation.

Union Representatives

Organizational change is often a disruptive process, not only resulting from technology modernizations and business process improvements, but many times it could prove disruptive to the organization's workforce. If the organization is represented by a labor union, then union representatives emerge as an important stakeholder group, since they will be involved in negotiations to ensure that the change is executed in accordance with collective bargaining agreements.

Union representatives also work as employee advocates, and during organizational change initiatives, they actively work to address concerns, assess negative workforce impacts, and negotiate other downline consequences resulting from the change. While unions in general receive negative perceptions for the work they do, their work is not primarily adversarial. Union representatives often collaborate with management to find solutions that are mutually beneficial. They also engage in collaborative problem-solving, constructive dialog, and pursue alternatives to mitigate potential adverse effects on its members. Throughout the organizational change process, union representatives therefore support change initiatives in a variety of ways, including but not limited to:

Representation and Negotiation: Union representatives serve as the voice of its members during organizational change-related discussions and negotiations. They represent the union members' collective interests, needs, and concerns, and ensure that their perspectives are heard and considered. They present collective bargaining interests and negotiate with management to obtain fair and equitable outcomes for its members. Negotiations often consider the impact of the change as it relates to job responsibilities, wages, benefits, and working conditions, with the primary objective being to secure favorable terms and protections for its members. There are times when grievances result from the change initiative, and during these times, union representatives play a crucial role to mediate disputes and help to resolve conflicts. They assist union members in filing grievance documentation and ensure that correct procedures are followed while advocating for equitable resolutions.

Information Sharing: Union representatives not only work to negotiate outcomes that are advantageous to its members, but they also work to provide clarity around the organizational change initiative, assess possible impacts to bargaining arrangements, and communicate helpful and pertinent information regarding proposed changes. They often liaise with management to gather timely and accurate information to provide members with updates on the change initiative, clarify ambiguities, and respond to inquiries and/or concerns. Their role throughout the transformation process is central to giving voice to members' needs and interests, so they employ effective information-sharing strategies to ensure transparency, maintain trust, and broker channels of communication to keep the workforce informed.

Training and Support: As an extension to information sharing, union representatives often facilitate professional development activities by offering training and support to its members for them to effectively navigate the change. Training focuses on developing competencies (i.e., skills, attitudes, and knowledge) needed to adopt desirable change outcomes, and to provide support for newly implemented policies, procedures, or job requirements. In the process, union representatives equip members with relevant and timely information, provide access to resources, enroll members in support networks, and provide assistance as necessary to navigate the organizational change process.

Shareholders and Investors

Organizational change is meaningless unless it provides tangible benefits to the organization, and to those who are mostly invested in its products, services, and the organization's viability. When considering stakeholder groups, there is no group that is focused on profitability than shareholders and investors. These are groups of individuals that have made financial investments in the organization and therefore have a vested interest in its operations and prospects for the future. When considering organizational change, stakeholders and investors will be interested in knowing the reasoning necessitating the change, along with the potential impacts, particularly in relation to the company's financial performance. Because they have a financial stake in the organization and seek to protect and optimize their investments, shareholders, and investors influence organizational change management initiatives in a variety of ways, some of which include the following:

Decision-Making and Approval: Shareholders, especially those with substantial ownership or voting rights, are able to significantly influence and approve organizational change goals and objectives. Their influence is often most exerted when changes related to management strategy, market positioning, profitability, and key strategic decisions (i.e., mergers, acquisitions, divestitures, and reorganization efforts) are undertaken. Executives responsible for crafting the vision that guides the change initiative will often seek the assent of this critical stakeholder group since the change outcomes invariably affect the organization's financial position or governance structure. Shareholders and investors also often evaluate the organization's performance and make projections about the impact of the change on the organization's value and growth potential. They do this by analyzing financial reports, assessing key performance indicators, and monitoring other relevant metrics to evaluate feasibility, promote transparency, and instill accountability early in the organizational change process. They also evaluate organizational change risks along with the prospective impact on financial stability, competitive positioning, and long-term viability of the organization.

Engagement and Communication: Given the visibility, interests, and influence of this critical stakeholder group, shareholders and investors require transparent communication regarding the change initiative's goals, expected outcomes, and detailed analysis of possible impacts (both negative and positive) that can affect the organization. While their interaction with the organizational change management team is often limited and less frequent than with executives, shareholders, and investors communicate with the organization's management team through annual general meetings, investor conferences, and other forums to convey their opinions, raise concerns, or request additional information about the change. During these meetings, effective communication is critical to build trust, facilitate dialog about the organizational change initiative, and align shareholder expectations with the strategic direction of the organization.

Long-Term Value Creation: Ultimately, shareholders and investors are primarily concerned with maximizing their returns and creating long-term value. They assess the organization's change initiatives based on their potential to boost profitability, improve market positioning, and maximize shareholder value. For this reason, they require that management have a well-defined strategy and implementation plan that articulates how the change will generate sustainable growth and long-term financial success for the organization.

Communities and Local Authorities

Organizational change outcomes often trickle down and affect local communities in a variety of ways. For this reason, local communities and authorities have an interest in the goals and expected outcomes of the change initiative, particularly in large-scale projects that carry significant social or environmental repercussions. Communities and local authorities are therefore an important stakeholder group since they represent the interests of residents and local enterprises, while also serving as consumers of products and services rendered by the organization. Effective engagement is critical for this stakeholder group, and failure to manage expectations, solicit their input, analyze feedback, and conscientiously address their concerns will ultimately threaten the success of the change initiative, and in some cases completely derail it. For these reasons, proactive change management planning must consider requirements from this stakeholder group, and carefully assess the collective aspirations that provide meaningful and tangible benefits for the community at large. Early engagement in the organizational change process is critical for long-term success; therefore, when undertaking organizational change, it's imperative to enlist the support of this stakeholder group since they are key participants in the following change-related functions:

Impact Analysis and Assessment: Communities and local authorities have first-hand knowledge of activities that provide benefit to the wider community, along with those activities that threaten the long-term interests of the community. As a collective, this stakeholder group can assess social, economic, and environmental effects of the change initiative and provide insight into employment, infrastructure, services, and residents' overall quality of life. This assessment allows organizational change leaders to make informed decisions and, if necessary, define and implement mitigating measures that risk long-term societal benefits.

From a regulatory perspective, local authorities have the burden of overseeing regulatory compliance in areas such as zoning, building permits, environmental regulations, and licensing. They are therefore positioned to exert influence on the change initiative by taking the needs and requirements of the wider community into account. Consequently, organizations must work in harmony with this stakeholder group to meet regulatory compliance and comply with all applicable laws and regulations.

Infrastructure and Resources: Organizational change never occurs in a vacuum: it often requires close collaboration across a variety of stakeholder groups. This is true for community and local authorities as well, since this group provides critical subject matter expertise necessary to successfully guide organizational change initiatives. Local projects may also require change management teams to gain access to critical infrastructure and technical resources that can significantly inform requirements gathering, business process analysis, and provide technical project implementation guidance. Additionally, local authorities may also facilitate obtaining construction permits, coordinate transportation logistics, assist in provisioning utility services, integrate legacy systems with new technology systems, and broker technical coordination sessions with local groups. Close collaboration between the organization and the community requires careful and strategic alignment so that organizational change goals are congruent with local interests and aspirations of the local community.

Economic Development: Communities and local authorities must work collaboratively with the organization in areas pertaining to local community development and are thus motivated to continuously explore creative ways to improve the general well-being of their residents. During the organizational change process, collaboration between the organization and local authorities often results in identifying new opportunities that improve community amenities, encourage social responsibility, and support expansion of existing community initiatives. However, one of the most important drivers for organizational change is fiscal expansion of local economies. This is another critical role that communities and local authorities play in the organizational change management continuum. Therefore, since organizational change often has significant effects on economic development and employment in local communities, local governments are incentivized to support and collaborate with organizations to promote employment creation, workforce development, and economic expansion. Additionally, local authorities can also provide organizations with resources, incentives, and assistance to help them adapt to local environments, and ultimately become a meaningful contributing entity to the local economy.

Crisis Management and Emergency Response: Finally, local authorities play a crucial role in crisis management and emergency response when the change process poses potential hazards or emergencies. They may provide direction, coordinate emergency services, or collaborate with other organizations to mitigate risks to ensure the safety of the community. This shared vision of building safe and communal environments is paramount for this stakeholder group, since local communities represent a group of people who live, work, and commune together, and share a variety of shared interests, needs, and goals. Therefore, communities and local authorities help to facilitate stakeholder engagement, conduct impact assessment, ensure regulatory compliance, facilitate infrastructure development, and foster resource collaboration. They also support economic development and employment, contribute to community development activities, and provide emergency response during times of crisis management. Organizations must actively engage with communities and local authorities to ensure that change initiatives align with community requirements, regulations, and community aspirations, thereby fostering positive relationships and sustainable outcomes for both the organization and the local community at large.

How to Define a Purpose Statement

In the previous sections we established why it was important to define the purpose of an organizational change management effort. We also established that this was central to communicating what changes were being undertaken so that those impacted by the change would comprehend, accept, and adopt new organizational states. We also established that defining a clear sense of purpose was the first of five essential change management pillars that articulate executive vision: a critical step necessary to legitimize and explain organizational change and the attainment of its goals.

The process of defining a clear change management purpose provides several benefits, including providing stakeholder alignment, facilitating activity prioritization toward goal attainment, fostering improved decision-making, and enhancing stakeholder commitment. Further, a well-defined purpose communicates authenticity, builds trust, fosters long-term relationships, and sets in motion the acquisition of new skills, methods, tools, and techniques necessary for effective change adoption.

Having established the rationale and the list of benefits, what are the practical steps needed to define a clear purpose statement? The remainder of this chapter will be devoted to outlining a series of steps to provide a useful framework for developing an organizational change management purpose statement.

Step #1: Clearly define the objective of your change management initiative. An objective is a specific, measurable, and time-bound goal that the organization seeks to achieve. The goal must include specific details around desired changes (i.e., business process optimization, technology system deployment, workflow automation, workforce expansion, legacy system enhancement, revenue maximization, etc.). The objective must also address current organizational "pain points" that if left unaddressed, result in negative outcomes for the organization. The objective should also be forward looking and provide clarity around the desired "end state" of the initiative, along with expected outcomes, a thoughtful projection of organizational and individual benefits to be derived, and a listing of anticipated improvements that aligns with the scope of the initiative. Finally, the objective must appeal to stakeholders to the degree that it compels action, creates motivation for change, and anticipates a future state where stakeholders envision themselves thriving and growing with the organization.

Step #2: Identify all relevant stakeholders and determine their roles in order of significance as it pertains to influencing the implementation of the change initiative. Stakeholders previously discussed include project teams, customers & clients, suppliers, regulatory agencies, union representatives, shareholders & investors, and communities & local authorities. Recognizing interdependencies between stakeholder groups affects the order in which change is executed; therefore, documenting short-term and long-term requirements for each of the affected stakeholder groups will aid in developing critical path activities; a crucial outcome from the planning phase on the change implementation. While planning is the next pillar in the change continuum, understanding stakeholder requirements is central to formulating a cohesive purpose statement that considers the collective interests, needs, and concerns of the wider community.

Step #3: Now that you have developed strategic objectives and have identified the various stakeholder groups influencing the initiative, it's now time to put "pen to paper"! The first step involves crafting a clear and concise opening sentence that summarizes the purpose of the change initiative. The opening sentence needs to appeal to the basic premise of continuous improvement and be written in a way where the reader envisions themselves learning, growing, and improving with the organization. The statement must be straightforward and utilize action-oriented language with expected results within a specified time period.

For example, this brief purpose statement supports process optimization following a technology implementation:

Our purpose is to streamline processes, empower employees, and drive innovation for our customers and clients in order to achieve sustainable growth within the first 8 months following the deployment of the new technology solution.

The next example provides more details and seeks to address culture transformation as part of the organizational change management goal:

Our purpose is to transform our company culture by embracing a customer-centric approach, fostering collaboration with internal and external stakeholders, and promoting continuous learning across our departments and individual teams. Through this change initiative, we aim to enhance employee engagement, drive innovation through our customers, clients, and supplier networks, so as to deliver exceptional customer experience that maximizes shareholder value and ultimately positions our organization as a leader in the industry within the next twenty-four months.

Step #4: While organizational change is focused on improving specific areas within organizational life, it's important that goals align with the organization's mission, vision, and strategic objectives. In so doing, the change management initiative will serve as a catalyst that advances the long-term goals of the organization and contributes to the attainment of the organization's larger objectives. Alignment also entails reconciling stakeholder input with change goals, and ensuring that input and feedback are incorporated in the change management planning process. Finally, alignment requires that change leaders make adjustments where there are discrepancies, so that the purpose statement accurately embodies the initiative's objectives and aligns with stakeholder aspirations.

Step #5: Now that the purpose statement has been finalized, it's time to disseminate it across the organization. This communication process is essential to establishing proper stakeholder orientation, and to elicit their commitment and participation in the change process. Clear articulation of the change's objectives and anticipated benefits will also encourage participation, deepen understanding, and enlist support for the change initiative. In summary, the purpose statement serves as the governing principle and overarching statement that guides the entire change initiative, providing clarity and direction to all stakeholders involved and affected by the change.

Now that we know what a purpose statement is, let's lay out the steps, activities, and milestones that will be needed to achieve the stated goals. To do that, change leaders need to carefully plan all aspects of the organizational change management initiative. This is the topic of the next section, in which we will introduce the framework that governs planning activities around the organizational change management initiative.

Chapter 2

Planning

Introduction

It's June 2023, and my family and I have just returned from a *Royal Caribbean* cruise. While sailing we learned of a new ship that was getting ready for launch: "The Icon of the Seas." Recalling our recent voyage, we started to recount the many features of our vessel ("The Vision of the Seas") and how it contrasted with what was being advertised in this new megaship. Sure enough, there were some significant differences in gross tonnage, physical dimensions, number of passenger decks, size of the crew, and the total number of passengers, just to name a few. But besides the sheer vast opulence that these vessels commanded, what struck me most was the degree of planning that was needed to successfully construct arguably the world's largest cruise ship.

Meticulous planning allows architects to envision the "Icon of the Seas" in its entirety before a single plank is laid. Ship designers and architects carefully mapped out every intricate detail, identified design challenges, explored opportunities, and made informed decisions that streamlined and optimized the construction process.

DOI: 10.4324/9781003544883-3

Similarly, in organizational change management, effective planning empowers change leaders to "see the end from the beginning," foreseeing obstacles, defining effective risk mitigation strategies, and ensuring that—like the "Icon of the Seas"—the project sails smoothly toward its completion. In this regard, planning serves as the compass that guides us through the vast ocean of possibilities, ensuring a smooth voyage to our charted destination.

At the most foundational level, what is planning, and what are the essential criteria that establish an effective plan? Let's get to it by defining what planning is.

Definition of Planning

Organizational change planning is a methodical process used to detail a series of activities and steps needed to achieve the organization's strategic objectives. The process requires a careful and intentional coordination of resources, actions, and schedules to articulate and attain short and long-term goals. Organizational change planning requires anticipating and addressing obstacles, mitigating risks that threaten

> Planning defines actions that aligns with OCM goals while mitigating potential risks.

change goals, and devising creative strategies to maximize intended outcomes. Taking an expanded view, planning is the process through which individuals or groups define actions that align with the purpose of the organizational change initiative by strategically anticipating and mitigating risks that threaten the attainment of stated change goals. It involves a two-fold focus (i.e., task definition and risk mitigation) that enables change leaders to make educated decisions, effectively allocate and manage resources, execute cohesive action plans with timebound activities, and monitor the initiative against measurable outcomes, all while being flexible to unanticipated obstacles in order to ensure the attainment of both short-term and long-term goals. Based on this definition, what are the essential criteria for defining an effective organization change plan.

Effective Planning Framework

Several important considerations determine the extent to which organizational change activities are successful thereby requiring change leaders to objectively think about methods, processes, and tools needed to successfully effect change.

An effective planning framework,

- facilitates the transformation of intangible concepts into concrete steps and actions, and provides a roadmap to facilitate the attainment of organizational change objectives.
- outlines processes for defining clear objectives, resource availability, threats, and risks, and defines measures for effective stakeholder engagement.
- seeks to ensure long-term adoption of systems, tools, techniques, and processes, and provides strategic direction that bridges current capabilities and future objectives with clarity, objectivity, and adaptability.

In keeping with these strategic imperatives, the following establishes a series of steps aimed at defining an effective planning framework when undertaking organizational change:

Step #1—Define a clear scope: The most important step in establishing an effective change management plan starts with defining a clear scope. Defining the scope entails establishing the actions, commitments, and critical outcomes that are necessary to achieve the strategic goals of the change effort. This also includes detailing required deliverables, establishing schedules and implementation milestones, allocating personnel and resources, and defining interdependencies that would determine the critical path for the initiative. Conversely, scope definition also entails delineating activities, expectations, and outcomes that will be excluded from the execution of the change initiative. Defining scope exclusions is important as it establishes activities that will not be considered a part of the effort, thereby enabling change leaders to focus, effectively plan, allocate resources, and define implementation tasks only for activities considered "within-scope." Focusing on activities within the scope of the initiative provides implementation clarity and ultimately increases the likelihood that the change initiative will successfully focus and achieve its stated objectives.

Step #2—Define Key Performance Indicators: Another critical step in establishing an effective change management plan includes defining key performance indicators (KPI). A KPI is a measurable value that demonstrates how effectively an organization is achieving stated objectives. While we will delve into KPIs in the chapter on "Performance," KPIs serve as focal points for the improvement of both strategic and operational processes, provide an analytical foundation for decision-making, and ultimately direct attention to the performance of metrics deemed critical for the measurement of organizational change outcomes. The process of formulating KPIs is an essential component of strategic planning, as it is often relied upon by management to measure the degree to which organizational change objectives are being met. The scope of KPIs and how they are developed exceeds the focus of this section, however, the following serves as a brief summary on how to define KPIs:

a. *Align KPIs with Strategic Goals*: KPIs must first and foremost be aligned with the strategic goals of the change initiative, and by extension, KPIs should also be clearly associated with the strategic goals of the organization at large. They should provide an honest and unbiased measurement of progress for decision makers to fully comprehend how the initiative is progressing. Before KPIs can be aligned with the organization's strategic goals, develop a prioritized list of your initiative's most important goals first. This will then inform how goals will be evaluated relative to reported progress of the change initiative.

b. *Identify Critical Business Areas*: The prioritized list from the previous step will help to identify the critical business areas that will be affected by the change, for which your initiative will need to closely monitor. Critical business areas represent departments, business units, or other areas within the organization that are identified as the most important areas that will be affected by or need to adopt the outcomes of the change initiative. For example, the implementation of a cloud-based solution may be central to increasing revenues from the Sales and Marketing Departments. In this example, the Sales and Marketing Department would be considered a critical business area, as performance metrics will inform the degree to which sales have increased following the implementation of the technology solution. Other examples may include increasing response time for customer service, increasing production yields, or increasing charitable contributions within religious and/or non-profit organizations.

c. *Define Measurable Metrics*: Once the business area is identified, the next step will be to define a measurable metric that aligns with tangible/

observable performance. For example, management needs to monitor customer sentiment over a three-month period. One possible metric would be to quantify the number of positive reviews over the three-month window. Negative reviews would also factor into the evaluation, since the ratio of positive to negative reviews would provide a percentage value that can then be used as a metric of customer sentiment. Another example could be to use the results of a customer satisfaction survey to gauge the level of customer satisfaction in relation to the organization's products or services.

d. *Set Targets*: Now that metrics have been defined, prioritized, and aligned with critical business areas, it's now time to define thresholds and/or performance targets for each metric. This equips management with decision-making and analytical tools to objectively scrutinize the performance of defined metrics relative to stated goals. From there, corrective measures can be taken for improvement or course correction.

e. *Review Regularly*: KPIs have been defined, metrics established, and targets set. At this stage in the process, management can now frequently monitor KPI performance against established targets. In so doing, timely, relevant, and verifiable data relative to how the initiative is progressing can be quickly analyzed. Management may also make the determination to adjust if a KPI is routinely and easily achieved. This would signal that the performance standard is not rigorous enough and thus may require adjusting to ensure that the team is consistently pushing toward quality goals versus meeting easy targets. Conversely, if a KPI is routinely missed, this may also signal that the threshold is not achievable, that the goal is overly optimistic, or that there are underlying problems that need to be addressed and remedied. For this reason, KPI review and monitoring are essential to strategic and operational improvement of the change initiative.

Step #3—Develop a Schedule: Another important step in defining an effective change management plan is to develop a schedule that considers all relevant deliverables required for the change initiative's completion. This process is aided by the development of a Work Breakdown Structure (WBS) that defines all physical and tangible assets (i.e., work packages) to be produced and accepted as part of the implementation. Schedule development further involves defining critical delivery dates, establishing resource availability, completing task allocation, and defining project interdependencies that inform critical project milestones and deadlines.

In developing the WBS, there are a few considerations to be heeded to ensure work packages are properly defined. These considerations are answered with the following questions:

- Can change leaders accurately estimate the resources needed to produce work packages?
- Can leaders estimate how long the work packages will take to produce?
- Are work packages self-contained to the degree that if work needs to be reassigned, scope and delivery expectations are fully understood?
- Does the delivery of work packages fully constitute project completion?

These questions are foundational in defining the boundaries of the change initiative; thus, when developing an effective organizational change management plan, it's critical to establish clarity around work package definitions and implementation delivery expectations.

Finally, schedule development is an action-oriented activity that details a list of activities or tasks to be accomplished, along with establishing relevant tasks relationships, estimating task durations, and making resource assignments based on availability. However, to keep the initiative on schedule, it is often advised to include schedule contingencies to allow for uncertainty and associated implementation risks. Scheduling contingencies provide additional time allocation beyond estimated durations to minimize downline impacts to other related tasks and activities.

Step #4—Evaluate Resource Constraints: In the previous section the concept of resource availability was introduced; however, while discussions around this topic are often limited to personnel availability, a resource is a much more encompassing term. Therefore, effective organizational change planning must go further and establish a comprehensive view on how resource availability can impact organizational change initiatives. Resources are defined as assets, materials, tools, or personnel required to successfully execute the change initiative. Resource constraints, therefore, describe limitations or impediments that inhibit their use and thus impact the execution of the change initiative. A summary of resources includes the following examples:

a. Human Resources: These include organizational change stakeholders who serve in the roles of project administrators, team members, subject matter experts, and any other project participants. Human resources provide the necessary knowledge, abilities, and expertise necessary to complete assigned duties.

b. Financial Resources: This is one of the most important assets that can alter the execution of the change

initiative. Financial resources represent the project's
spending authority and are the source from which
project-related expenses are drawn. Financial resources
enable the acquisition of equipment, technical services,
and other project-related services necessary to achieve
organizational change objectives.

c. Physical Resources: Physical resources facilitate
the execution of project activities and represent
tangible assets that are needed to support daily
operations. Physical resources may include office
space, equipment, machinery, vehicles, technology
infrastructure, and other tangible assets required to
support the change initiative.

d. Information and Knowledge Resources: Information
and knowledge resources enable organizational change
execution by facilitating decision-making, analysis, and
intra-organizational communication. These resources,
which often include technology systems, include
database repositories, software systems, project and
organizational documentation, research materials, and
other sources of information that enable the success of
the change initiative.

e. External Resources: These are resources acquired from
outside the organization to provide essential services,
technical expertise, and necessary products to facilitate
the attainment of organizational goals. External
resources may include consultants, contractors,
suppliers, vendors, and other external entities
who are relied upon to ensure successful change
implementation.

Effective organizational change planning therefore
considers the availability of resources along with their
associated constraints, to devise strategies to ensure
that organizational change goals are achieved. Failure

to account for resource constraints may ultimately result in implementation delays, quality concerns, budget overruns, and personnel-related issues. For this reason, effective resource management requires defining all necessary resources needed to support the initiative, estimating their availability, acquiring and allocating them appropriately, and

> **Effective resource analysis enhances project efficacy, mitigates risk, and increases the project's probability of success.**

ultimately ensuring their optimal utilization. Ultimately, effective resource analysis enhances project efficacy, mitigates risk, and increases the probability of success for the change initiative.

Step #5—Management of Risk: Risk management, at its core, is the process that identifies potential impediments, threats, and uncertainties that could threaten the success of the change initiative, while employing measures and/or solutions to lessen their likelihood of occurrence. Within the context of organizational change, risk management refers to the systematic process that is aimed at identifying, assessing, and reducing the negative impacts associated with the change. The process proactively adopts strategies that anticipate obstacles, challenges, and complex reactions that emerge during the change process. The key elements involved in an effective risk management strategy are summarized in the following:

a. Risk Identification: The process that identifies risks and weaknesses resulting from internal and/or external factors that may impede the change initiative.

b. Risk Assessment: The process of evaluating the likelihood, impact, and severity of occurrence for each risk identified, and ordering risks in order of importance.

    c. Risk Mitigation: The process of developing strategies and actions aimed at reducing or eliminating the chances of identified risks occurring.

    d. Risk Monitoring: The continuous process of monitoring and reassessing risks throughout the change initiative to ensure that new risks are mitigated. Previously identified risks are kept under close watch.

Given that organizational change introduces a fair degree of uncertainty and disruption within the organization, risk management is a critical planning exercise with its singular focus being to minimize negative consequences associated with the change while utilizing methods to maximize organizational change success.

Step #6—Stakeholder Management: The first pillar in the organizational change continuum explored the criticality of defining a purpose statement, and in that chapter, an exhaustive review of various types of stakeholders was performed. Within context of this chapter that is focused on change management planning, development of a stakeholder management plan is central to codifying stakeholders' expectations, address their concerns, and taking proactive measures to ensure active involvement in the decision-making process. For this reason, stakeholder management is a critical planning process that requires an efficient strategy that solicits participation from all pertinent stakeholders affected by the initiative. The stakeholder management plan therefore documents stakeholder requirements, expectations, aspirations, and suggestions. The plan is conceptualized very early in the planning stages, to encourage teamwork, validate stakeholder input, and solidify buy-in needed to increase the chances of success for the initiative.

Finally, and in addition to providing structure and direction, a well-developed stakeholder management plan anticipates changes, and provides flexible and adaptable processes to facilitate changing stakeholder requirements.

Feasibility and Sustainability Analysis: The final step in developing an effective planning framework concludes with assessing the plan's feasibility and sustainability. An efficient plan considers both feasibility and sustainability components, while taking into account environmental, social, and economic considerations. This expansive viewpoint is needed to guarantee that the plan is in line with long-term sustainability goals, and by extension, the organizational change initiative's objectives. In so doing, long-term success is much more likely to be achieved by adopting a strategy that prioritizes stakeholder interests and promotes responsible business practices, thereby increasing the chances of success for the organizational change initiative.

Models, Frameworks, and Methodologies

The corporate world is constantly evolving, and with it, organizations must adapt and embrace change to stay competitive and adjust to new environments, whether that change is prompted by new technologies, shifting markets, or internal enhancements. To successfully undertake organizational change initiatives, organizations often employ change management methodologies that guide their change process.

> Long-term success is more achievable through a strategy that prioritizes stakeholder interests and promotes responsible business practices.

Selecting the most appropriate change methodology is not a random undertaking, but rather a deliberative process that is aligned with the organization's strategic goals and embedded culture. Since choosing the right methodology establishes the groundwork for implementing a systematic and productive organizational change strategy, change leaders need to be familiar with the various theoretical constructs, strategies, and diagnostic tools, while fully grasping their advantages and differences. It is therefore imperative for change leaders to develop a thorough understanding of these constructs since the chosen strategy will ultimately influence all aspects of the change initiative.

While a detailed exposition of all the possible change management theories is well beyond the scope of this chapter, a summarization of proven models, that includes a discussion around the underlying principles, methods, techniques, and processes, is pertinent to empowering change leaders with the requisite skills and knowledge necessary for their adoption. Therefore, the following is a summary of some of the most effective constructs, strategies, and diagnostic tools that are often employed during organizational change, providing change leaders with critical information needed to inform key decisions pertinent to organizational change management planning. The first model for discussion is The Lewin's Change Management Model.

The Lewin's Change Management Model

The Kurt Lewin's Change Management Model is one of the most widely recognized and influential frameworks for understanding and managing organizational change. Developed in the 1940s by social psychologist Kurt Lewin, this three-phase model emerged from Lewin's study of force field analysis that examined both "driving" and "resisting" forces associated with change initiatives. Driving forces are motivating levers that create the necessary desire to adopt change. Conversely, resisting forces act as impediments and barriers that oppose change. While Lewin's model provides a structured approach that guides individuals, teams, and organizations through change, Lewin contends that for change to occur, driving forces must outweigh resisting forces, and this "force-field" imbalance is central for making positive behavioral shifts by instilling a feeling of urgency, followed by change instantiation, and culminating with the assimilation of the new state within the organization.

> In Force-Field Analogy, driving forces must outweigh resisting forces to achieve lasting change.

Lewin summarizes these core activities in three phases: (a) unfreezing, (b) change initiation, and (c) refreezing.

The underlying principle that governs driving and resisting forces is predicated on the notion of homeostasis. According to Cameron and Green, homeostasis is the tendency for an organization to maintain its equilibrium in response to disruptive organizational changes, to the degree that when change confronts an organization, internal forces are exerted that seek to maintain the organization's status quo by normalizing and eliminating the threat of disruptive change. Therefore, to ensure change permanence, Lewin contends that new organizational states must be intentionally defined, pursued, and implemented while moderating the counterbalancing forces that resist its adoption.

It's against this backdrop that Lewin's model provides guidance by laying out a structured approach that guides individuals, teams, and organizations through the process of change. This process is first initiated by instilling a sense of urgency to establish the premise for the change effort (unfreezing), followed by tactical execution of activities that operationalize the change (change initiation), and finally, culminating with the consolidation of the new organizational state that establishes new ways of thinking, acting, and operating (refreezing). These three stages are further described in the following:

> *Unfreezing*: In this stage, the status quo is challenged and the case to adopt new systems, processes, or enhancements is advanced. In this unfreezing stage, the problem statement compels action and prepares individuals and the organization for imminent change. The preparation involves creating a psychological state of readiness that illuminates a desired future state, while dismantling the mindset of dysfunction that has resulted in inefficient processes, methods, or systems. The underlying premise in this stage is centered on the fact that individuals, and by extension the organization, will likely embrace the case advanced for change if the benefits are clearly understood, and people are individually willing to let go of old behaviors and attitudes as reified by the status quo. This stage is very important in shifting the culture of the organization; thus, here are four key tenets for this transitional stage of unfreezing:
>
> a. *Make the Case*: Leaders make the case for the change by creating a sense of urgency. They do this by articulating a compelling reason for the change, while highlighting the risks and opportunities associated with maintaining the status quo.
>
> b. *Build the Case*: Advocacy becomes the next critical activity after the case is advanced. In this step, change leaders build a coalition from executives, business sponsors, and other influential stakeholders who can advocate for change and provide timely support throughout the continuum of the change process.
>
> c. *Support the Case*: In this stage, change leaders solicit and collect feedback about the change process, benefits to be realized, and the tangible improvements that are being undertaken across the organization.

This process creates awareness about the change
and solicits individuals from across the organization
to share their perspectives, concerns, and sources of
concern that can impede the change. This is critical as
it fosters trust and conveys the impression that change
is being done *with* you, versus *to* you.

d. *Implement the Case*: Before the change goes into
effect, people must not only know about it, but
they must be prepared to adopt it. This requires
providing education and training across all areas of the
organization that will be impacted by the change, to
equip them with the necessary knowledge and skills
to adapt to forthcoming changes.

Since Lewin introduced his three-stage model, other
change pioneers have referenced and elaborated upon this
seminal work, one of whom is Edgar Schein. Schein's Model
of transformative change gained popularity in the late 1990s
with his published works *Process Consultation* (Schein, 1969)
and *Organizational Culture and Leadership* (Schein, 2004).
Drawing from the discipline of clinical psychology and group
dynamics, Schein's model influenced the field of organizational
development by providing a wider perspective to Lewin's
organizational unfreezing, changing, and refreezing construct.
Schein expanded on these three phases recognizing that
stakeholders who are going through change not only wrestle
with the organizational context but must also reconcile the
change through the lens of an individual. For this reason,
Schein argues that the individual must first go through the
difficult and sometimes uncomfortable process of unlearning
legacy methods, processes, and tools associated with the
status quo—similar to Lewin's unfreezing stage.

The process further requires the individual to confront
two forces; the first is the force of learning anxiety, and the
second is the force of survival anxiety. Learning anxiety is

described as the fear that is associated with adopting new states of being that requires learning new skills, methods, tools, and processes to become a proficient and effective organizational contributor. In their book, "Making Sense of Change Management," Cameron and Green posit that individuals grappling with learning anxiety often ask themselves evaluative questions such as: Will I fail? Will I be exposed? (Cameron & Green, 2015). These questions are precursors to the next competing force: the force of survival anxiety. While learning anxiety is premised on the need to learn, survival anxiety is predicated by the pressure to change. Thus, individuals ask a different set of questions, which include: what if I don't agree, conform to, or simply don't change? These questions are more probative to the extent that individuals assess consequences relating their response to external demands for change. Questions such as, what consequences will I face? Will I lose place within the organization? Will I get left behind? Will I be fired? These fears often bear tangible impact and result in a flood of individual introspection, the outcome of which yields behavioral conformance. While the individual may adjust to avoid negative consequences, their adherence must not be confused as agreement, but rather as an avoidance strategy to defer untimely and unwanted negative consequences. The astute change leader will recognize this difference and cater to the concerns or issues that undermine future loyalty in the next phase of change initiation.

> *Change Initiation*: The changing stage is where the proverbial "rubber meets the road," since it is the stage where change leaders begin the arduous process of implementing changes that require adopting new behaviors, processes, systems, or new organizational structures. This is the stage of turbulence, as the status quo is often difficult to upend. In addition to upending

the status quo, managing active and passive resistance, optimizing stakeholder engagement, and utilizing communication strategies to combat disinformation can often make this stage challenging. Change leaders therefore employ several strategies during this stage, some of which include:

a. *Communicate the vision*: As was done in the unfreezing stage, leaders articulate the reason for the change, highlighting the risks and opportunities associated with maintaining the status quo, but go a step further and paint a clear picture of a future state along with the benefits that will accompany it. This does two things: it recapitulates the organizational change objective that is grounded in a business case for the change, and second, it brokers the opportunity to create a shared vision that aligns individuals within the organization with the strategic goals of the change initiative.

b. *Empower the team*: One of the most important ingredients in the change process is ownership. Ownership fosters commitment to the extent that individuals become more committed to the success of the initiative when they are personally invested in its outcomes. Ownership also helps to quell resistance. This is particularly significant when individuals are included in the decision-making process and are able to give voice to the outcomes of the change process. This notion is predicated on an important principle: People are more likely to embrace the change, versus resist it, when they have given input into shaping the outcomes. Ownership also provides opportunities for accountability, collaboration, and participation: all of which serve as enablers to the change initiative by empowering individuals and teams to implement, adopt, and champion the outcomes of the initiative.

c. *Remove barriers*: In any change initiative, there are often barriers to success. Some common barriers to organizational change include: lack of sponsorship, inadequate communication, active/passive resistance, rigid organizational culture, lack of interest and thus commitment from those required to embrace the change, insufficient number of resources, just to name a few! Lewin's model recognizes the impediments that these barriers impose and thus requires change leaders to identify and take requisite action to remove obstacles that may hinder the change process. Actions often require finding creative ways to improve human-social interaction across the organization, taking decisive action to revise restrictive policies, prioritize and reallocate critical resources, and providing additional support through coaching and mentoring to help people navigate challenges while building confidence in adopting new ways of thinking and working.

Schein's Model of transformative change further expands on Lewin's two remaining stages of "changing" and "refreezing." In the changing phase, Schein explains that new concepts and new meanings for old concepts are pursued. During the "changing" phase, individuals begin to decouple the previous organizational state from the future state and begin the process of identifying and imitating new roles within their new organizational construct through trial and error, (Cameron & Green, 2015). In the final stage of refreezing, individuals internalize new concepts and meanings and find new ways to incorporate self-concept and identity while forming new relationships within the organization.

A close examination of Schein's model highlights the centrality of the "individual," the need to understand their unique journey through change, and their need to confront anxiety and fears. In addition to confronting individual learning and survival anxieties, Schein further lists four fears that the individual must overcome that are pivotal to change adoption:

■ Fear of temporary incompetence: The awareness of one's lack of competence to adequately adjust, adopt, and fulfill organizational responsibilities following the change effort;
■ Fear of punishment for incompetence: One's apprehension of being identified, singled out, or embarrassed for not being adequately skilled or competent to undertake new organizational roles or duties;
■ Fear of loss of personal identity: The internal turmoil one feels when their sense of self, as defined by their perceived role in the organization, is changed, threatened, or diminished because of the role no longer being valued or needed.
■ Fear of loss of group membership: The destabilizing effect of losing access, privilege, affiliation, and benefits from a group once served. The loss of membership may be due to organizational shifts in priority for the role, thereby affecting one's identity within the organization, and ultimately group memberships.

Each of these fears must be confronted to set in motion the next phase of refreezing.

Refreezing: Refreezing is the final stage in Lewin's Change Management Model. The refreezing stage seeks to provide continuity and stability from the earlier stage of conflict and aims to integrate new and permanent changes into the organization's culture and operations. Refreezing involves establishing new behaviors, reinforcing positive outcomes, and implementing processes to sustain the change in the long term. The methods employed in the previous stages to manage resistance, enlist leadership support, communicate regularly and accurately, and utilize strategies to build effective human-social collaboration, are all critical for this stage. Change leaders therefore employ strategies to foster change permanence during the refreezing period, some of which include:

a. *Celebrating successes*: During this stage, change leaders recognize and celebrate achievements resulting from the change. These achievements are often tied to KPIs discussed earlier and seek to provide a quantifiable basis for measuring change permanence. Additionally, celebrating successes serves to reinforce positive behaviors, boosts morale, and act as a "bonding catalyst" that glues the team together. When successes are celebrated, it further increases the likelihood that others within the organization will be motivated to perform/repeat behaviors and/or activities that are deemed positive. When acknowledgment of individual successes is carefully and strategically implemented, it ultimately motivates individual adoption of new behaviors and/or systems across the organization, and brokers change one person at a time.

b. *Embedding changes in culture*: In continuation to celebrating successes, finding creative ways to achieve change permanence is critical to making the desired changes a part of the organization's culture and values. Change leaders employ a variety of methods to ensure change adoption, including aligning policies, processes, and performance management systems to support and sustain the change, and taking the necessary steps to encourage human-social collaboration before and after the change initiative. Human-social collaboration emphasizes the value and power of collective intelligence, engagement, and collaboration needed to achieve successful change outcomes. Therefore, by fostering collaboration, organizations tap into the collective capabilities of their stakeholder groups, enhance problem-solving and innovation, and create a supportive and collaborative culture that embraces change.

c. *Providing ongoing support and reinforcement*: In the earlier section of "unfreezing," we discussed the need to prepare people to adopt change. The preparatory work that included providing education and training across all areas of the organization is recapitulated in this final stage. Thus, providing ongoing support and reinforcement, providing access to on-demand learning, and providing escalation methods for on-demand support all serve as critical enablers for change permanence. In the end, people will feel ready to adopt the change they were prepared to make!

d. *Evaluating and learning*: In addition to taking the necessary steps to ensure change permanence, effective change leaders implement measures to assess the effectiveness of the change implementation by gathering and analyzing individual feedback from across the organization. In so doing, leaders can collate various data points from which information can be derived to inform areas for improvement and learning for future change initiatives.

Lewin's Change Management model systematically navigates the stages of unfreezing, changing, and refreezing, to increase the likelihood of successful change implementation. While Lewin's model emphasizes the importance of engaging people, confronting sources of resistance, and creating a supportive environment utilizing three specific phases of engagement, other models build upon the central tenets of human-social interaction as the foundation for adopting an effective organizational change management methodology. One such example is Kotter's 8-Step Change Model, a model that we will review next.

Kotter's 8-Step Change Model

The Kotter 8-Step Change Model, introduced by John Kotter in 1995, was derived from his analysis of 100 different organizations going through change. The model provides a linear and structured approach to organizational change, highlighting eight fundamental lessons that serve as the backdrop for his famous 8-Step model. The model conceptualizes essential power levers that are critical for change enablement while underscoring the importance of creating a sense of urgency and articulating a clear vision for all affected stakeholders across the entire organization (Cameron & Green, 2015).

In his book "A Sense of Urgency," Kotter makes the case that creating a sense of urgency is the predicate for successful organizational change. Against this backdrop, Kotter provides a practical framework that helps leaders manage change systematically, reduce the likelihood of failure, and increase the odds of success by providing clear steps and processes. The model therefore places an emphasis on building a sense of urgency, putting together a steering coalition, conceiving a clear vision, delegating authority to people, and managing the change effort through a series of steps. As will be expanded upon shortly, each step in Kotter's 8-Step Model focuses on a different aspect of the change process, thus, neglecting any step may significantly impact the effectiveness of the overall change initiative. Following is a summary of Kotter's 8-Step Change Model:

Step #1: Create Urgency. The first step in Kotter's 8-Step Change Model, "Create Urgency," is arguably one of the most crucial parts of any change management initiative, since it lays the groundwork to assess the organization's openness and readiness to adopt change, while articulating the case why change is urgently needed. Creating urgency therefore describes the process of persuading individuals that a change is indeed required, and that it must take place immediately. Change leaders articulate urgency through a clear and sincere recognition of market realities, competitive forces, or legal obligations that mandate change, thereby encouraging individuals to abandon the status quo in pursuit of a more efficient and effective organization. While creating too much urgency can backfire and result in panic and confusion, here are a few strategies leaders must consider when creating urgency for change:

- *Initiate Open Dialogue*: Facilitate open and honest dialogue with stakeholders about the need for change, along with frank discussions around consequences if ignored.
- *Present Convincing Reasons with supporting evidence*: Provide honest and convincing reasons to get people thinking and talking about what needs to change. Discussions can start with reflections about market conditions, changing competitive strategies, declining consumer sentiment, compliance with city or state mandates, or simply the need for revenue maximization and cost containment.
- *Articulate Dangers of Status Quo*: Articulate the business case for the change so that individuals can identify and experience the pain of maintaining the status quo, while yearning for resolutions to prevailing business problems.
- *Engage Key Stakeholders*: Build a change coalition that includes important stakeholders in the early stages of the change process. Stakeholder involvement will lend credibility to the change initiative and increase the likelihood that others in the organization will also perceive the business case as credible and critical.
- *Communicate Consistently and Regularly*: Provide frequent communication about the urgency for change to create and maintain momentum. Since messaging is

critical in this step, change leaders should discuss the urgency in large forums, small meetings, and in one-on-one conversations to reiterate the urgency around the change initiative.

Step #2: Form a Powerful Coalition: Step two of Kotter's 8-Step Change Model requires forming a powerful coalition that includes a wide range of organizational stakeholders to support and drive the change process. This group is focused on conveying accurate and consistent messaging around the change initiative and serving as "champions" of the change initiative. Since organizational change cannot be implemented by a single person, an effective coalition of influential stakeholders facilitate critical recruitment activities necessary for garnering support from across the organization. They do this by:

■ *Identifying Influencers*: These are organizational leaders who can influence their peers and subordinates to embrace change based on their positions of influence within the organization.

■ *Engaging with Fellow-Change Champions*: These are stakeholders who are passionate about the change, either due to the risk of loss, incentive for financial gain, or are simply committed to the change due to their track record of supporting organizational innovation.

■ *Ensuring Diversity*: The coalition, ideally composed of stakeholders from all levels of the organization, brokers effective communication, facilitate diverse perspectives, and inspire others to participate in the initiative.

■ *Building Trust*: A powerful coalition relies on trust among its members. This can be built by having open and honest discussions, acknowledging contributions, addressing concerns, and following through on stakeholder commitments to meet their expectations.

- *Developing a Shared Vision*: While messaging is critical, defining a shared vision is essential. The coalition must therefore have a shared understanding of the change initiative, sufficient to guide collective actions and decisions in pursuit of the group's shared interests and goals.
- *Empowering the Coalition*: Armed with a shared vision and a diverse team of change champions, the coalition must be entrusted with the power to lead the change initiative. This is conveyed through funding appropriations, personnel assignments, access to information systems, and provisioning of organizational assets that equip them to successfully effect change across the organization.

Step #3: Create a Vision for Change: Creating a clear and easy-to-understand vision is essential to convey a picture of the future that ultimately will garner stakeholder interest and support. As noted earlier, a clear vision clarifies why the change is being undertaken while highlighting the various impacts and consequences of maintaining the status quo. It further codifies the roles that individuals will play post the change initiative, to recruit support, build desire, and ultimately secure willingness for its adoption. To meet this standard, effective change leaders include many—if not all—of the following attributes when developing vision statements:

- *Clarity*: Articulate a vision statement that clearly and concisely defines where the organization is headed, how it will look after the change, and how it will be different from the current organizational state.
- *Inspirational*: The vision statement should inspire and motivate stakeholders to action, leveraging emotions and the sense of excitement about future possibilities amidst current challenges.

- *Future-oriented*: The vision statement must be future-oriented, challenge the status quo, and encourage stakeholders to think beyond present circumstances.
- *Strategic Alignment*: The vision must align with the organization's strategic objectives and be consistent with the organization's mission, values, and long-term goals.
- *Realistic and Achievable*: While the vision should be aspirational, it should also be realistic. Therefore, an effective vision statement must be grounded in the capabilities and resources of the organization and should be achievable within a defined timeframe.
- *Easily Communicated*: The vision should be "crisp" and easy to share without distortion or distraction.

Step #4: Communicate the Vision: The fourth stage of Kotter's 8-stage Change Model, "Communicate the Vision," involves communicating the change's vision throughout the organization. Once the vision for change has been created, it needs to be communicated frequently and powerfully and embedded into everything the organization does. Communication is an essential ingredient for organizational change since it facilitates the dissemination of the initiative's purpose, process, methods, and intended benefits to affected stakeholders. To ensure that the vision is not only known but also understood, accepted, and implemented, change leaders utilize the following strategies to ensure its dissemination across the organization:

- *Simplicity*: Express the vision as simply as possible in order to assure clarity and prevent confusion by avoiding technical jargon and obscure terminology.
- *Consistency*: Continually seek ways to share the vision across the organization with a high degree of frequency, leveraging communication channels, key leaders, and essential stakeholders from across the organization.

An important tenet of effective communication is to communicate frequently. This ensures that messages are heard, but more importantly, remembered and understood across all stakeholder groups.

■ *Multiple Channels*: In addition to communicating consistently, change leaders must also leverage all available communication channels, including meetings, emails, newsletters, internal print materials, social media, etc.

■ *Interaction and Dialogue*: Encourage discussion about the vision, solicit input, and utilize shared comments to help frame the decision-making process.

Step #5: Remove Obstacles: The fifth stage of Kotter's 8-Stage Change Model focuses on identifying and removing obstacles that impede the change initiative. Obstacles take many forms, including obsolete processes, systems, and structures, as well as active and passive resistance to adopting change objectives. Kotter's fifth step therefore seeks to identify people or processes that may resist change, and work to remove these barriers utilizing the following strategies:

■ *Identify Potential Hurdles*: Change leaders begin by recognizing potential hurdles to change. These impediments may include physical limitations such as outdated technologies, procedures, or structures, or intangible limitations such as attitudes, anxieties, or the general aversion to adopting the change.

■ *Address Structural concerns*: Review and redefine organizational structures, job duties, performance systems, or incentive programs that are not aligned with the organization's strategic imperatives.

■ *Address Resistant Attitudes*: Stakeholder attitudes and actions rooted in fear of the unknown, loss of control, or even uncertainty about the viability of the change can all cause resistance. Leaders should address these concerns openly, and provide assurances in order to build trust and commitment to the change.

■ *Empower Action*: Provide incentives that encourage stakeholders to take action. Recognize and reward people who, through their actions, exemplify the change initiative's vision. This serves as an essential motivator, inspiring individuals to do the same since they are less likely to reject change if they believe they have the power to impact it.

■ *Provide assistance and training*: Provide many training opportunities for stakeholders to develop the new skills needed for change adoption. This enables individuals to assimilate into new positions and assume new roles for which the acquisition of new skills is required. Ultimately, training programs facilitate the development of critical workforce competencies to narrow skill gaps and facilitate the adoption of new organizational systems and processes.

■ *Address Organizational Culture and Norms*: If existing organizational culture and norms are not supportive of change, they can be significant impediments to the initiative. Therefore, effective change leaders create a culture that promotes change, encourages creativity, and provides the necessary support systems required for individual and collective adaptation.

Step #6: Create Short-term Wins: Nothing motivates more than success, and that is the premise of Kotter's sixth step. Creating short-term wins is predicated around the concept of celebrating small, tangible victories early and often throughout the change process. These small victories, punctuated milestones, or short-term wins represent accomplishments, desired outcomes, or behaviors that are consistent with the change initiative's goals. Creating short-term wins is an essential enabler for long-term change adoption, as it serves as a motivating catalyst, provides confirmation that the initiative is achieving intended results, and inspires action that builds momentum toward additional change adoption.

Change leaders often create short-term wins by adopting one or more of the following strategies:

- *Plan for Success*: Intentionally seek areas for improvement that are easily achievable and consistent with the change initiative's strategic objectives.
- *Pick Simple Targets*: Go after "low hanging fruits" by looking for opportunities in which the team can make immediate and tangible improvements.
- *Communicate Wins*: Celebrate progress immediately and share victories with the entire organization. Be intentional to thank those whose efforts made the victory possible to inspire similar action across the organization.
- *Analyze Successes*: Use short-term wins as a learning opportunity by analyzing what led to the success and how it can be replicated.
- *Build on Success*: Use recent successes as a springboard for future action, decision, and planning; since, each victory can ultimately inspire greater change and thereby create momentum for the initiative.

Step #7: Build on the Change: While the prior step emphasizes the importance of celebrating early wins, Kotter argues that many change projects fail because victory is sometimes declared too early. While celebrating "quick wins" help to inspire momentum and demonstrate that the change initiative is progressing, real lasting change requires cultural reorientation that only occurs after the desired change, behaviors, and processes are frequently repeated with confidence. Therefore, each success must serve as the building block for developing and deepening competencies while building confidence to adopt successive levels of planned change. For this reason, effective change leaders are careful to:

■ *Build and Maintain Momentum*: Celebrate short-term wins, but ensure that they are seen as building blocks toward the long-term attainment of organizational change objectives.

■ *Learn from Successes*: Cultivate an environment of continuous learning by identifying success enablers, and finding creative ways to leverage their use for future activities.

■ *Drive Deeper Change*: Leverage goodwill based on previously celebrated wins, and use earned credibility to confront deeper-seated organizational norms, entrenched attitudes, and behaviors, while proposing new and more efficient organizational structures.

■ *Build Capacity*: Deepen the resource pool by hiring and/or promoting individuals from within the organization who align with the change initiative's strategic objectives and who can provide additional value in accelerating change permanence.

Step #8: Anchor the Changes in Corporate Culture: In order to achieve change permanence, steps must now be intentionally taken to engrain new processes, systems, tools, and techniques into the fabric of the organization. This is essential since cultural change is often the hardest and most resistant part of the change process. Achieving lasting change, therefore, requires time, patience, consistent effort, and commitment from leadership to see the change through and to maintain it over time. The entire cross-section of the organization is needed to adopt new organizational norms, embrace shared values, adopt new technology and performance systems, and codify behaviors that warrant individual rewards. Therefore, to achieve these goals, effective change leaders employ a variety of strategies that aid in facilitating long-term change adoption, some of which include:

■ *Align Culture with Change*: This is a recurring theme from the first pillar of "Purpose Definition"; thus, change activities must support useful components of the organization's culture while seeking to transform elements that are not.

■ *Reinforce Desired Behavior*: Implement processes to facilitate long-term adoption of new processes, methods, tools, and techniques. This is critical, since change permanence is dependent on equipping individuals with change-supporting behaviors that lead to require changes being engrained in the culture of the organization.

■ *Integrate Organizational Practices*: In addition to behavioral alignment, organizational process realignment—ranging from recruiting, training, and technology and workflow adoption—will be necessary to consistently reinforce organizational changes, until required changes become ingrained in the organization's daily functioning.

■ *Communicate Regularly*: Identify and communicate the relationships between new behaviors and organizational change adoption successes on a regular basis.

■ *Leadership Support*: Finally, leaders should model the change they want to see in their subordinates as they continue to support and champion the change across all levels of the organization.

Both Lewin's Change Management Model and Kotter's 8-Step Change Model are widely respected frameworks for managing change. Even though each model is unique in some ways, they share one important similarity: focus on the "organizational view" perspective.

The next model—the ADKAR model—departs from this perspective and provides an individualized approach to embracing change and will be the topic of our next section.

The ADKAR Model

The ADKAR change management model, developed by Jeff Hiatt and the Prosci research organization, provides a unique perspective on change adoption by emphasizing the centrality of the individual's capacity to embrace and adopt change. ADKAR, a well-respected model in the change management discipline, represents the stages that people go through when adjusting to change. The stages—Awareness, Desire, Knowledge, Ability, and Reinforcement, provides a simplistic, practical, and linear approach that serves as the foundation of organizational transformation.

> ADKAR provides a simplistic, practical, and linear approach to organizational transformation.

The central tenet of ADKAR recognizes that organizations are made up of individuals, thereby requiring individuals to undergo change individually before change can become entrenched organizationally. Since change leaders must effectively articulate the purpose and urgency for change, let's examine each of these stages from an individual's perspective.

- *Awareness:* Awareness represents the first and most important building block of the ADKAR model, as it emphasizes the need for individuals to comprehend and embrace the reasons why change is, in fact, needed, and by extension, its derivative benefits and risks. In this step, it is vital for change leaders to provide honest, transparent, and succinct communication for the individual to accept the first step in traversing the change continuum. Effective change leaders broker discussions around the potential effects on the organization and articulate the potential effects that the change may have on the individual. This discussion not only entails changes that are positive, but also necessitates frank and honest dialog about the possible consequences that may result if the change is not implemented. At this stage, individual receptivity to the message of change is vital; however, while receiving the message of change is important, awareness by itself does not imply individual acceptance of the change initiative. For this reason, the model requires advancing to the next stage to influence individual openness by building their desire for the change.

■ *Desire* Now that there is awareness of the need for change, the next step is to build desire. The process of building desire focuses on creating a personal drive to support and participate in the change initiative. This stage requires personal reflection, as the individual must consider the benefits, threats, and opportunities in order to assess the value of the change to themselves. They perform this assessment seeking to answer the fundamental question "what's in it for me?." Answers to this probative question demonstrates how the change initiative aligns with their personal values, goals, and desires. For this reason, effective and influential leadership that emphasizes the benefits of change plays a crucial role in fostering individual desire to embrace and participate in the change. Recognition of the change, and building desire to support the change are two important milestones along the ADKAR change continuum; however, change leaders must be able to answer the questions "who, what, where, why, and when" to fully appreciate the scope and impact of the change. Establishing this framework is critical in developing knowledge about the change, and thus the focus of the next building block—knowledge.

- *Knowledge* This phase in the ADKAR model focuses on equipping individuals with the necessary information and skills to navigate the change successfully. In this stage, individual training sessions are provided to facilitate learning new skills, adopting new behaviors, or assuming new roles in the organization. This stage also marks an important inflection point as individuals begin to make the mental shift from "change is coming" to "change is here." To achieve success in this phase, it is, therefore, necessary to have a variety of training and support resources tailored to the specific roles that individuals will be required to assume at the conclusion of the change initiative. As a predicate to combating misinformation in the organization, it may also be advantageous for individuals to understand not only the technical aspects of the change, but also grasp the underlying management concepts and principles requiring its adoption. This equips the individual navigating the change process with the requisite ability to respond to technical, ideological, and philosophical oppositions they may encounter from those opposing the change within the organization. While knowledge is essential for change adoption, developing the requisite ability to sustain the change is essential for change permanence, and that is the next building block.
- *Ability* Building on the acquired knowledge, individuals are now equipped to apply their new skills effectively, putting their newly acquired information into practice, and demonstrating competencies necessary for long-term success. Recognizing that individuals are emerging from the learning process, change leaders provide support, coaching, and mentoring to help individuals overcome any obstacles or challenges so that new roles, duties, and responsibilities can be successfully assumed. Further, effective change leaders foster an environment that

encourages experimentation, learning, and continuous improvement for individuals to develop skill-mastery for the new roles and duties they will assume. The adage, "it is one thing to comprehend what is required, but it is an entirely different thing to be capable of doing what is required" is most certainly true in the field of change management. It is this truism that requires effective change leaders to provide opportunities for continuous learning that aids in reinforcing the skills and abilities needed for organizational change success, and thus the topic of the last building block—reinforcement.

■ *Reinforcement* represents the final stage in the ADKAR model and involves taking the necessary steps to ensure change permanence. This stage not only requires skills-maintenance, but also involves employing strategic reward processes to aid in long-term change adoption. This final stage of reinforcement therefore requires change leaders to celebrate achievements and reward positive behaviors that lead to long-term change adoption. For this reason, consistent communication, along with frequent, visible, and genuine support from leadership, all play a crucial role to prevent individuals from reverting to old habits and behaviors, especially when under pressure or placed in challenging situations.

The ADKAR model's strengths are its simplicity, flexibility, and its focus on the human side of change. The model can be used to make both small and big changes, and it is easy to understand and put into practice. Also, by focusing on the human side of organizational change, ADKAR makes the point that effective lasting change is predicated on individual acceptance and adoption of change, since change happens "one person at a time."

Like all models, ADKAR is not devoid of its own set of limitations. In fact, that which is considered its strength—its simplistic and linear ease of use—often makes it hard to confront complicated and deep-seated changes that are needed in the organization. Further, while ADKAR focuses on individual change as the building block of organizational change, it may not adequately account for the complexities around group dynamics that often accompany realignment of organizational structures or systems. Notwithstanding, the ADKAR model is a strong and easy-to-use model that shows how important it is to understand and help people navigate the various stages of organizational change. Although the ADKAR change management model offers a structured and step-by-step approach to managing change at both the human and organizational levels, the increasingly dynamic nature of today's corporate environment frequently necessitates an approach that is more iterative and adaptable. The Agile change management model seeks to meet this objective and is the subject of our next section.

Agile Change Management

The Agile change management model represents a unique approach to change management that draws from Agile software development processes and applies relevant techniques to organizational change management. The result is an innovative approach that places an emphasis on adaptability, flexibility, and stakeholder involvement with the goal of achieving incremental progress through effective teamwork. The model emerged in a response to the limitations encountered by other conventional change management models that prescribed the linear implementation of a series of steps to achieve change objectives. Conventional models often assume linearity, predictability, and organizational stability, to the degree that change leaders wrongly assume that the organizational environment will remain stable over the life of the change initiative. Given the ever-changing, dynamic, and fast-paced organizational climates through which change initiatives are undertaken, proponents of the Agile change management model contend that conventional change models fall short of meeting expectations, thereby requiring a different approach that succeeds even in difficult and uncertain organizational contexts.

While this observation has merit, there are some striking similarities between the Agile change management model and other conventional models. One is the need for planning. Critics of Agile methodology often wrongly assert that Agile methods are devoid of effective planning processes; however, proponents argue to the contrary, citing that Agile change management, by definition, employs an iterative cycle of planning, executing, and monitoring the implementation of change processes, albeit utilizing shorter cadences. The benefit of this approach, and thus one of the fundamental attributes of the Agile change management paradigm, is that meaningful outcomes are realized more quickly than other traditional change models. When Agile change management techniques are employed, work is undertaken utilizing smaller action plans to achieve very specific change outcomes. Herein lies the contrast to conventional change models that often require the development of comprehensive change documentation at the start of the change initiative. In the end, the Agile change management model facilitates change adoption by achieving smaller, more manageable objectives with the goal of building upon previous successes each iteration until the scope of the change initiative is achieved. In terms of cadence, an iteration represents a period in which work is undertaken to achieve the specified objective, and usually lasts between two to four weeks. Therefore, at the conclusion of each iteration, the change leader facilitates a review session with the team to

> Agile change management focuses on building on previous successes, iteratively.

extract lessons gleaned during the process, while leveraging new insights to guide the implementation of the next iteration.

Another important tenet of the Agile change management model is the centrality of human-social collaboration. As described earlier, human-social collaboration emphasizes the value and power of collective intelligence, engagement, and collaboration needed to achieve successful change outcomes. Therefore, and consistent with this objective, the Agile change management model places significant focus on organizational communication and effective stakeholder cooperation as two of its fundamental principles. In so doing, the model promotes continuous conversation between the change management team, stakeholders, and those whose lives will be affected by the change initiative.

Change leaders hold regular meetings, typically daily, to discuss the progress that has been made from the previous day, find solutions to any problems that have arisen since the last meeting, and revise plans as necessary for the next phase of the implementation. Because of this continuous review cycle, the team can more effectively respond to new challenges almost in real-time and confront and mitigate obstacles as they arise.

Another similarity between the Agile change management model to other conventional models is the need to develop and communicate the vision for the initiative across the organization. This critical function is performed by the "change owner." The change owner, who is typically a senior leader within the organization, is responsible for communicating the vision for change, providing the required resources to carry out the change, and developing solutions to remove impediments that threaten to derail the change initiative. The change owner therefore ensures that the strategic goals of the organization are aligned with those outlined for the change initiatives, and champions the change initiative to its completion.

In addition to the change owner, the change initiative often recruits one or more change agents to play significant roles in the change initiative. These roles are often filled by middle-level managers, influential department leaders, and advocates who are responsible for initiating the initiative, facilitating communication, and providing support for individuals whose lives are being upended by the change. This is another similarity to other conventional models that require building a leadership coalition from executives, business sponsors, and other influential stakeholders to advocate for change.

Drawing inspiration from Agile principles typically used in Agile software development, the Agile change management model is designed to embrace fast-paced, uncertain, and complex business scenarios that organizations frequently navigate. It recognizes that change is not always a linear process and that new insights or changes in context can arise, requiring adjustments and realignments. Thus, to keep track of planned activities, change leaders often rely on visual management tools often used in Agile software development to monitor progress, draw attention to problems, and graphically display the flow of tasks. This transparency helps the team establish a shared understanding of activities being undertaken and ensures that all parties involved are on the "same page," and are aligned with future next steps.

One important and distinctive concept that guides Agile change management is organizational agility. Organizational agility is the ability of an organization to adjust quickly and efficiently to changes in the business environment, as demonstrated by the organization's ability to define, accept, and respond to the need for change. Organizational agility also represents the keen willingness of leaders to adapt the organization's operations to seize new opportunities, improve efficiency, and inspire stakeholders to pursue a future with mutually considered benefits. This keen mentality for (a) prioritizing responsiveness over comprehensive preplanning, (b) collaboration over working in isolation, and (c) iterative learning over progression in a linear fashion represents the distinctive differentiators of the Agile change management model. Organizations with high degrees of agility therefore often embrace Agile change management methods; as these organizations often have a culture that is open to change, supports learning, and makes open communication a priority in pursuit of achieving organizational efficiencies. Further, organizations that embrace this Agilist mindset often thrive in environments where rapid change is the norm. They are able to demonstrate the ability to quickly adjust when thrusted into initiatives where adaptability is of the utmost importance. Adoption of this model invariably will help organizations manage change more successfully, reduce resistance to change by identifying roadblocks sooner, promote stakeholder participation, and achieve desired objectives more quickly when it is correctly applied.

While the Agile change model certainly provides advantages for well-suited organizations, that is not to suggest that other linear models are incapable of achieving lasting and meaningful change. In fact, to the contrary, change strategists often employ a hybrid approach that leverages the benefits of the Agile change management model with other linear models, such as the ADKAR model. Organizations that utilize a hybrid approach that blends ADKAR's foundational principles of individual change, with an Agile iterative framework that emphasizes continuous improvement, iterative learning, and the ability to respond to change more swiftly, offers the best of both worlds, and thus, significant benefits to the change initiative. The ADKAR model offers a roadmap for the linear progression of change, while the Agile change management model provides the flexibility to adjust as circumstances evolve, thereby encouraging teams to experiment, learn, and adapt, while fostering a culture of resilience and innovation that can drive sustainable change at the individual level.

While the hybrid approach offers value, the Agile change management model is not linear. Rather, it involves repeating and revisiting several stages as the organization learns and adapts throughout each change cycle. It therefore requires adaptability, a willingness to learn, and the ability to effectively respond to new information and shifting circumstances. For these reasons, change leaders often implement the Agile change management model utilizing the following steps:

■ *Step 1: Articulate the Need for Change*

The first stage is to articulate why the change is being undertaken. Consistent with other models, change may be a response to external causes such as market competition. It can also be a reaction to internal reasons such as performance improvement or the adoption of new technology.

■ *Step 2: Develop a Vision Statement*

The change owner must articulate a clear and compelling vision for the change. This vision should define the intended future condition as well as the benefits it will provide to the organization. The vision statement serves as the guiding light for the entire change initiative.

■ *Step 3: Create a Change Team*

Create a dedicated change team comprised of change agents and other influential stakeholders. These people will be responsible for implementing the change, while fostering communication among all affected stakeholders.

■ *Step 4: Determine Change Increments*

Break the change process down into manageable amounts or ""sprints." Each sprint should have clear targets that are in line with the overarching change vision. This stage also entails ranking these increments in terms of their prospective impact and feasibility.

■ *Step 5: Schedule the First Sprint*

Plan the first sprint in detail once the increments have been selected. Determine the tasks that must be completed, allocate responsibility, and establish a completion date.

■ *Step 6: Carry out the Sprint tasks as scheduled*

During this stage, regular communication is essential. Utilize daily stand-up meetings to share progress, resolve difficulties, and, if required, amend plans as needed.

■ *Step 7: Review and Learn*

At the end of each sprint, hold a review session to evaluate the results. Assess what was effective, what could have been improved, what unanticipated difficulties arose, and what lessons can be applied for future sprints. Use these findings to guide sprint planning for the upcoming sprint.

■ *Step 8: Communicate Progress and Recognize Success*

Keep all stakeholders apprised of the initiative's status and celebrate the completion of each sprint and milestone. This is critical to maintain momentum, inspire motivation, and facilitate stakeholder engagement.

■ *Step 9: Iterate*

For each successive sprint, repeat the cycle of planning, executing, reviewing, and learning.

■ *Step 10: Embed the Change*

Once the intended change has been achieved, work to integrate it into the organization's culture, procedures, and systems. To ensure the sustainability of the change, policies may need to be changed, training provided, and other supporting measures implemented to ensure change permanence.

In today's ever-changing and unpredictable business climate, the Agile change management model offers numerous benefits. It encourages teamwork and a flexible approach to change management that relies on small, incremental improvements. A culture of shared ownership and accountability is fostered through individual adaptability and stakeholder participation, which in turn enables organizations to achieve change permanence. However, there are times when organizations need a change management strategy that places a heavy emphasis on enhancing processes and decreasing variability. The Six Sigma organizational change model quickly comes into focus since this model focuses on achieving process excellence, minimizing waste, and utilizing a structured data-driven approach to organizational change. In view of these insights, we'll explore the Six Sigma change management model in the next section.

Six Sigma Change Management Model

Six Sigma is a structured, statistical, and data-driven methodology that is often used to improve business processes by seeking to reduce defects and variations. The model was developed by Bill Smith and continues to be one of the more well-established models for process improvement. The Six Sigma Change Management model, by extension, builds on the analytical and problem-solving attributes of Six Sigma by infusing change management principles, resulting in a blended approach that focuses on achieving organizational process improvements.

The model was first established for the purposes of quality management; however, given its structured DMAIC approach (DMAIC—Define, Measure, Analyze, Improve, Control), change leaders have adopted its use to help identify root causes of problems, assist in making data-driven decisions, and optimize complex organizational processes. Its use is governed by the need to locate and eliminate organizational process inefficiencies, which in turn makes organizational change and business process optimization easier to implement. Together, the analytical rigor of Six Sigma coupled with the human-social collaborative attributes required for organizational change yields a cohesive and blended approach that highlights the need to effectively manage the soft side of change (i.e., people's emotions, attitudes, and behaviors), while employing data-driven and problem-solving strategies to improve organizational functioning. Similar to other change management models already discussed, change leaders use the model to facilitate organizational change by utilizing a structured approach that is comprised of the following steps:

Step #1: Conduct an Organizational Process Assessment

W. Edwards Deming is quoted as saying, "Without data, you're just another person with an opinion," and this principle is central to the school of six sigma. Six Sigma is premised on the use of data to drive decisions, and this is the reason why the first step in the model requires collecting data pertinent to areas in the organization where process improvements are needed. A variety of strategies are often

> **"Without data, you're just another person with an opinion"**
> **W. Edwards Deming**

employed to locate inefficient processes, some of which include formal business process analysis, business process reengineering, customer feedback, data analysis, the use of Six Sigma tools like SIPOC (Suppliers, Inputs, Process, Outputs, Customers), and Voice of the Customer (VOC) analysis. The outcome of this analysis will be instructive for the rest of the model that requires articulating the need for change and creating a sense of urgency for undertaking the change initiative.

Step #2: Create Change Urgency

The second step in the model requires creating a sense of urgency. Similar to Lewin, Kotter, ADKAR, and Agile change management models, the Six Sigma model also requires change leaders to develop a narrative that compels action for change. Creating change urgency, either in response to external pressures or the need for making internal improvements, require effective stakeholder engagement. During this engagement process, change leaders outline the potential benefits to be derived from the change, and conversely, the consequences associated with staying the same. Effective stakeholder engagement also solicits the requisite commitment needed from key organizational leaders, to achieve stated change objectives.

Step #3: Develop a Cross-Functional Team

The next step in the process requires enlisting the support of influential change agents to be a part of a cross-functional team to oversee the implementation of the change initiative. This team is often comprised of Subject Matter Experts (SME) who are experienced in utilizing Six Sigma tools and implementing organizational change management methods. This range of experience is critical as the Six Sigma change management model requires a delicate blend of quantitative data-driven strategies, and effective human-social collaborative approaches to successfully achieve change adoption.

Step #4: Defining Project Scope and Goals

With the cross-functional team assembled, the full scope of the change initiative must be defined utilizing SMART goals. As the Six Sigma model relies on quantifiable and data-driven strategies, goals must be Specific, Measurable, Achievable, Relevant, and Time-Bound. By extension, organizational change objectives must therefore be written in alignment with these goals and articulate the required organizational changes pertinent to business process optimization, technology system deployment, workflow automation, workforce expansion, legacy system enhancement, and revenue maximization, clearly and concisely.

Step #5: Utilize the DMAIC for Change Execution

The DMAIC approach allows change leaders to Define, Measure, Analyze, Improve, and Control the execution of the change management initiative. This process can be summarized as:

    a. Define: Change leaders establish a clear problem statement that articulates the organization's need for change, along with the associated goals and scope boundaries for the initiative. In this stage, change leaders further establish the key stakeholders required for sponsorship, and facilitate the development of strategic imperatives based on organizational requirements, along with critical issues and concerns that require mitigation.

    b. Measure: Change leaders perform an assessment of "as-is" processes by evaluating performance data relevant to current organizational processes in order to effectively evaluate change efficacy and its associated impacts on the organization.

c. Analyze: Change leaders perform an analysis to determine the underlying reasons for current organizational issues being tackled. In response, they then codify change related processes that take into account impediments and other sources of resistance that would affect change adoption, while taking preemptive steps to mitigate possible occurrence.

d. Improve: Change leaders brainstorm, develop, and execute remedies to foundational organizational issues while maintaining effective stakeholder engagement throughout the process to increase the likelihood of adoption by ensuring buy-in, ownership, and advocacy of proposed solutions.

e. Control: Change leaders finally define control measures that are needed to maintain proposed improvements. Leaders rely on cross-functional team members to monitor and respond to problems as they arise to maintain change momentum, establish new organizational standards, and ultimately ensure change permanence.

Step #6: Confront Resistance and Cultural Change

Woodrow Wilson once said, "If you want to make enemies, try to change something." That is true with organizational change as well. That's why resistance to cultural change must be anticipated and adequately planned for in order for the change initiative to be successful. Resistance is a natural and individualized response that stems from change uncertainty, fear of the unknown, and individual concerns around negative impacts following the execution of the change initiative. Individuals demonstrate resistance when they perceive an adverse effect on their well-being, their responsibilities, or their sense of perceived standing within the organization. In contrast, cultural change is more nuanced, and refers to the perceived shift in shared values, beliefs, norms, and behaviors; all of which are essential for long-lasting change across the organization.

Step #7: Monitor and Celebrate Success

Once the change has been implemented, change leaders actively monitor progress and seek opportunities for reinforcement by celebrating desirable behaviors. Monitoring and celebrating success therefore are essential practices for reinforcing positive outcomes, maintaining motivation, inspiring motivation, and ultimately achieving change permanence. Celebrating success also conveys to the team that success is a team effort, an important predicate for cultural realignment. A culture of achievement further promotes a continuous improvement mindset, and sets in motion the collective willingness to confront, adopt, and embrace change together.

While the Six Sigma change management model is highly effective in facilitating change in a structured and data-driven way, its adoption does require a significant investment of time, resources, and skilled personnel. Change initiatives that are devoid of these critical enablers often encounter implementation barriers despite its touted benefits. Another limitation focuses on the scope of change. Since Six Sigma focuses primarily on improving existing processes, the approach may not be best suited for initiatives that require implementing new organizational processes or those requiring radical change or innovation. Therefore, the decision to utilize the Six Sigma change management model must be influenced by the readiness of the organization to undertake change, the presence of an active and involved leadership coalition, and the delegation of adequately trained resources to provide training and implementation support during and after the change initiative. Notwithstanding, the Six Sigma model stands as a powerful tool to be reckoned with for data-driven organizational cultures undertaking process improvements.

Appreciative Inquiry Change Management Model

Of all the organizational change models discussed, the Appreciative Inquiry model presents a unique approach that is premised on discovering the organization's positive attributes as the basis for making change through human-social collaboration. Developed by David Cooperrider and Suresh Srivastva in the 1980s, Appreciative Inquiry is a discovery-based approach that seeks to define and amplify the organization's strengths and positive qualities as a predicate for motivating individuals to imagine and then implement positive change across the organization. Appreciative Inquiry endeavors to identify and amplify the best aspects of a company's culture, processes, and people to achieve organizational change goals. The model focuses on the identification

> Appreciative Inquiry amplifies the organization's strengths and positive qualities in order to motivate change adoption.

and comprehension of an organization's assets, successes, and positive experiences, as opposed to traditional problem-solving methods that emphasize remediating organizational inefficiencies and process-related shortcomings. Change leaders therefore implement Appreciative Inquiry through a series of steps that include:

Step #1: Discovery: During this phase, stakeholders engage in appreciative interviews, perform narrative development, and initiate data collection activities to identify and investigate the organization's positive attributes, along with characteristics that led to past organizational successes. The focus of this initial phase is to conduct interviews with stakeholders to identify organizational processes that work well and to engage in story telling activities to collect examples of times when the organization performed at its best. Stories serve to identify the organization's core strengths and potential, and help to create a supportive framework that can then be used to inform change related planning activities.

Step #2: Dream: While the discovery phase looked into the organization's past, the dream phase peeks into its future by encouraging stakeholders to imagine the optimal future for the organization. During this phase, stakeholders express their collective aspirations, desires, and dreams for the organization's future with the aim of developing a shared vision for the desired future state. "When we inquire into the best of 'what is,' we ignite the collective imagination and open pathways for positive change" (Gervase Bushe).

Step #3 Design: While the discovery phase articulated "what is," and the dream phase focused on "what could be," the design phase seeks to answer the question "what should be." The design phase often includes propositions or design statements that reconcile the best of "what is" with the collective speculation about "what could be." Change leaders therefore attempt to translate previous phases' discoveries and aspirations into actionable initiatives and strategies by defining specific objectives, prioritizing actions, and developing a comprehensive strategy to achieve stated organizational change goals.

Step #4: Destiny: The destiny phase is the culminating phase in which the design is operationalized, and change strategies are executed for the organization to fulfill its dream. In this final stage, changes are made, and the organization moves toward its envisioned future state.

Change leaders employ continuous learning, feedback analysis, and change adaptation to ensure continuous alignment with the evolving requirements of the organization.

These four phases of Appreciative Inquiry work together to unlock the full potential of individuals and organizations, making for an effective change management process. Improved employee morale, effective stakeholder engagement, and the attainment of shared organizational goals are just a few of the benefits that can result from implementing a process that emphasizes optimism, collaboration, and the pursuit of a shared vision. Further, Appreciative Inquiry provides for effective organizational change by promoting inclusivity, ownership, and effective stakeholder engagement. The approach is premised on the fact that individuals are more likely to support and adopt changes when their inputs are heard, validated, and valued. This culture of inclusivity is further enhanced through collaboration, trust, and innovation, and further deepened through individually shared organizational experiences.

Appreciative Inquiry sets the foundation for comprehending current organizational states while imagining desired future states. However, as organizations begin to implement changes, it is critical to overcome the inherent problems that transitions present. The Bridges Transition Model comes into play, providing a formal framework for managing and facilitating smooth transitions.

The Bridges' Transition Model

The Bridges' Transition Model is a powerful framework developed by William Bridges that focuses on the emotional and psychological components of individual and organizational change. Recognizing that the only thing that is certain in life, is that everything will always be subject to change, the Bridges

Transition Model provides a humanistic approach to change, whether the change is the result of a personal life event or a planned organizational change initiative transition. The model makes a distinction between "change" as an external occurrence and "transition," which describes internal psychological processing that individuals navigate before change adoption and change permanence are realized. Change, therefore, is considered situational and is not dependent on individuals transitioning from the status quo. Conversely, a transition creates psychological tension for individuals, as they must traverse a three-phase process that confronts the reality of change, its gradual acceptance, and ultimately its cultural adoption.

Given this three-phase process, the model places a strong emphasis on comprehending and effectively managing the human-social context as described by its three distinct inflection points: (a) Ending, Losing, and Letting Go, (b) The Neutral Zone; and (c) The New Beginning.

Understanding the primary aspects of the model, its progression, and the role it plays in managing transitions are essential enablers that equip change leaders with the requisite human-social skills necessary for navigating change, starting with the first phase—ending, losing, and letting go.

Phase #1: Ending, Losing, and Letting Go

In this initial phase, individuals are confronted with the reality of letting go of legacy systems, processes, and practices by acknowledging and releasing the status quo. During this phase, emotional turbulence, confusion, and role ambiguity emerge as individuals come to terms with the loss of something familiar. While individual responses often vary, individuals may experience resistance, denial, sadness, anxiety, and a host of other complex emotional states during this time. Effective change leaders must, therefore recognize, acknowledge, and discuss these complex emotional responses to broker honest dialog, process negative reactions, and seek ways to improve individual experiences so as to successfully attain organizational change goals.

Phase #2: The Neutral Zone

The neutral zone is often characterized as the proverbial "no-man's land" since it straddles two critical, but essential organizational states: the state where individuals must let go of the status quo, and the state of seeking a new norm, a new sense of belonging, and a new culture that has yet to take root. During this delicate period of uncertainty, individuals may feel disoriented and experience a lack of clarity about the organization and its future. Individuals may also question the overall mission and success of the change initiative. This state of ambivalence could undermine the chances for change permanence; thus, change leaders must be able encourage innovation and growth while at the same time wrestle with the human-social dynamics of individuals who are going through the neutral zone.

Phase #3: The New Beginning

The New Beginning phase is the final stage of transition and is characterized by acceptance, and an increase in excitement that signals the culmination of the transition. In this phase, individuals begin to embrace changes and adapt to the new organizational reality. Change is not only palpable, but real! Individuals publicly embrace the change, tout its benefits, and begin the process of rebuilding their identities with a new sense of purpose. Change leaders rally around individuals during this period of metamorphosis by reinforcing the positive aspects of the change, providing individual support, and celebrating successes of new beginnings.

While the Bridges Transition three-phase model provides a practical framework to provide psychological and emotional support at the individual level, the model is not devoid of criticism. One of which is the apparent linear process that predicts humanistic responses and outcomes to unpredictable change events. The oversimplification of emotional complexity that results from unpredictable human responses bear witness to the fact that organizational change occurs at the individual level first, before it can be reified at the organizational level. Despite its focus on the individual, the model still provides a unique perspective that equips change leaders with the requisite skills necessary to anticipate individual reactions, communicate effectively, and help individuals cope with complex emotional responses that often accompany organizational change.

Beckhard–Harris Change Model

Thus far, we reviewed various organizational change models and compared/contrasted their advantages and limitations; however, this analysis would not be complete without a discussion on the Beckhard–Harris Change Model—also referred to as the Beckhard–Harris Change Formula. This model, that resembles a diagnostic tool, is often used to assess the relative strengths of organizational forces at work during times of change. The model was adapted from the seminal work of Gleicher (1969) and provides a concise formula that describes the relationship between factors needed for change enablement. The formula states:

$$\text{Change} = [ABD] > X$$

where:

  A: Level of dissatisfaction with the status quo
  B: Desirability of the proposed change or end state
  D: Practicality of the change as described by the risk of
    organizational disruption
  X: The "Cost" of changing

This linear multi-variable model is predicated on the collective inter-relationships between dissatisfaction, desirability, and practicality when compared against the cost of maintaining the status quo. Cameron and Green (2015) cites Beckhard and Harris:

> Factors A, B, and D must outweigh the perceived costs [X] for the change to occur. If any person or group whose commitment is needed is not sufficiently dissatisfied with the present state of affairs [A], eager to achieve the proposed end state [B], and convinced of the feasibility of the change [D], then the cost [X] of changing is too high; that person will resist the change. Resistance is normal and to be expected in any change effort. Resistance to change takes many forms; change managers need to analyze the type of resistance to work with it, reduce it, and secure the need for commitment from the resistant party.

Mathematically, this formula provides a deceptively simple but useful tool to provide point-in-time assessment of the change effort. While the assessment is quickly done through simple multiplication of factors, the formula's outcome predicts one important reality: if any factor is zero or near zero, the product—that represents change enablement—will also be zero or near zero. Simply stated, the cost for change outweighs the rational put forward for change. The application of the formula would therefore suggest that resistance to change will be so formidable that change leaders will not be able to overcome it sufficient for lasting change to take effect. For this reason, Beckhard and Harris contend that change leaders would need to articulate a clear vision that highlights the need for change, sufficient to evoke levels of dissatisfaction with the current organizational state that ultimately incentivizes overcoming the resistance needed to maintain the status quo.

Now that we have reviewed several organizational change models and gained an understanding of their respective strengths and weaknesses, the next crucial planning activity requires the careful selection of a change management framework. Selection is based on suitability with the organization's culture, its distinctive capabilities relative to achieving organizational change goals, and its ability to account for the unique human-social nuances within the organization. The culmination of this planning activity requires change leaders to consider the human aspects associated with the change, lay out effective communication strategies, codify effective stakeholder management approaches, and outline a cogent approach to seamlessly navigate organizational change transitions. The artifact resulting from this planning exercise is a practical and comprehensive organizational change management artifact that is often referred to as the Organizational Change Management Plan.

The Organizational Change Management Plan is an essential road map that outlines in detail the strategic imperatives, planned activities, and required resources necessary to put the change into effect. It defines responsibilities and roles for everyone involved in the change initiative and defines who is responsible for what, when, where, and how the change process will evolve. The plan also details required communication channels and strategies; specify stakeholder interests, concerns, and desired outcomes; and provides a comprehensive narrative that seeks to preempt critical aspects of organizational change planning. Effective change leaders therefore utilize the Organizational Change Management Plan to ensure that change activities are well defined to ensure that the chosen change methodology is executed with fidelity. In so doing, organizations will invariably improve their chances for success by ensuring that the psychological and emotional aspects of change are effectively planned and managed throughout the entire change continuum.

Now that we have established the need for, and importance of, developing an Organizational Change Management Plan, we will now delve deeper into this topic and provide practical guidance for designing an effective organizational change plan, employing the insights gained from the change models previously discussed.

How to Develop an Organizational Change Plan

Creating an Organizational Change Management Plan is the first step change leaders take toward successfully implementing organizational change. Recognizing that each change initiative is unique, an effective plan addresses critical areas in the change initiative by providing clarity, along with articulating an effective approach necessary to achieve organizational change permanence. The change management plan is often regarded as the guiding document that informs all aspects of the change initiative. It further provides a roadmap to mitigate risk, minimize resistance, along with defining organizational change objectives, scope, required communication strategies, evaluation methods, and implementation milestones, to name a few.

While each change initiative is unique and offers varying degrees of complexity, the change management plan must be tailored to meet the specific needs of the change initiative. The following outline provides a detailed listing of sections that are often included in an organizational change management plan, along with a brief description of relevant content by section.

A) **Introduction**
   a. Outline the purpose of the Change Management Plan
   b. Articulate the need for change
   c. Develop a vision statement
   d. Provide a summary of the proposed change

    e. Introduce the selected change management model/
       strategy
    f. Analyze the organization's readiness for the change
    g. Identify potential barriers and resistance

B) **Background and Rationale for Change**
    a. Provide an overview of the current conditions and/or
       legacy systems or processes
    b. Describe the problems or limitations with current
       organizational conditions
    c. Describe the risks associated with not making the
       change
    d. Articulate the benefits and opportunities of the
       proposed change

C) **Change Objectives**
    a. Outline change goals and objectives
    b. Define KPIs
    c. Demonstrate KPI alignment with organizational goals
    d. Elaborate on selected change strategy and models

D) **Scope of the Change**
    a. Provide detailed description of what is within the
       scope of the initiative
    b. Define out-of-scope items that are not part of the
       change
    c. Provide high-level timeline for the change initiative

E) **Stakeholder Analysis**
    a. Develop a complete stakeholders list
    b. Define Strategies to engage and involve stakeholders
    c. Articulate Stakeholder's current and future States
    d. Outline anticipated reactions/resistance to proposed
       change(s)
    e. Articulate strategies to manage stakeholder
       expectations, concerns, and resistance

F) **Communication Plan**
   a. Define communication objectives
   b. Develop a communication strategy
   c. Align key messages with stakeholder groups
   d. Define communication channels
   e. Define engagement frequency
   f. Define feedback communication strategies

G) **Training and Development**
   a. Identify skill gaps and training needs
   b. Develop training and skill development plans
   c. Define coaching and mentoring support
   d. Develop employee engagement strategies
   e. Define reward and recognition programs

H) **Change Implementation Plan**
   a. Develop a detailed implementation plan
   b. Define roles and responsibilities
   c. Define resources needs
   d. Define resource acquisition strategies
   e. Select, onboard, and assign resources
   f. Develop timelines and implementation milestones

I) **Risk Management and Mitigation Plan**
   a. Conduct risk identification affecting the change
   b. Perform impact assessment of each risk
   c. Define risk mitigation strategies
   d. Establish crisis management procedures
   e. Define sources of resistance
   f. Establish methods to resolve stakeholder concerns
   g. Implement strategies to overcome resistance

J) **Celebrate Success and Recognize Efforts**
   a. Acknowledge early wins, achievements, and milestones
   b. Recognize employees' efforts and contributions
   c. Reinforce positive behaviors and outcomes

K) **Evaluation and Continuous Improvement**
   a. Evaluate outcomes against performance metrics and KPIs
   b. Define methods to integrate change into the organization's culture
   c. Define and provide reinforcement strategies
   d. Implement continuous improvement strategies
   e. Gather feedback and insights from stakeholders

L) **Conclusion**
   a. Recap the key points of the change management plan
   b. Emphasize ongoing evaluation and adaptation strategies
   c. Articulate next steps and required actions

With the change management plan in place, the next essential stage is to assess the organizational change process, as it provides valuable insights and allows change leaders to make strategy refinements as part of the groundwork for a successful and seamless change initiative. Organizational change assessment also seeks to evaluate the organization's preparedness by ensuring that strategies outlined in the change management plan align with the organization's change goals. Change leaders must, therefore, engage with key stakeholders to collect feedback, and to begin uncovering areas of dysfunction within the organization. This assessment, often conducted through surveys, interviews, and workshops, enables change leaders to glean insights into the organization's culture, structure, and existing processes to determine strengths and areas for improvement. This strategic analysis serves as the pretext for conducting detailed business process analysis, the topic of the next pillar in the organizational change continuum.

Chapter 3

Process

Introduction

In the previous chapters, we went into details on the first two pillars for the 5-Ps of Change. The first pillar dealt with the importance of defining the project's purpose by elaborating on the rationale for the change, the boundaries that define its scope, the critical success factors that inform what success looks like, and ultimately, the metrics for assessing the degree to which change adoption has taken place. The second pillar further extended this construct, focusing on why change was needed, and introduced methodologies, frameworks, and diagnostic tools to aid in planning change-related activities. Now that these frameworks have been introduced, and the scope of the change initiative has been defined, let's take a deep dive into the next pillar—*process.*

Grace Hopper, a computer scientist, mathematician, and United States Navy rear admiral, once said "A vision without a process is merely a dream; a process without a vision is just drudgery; but a vision with a process can change the world." It's against this backdrop that we build on the two

DOI: 10.4324/9781003544883-4

previous pillars and now take a detailed view on defining business processes, and how they affect all aspects of organizational functioning.

Defining the Process Framework

The term "process" is universally acknowledged within the discipline of change management as a critical enabler for improving organizational effectiveness. The term is frequently perceived as vague and enigmatic and is often subject to a variety of interpretations and applications. Ambivalence around its meaning is further amplified by nuance, since its interpretation is often affected by context, and how that context influences the achievement of the organization's strategic imperatives. The term also frequently conjures associations with bureaucratic procedures, excessive paperwork, and suboptimal systems that require assessment against efficiency and effectiveness metrics. Nevertheless, the implementation of a structured and systematic *process* is not merely an obligatory inconvenience nor a necessary evil, but rather a fundamental element in change management continuum that underpins the achievement of successful organizational transformation.

At its most basic level, a business process is a repeatable activity or set of activities that transforms inputs into outputs with the aim of achieving an organizational goal efficiently and effectively. Business processes are essential for achieving organizational success since they provide the roadmap that identifies the critical steps and resources that are needed to perform and maintain business operations. Business processes often span functional units within an organization and can be manual or automated (Davenport, 1993).

Efficient and effective business processes are critical to organizational success, as they equip individuals, teams, and business units with repeatable methods that provide predictably consistent outcomes. They also aid in reducing the likelihood for implementing ineffective workarounds or adopting dysfunctional operational procedures that often lead to waste, service interruptions, reduced productivity, and increased error rates.

The ability to accurately assess process efficiency and effectiveness is critical to identifying bottlenecks, dysfunction, and suboptimal organizational procedures that impede high levels of performance. This is why business process analysis and business process management are so important, as they provide a structured way for the organization to achieve increased organizational performance. Against that backdrop, let's delve deeper and further define a few more relevant terms.

The term "process" is often viewed through a variety of lenses, thus representing a multivariate topic that:

■ Bridges the optimization of legacy methods, tools, systems, and workflows,

■ Is layered by organizational decisioning methods, tools, and role assignments that all work to influence organizational efficiencies and effectiveness,

■ Is prescriptive for future implementation of enhanced methods, tools, systems, and workflows that aim to increase organizational efficiency and effectiveness.

Further, and given the breadth and depth of its application, the term also conveys a dynamic versus static interpretation. This is due in part to the fact that the need for process-related change is often (a) a direct response to technology changes, emerging market trends, and conditions, (b) changes to organizational leadership, and by extension the direction of the organization, and (c) finally, leadership's response to the gradual changes affecting organizational life and culture. Process therefore represents a variety of complexities that require adaptability, human-social collaboration, and an honest assessment of the effectiveness of interconnected systems, applications, and procedures with the aim of optimizing organizational functioning. In view of these complexities, the term "process" can be viewed both as a noun and as a verb, so let's first explore these differences before delving deeper into this chapter.

The Role of Process as a Noun

When used as a noun, the term "process" refers to an organized sequence of actions, steps, or tasks that are intended to generate a particular result, based on a set of inputs (Davenport, 1993). This sequence is often regarded as a workflow, as it details what must be done in the context of expected outcomes, along with the roles, resources, and relationships of individuals who are involved in its execution. Later in this chapter, these roles will be further expanded upon, along with the concept of actors, inputs, and outputs and their associated interrelationships.

The study of an organization's processes provides a unique glimpse into the organization's functioning and brings into view the framework within which actions, decisions, and value-creation activities influence the delivery of the organization's products and/or services.

The Role of Process as a Verb

The term "process" takes on a completely different meaning when used as a verb. In an active sense, "process" refers to an activity that executes a sequence of events, changes, or functions with the goal of arriving at a specific outcome. The verb form of the term is where organizational action is conceptualized. In the context of change management, "process" therefore refers to "executing change" by implementing, managing, and monitoring change-related activities either through iterations (i.e., using the Agile methods of change), or by adopting a series of stages that govern the successful attainment of organizational change goals. It is the verb form that requires open communication strategies that ensure that all relevant stakeholders understand the scope of the change, why it is being undertaken, and establish clarity around their various roles, responsibilities, and obligations as part of the change process. Going one level deeper, the verb form of the term "process" implies decisive action that moves the organization, either by making logistical restructuring of legacy systems, tools, and methods to yield optimized procedures, or by the instantiation of new applications, workflows, and methods aimed at improving organizational functioning through methods such as *business process analysis, business process management,* and *business process re-engineering.* Let's take a brief look at the first term— business process analysis.

> *Business Process Analysis* (BPA) is the systematic analysis and mapping of existing processes to acquire insights into their operation by identifying areas of inefficiency or bottlenecks (Ould, 2005). BPA requires deconstructing business processes into their constituent elements to obtain a comprehensive understanding of their operations, interdependencies, inputs, outputs, actors, and thus, opportunities where enhancements can be achieved. By virtue of its detailed view into organizational processes, BPA is often the initial stage of organizational process optimization that then leads to subsequent decisions and actions.
>
> *Business Process Management* (BPM) refers to a methodical technique used to define, optimize, monitor, and manage business processes with the

goal of enhancing organizational performance outcomes and operational agility (Weske, 2012). While BPA focuses on the decomposition and assimilation of organizational processes, BPM extends its scope by providing effective management of these processes throughout their lifecycle. BPM provides rich process information first by creating a model of the process, monitoring its execution, observing performance and outcomes, and taking the necessary steps towards performance optimization. The central objective of BPM, as will be expanded upon later in this chapter, is to ensure organizational alignment between the organization's processes and goals, while monitoring the degree to which processes produce intended outcomes.

Business Process Reengineering (BPR) refers to the complete restructuring of business processes with the aim of achieving substantial improvements in performance metrics such as cost, quality, service, and speed (Hammer & Champy, 1993). BPR is not interested in making minor or incremental enhancements; to the contrary, BPR seeks to completely revamp existing processes, or create wholly new ones, to fundamentally rethink how business is to be conducted to achieve immediate and significant business improvements.

These well-established procedures not only serve as benchmarks against which legacy processes are assessed, evaluated, and optimized, but they provide the catalyst needed for leaders to uncover areas of dysfunction, thereby bringing focus to areas that require optimization, enhancement, and adjustment. With these tools and blend of approaches, organizational process optimization will ultimately minimize risk, instill accountability, and ensure the reliable and consistent delivery of the organization's products and services.

Business process analysis, management, and reengineering form the backbone for achieving operational excellence.

> **Business process analysis, management, and reengineering are essential to achieve operational excellence.**

Each offers a unique lens through which to optimize performance. Business process analysis lays the groundwork, diving deep into existing processes to identify inefficiencies and areas for improvement. Once these processes are mapped and understood, business process management steps in, providing the tools and methodologies to monitor, control, and continuously improve these processes. Meanwhile, business process reengineering takes a more radical approach, rethinking and overhauling processes from the ground up to achieve transformative changes.

The degree to which each of these three methodologies is deemed successful is predicated upon their alignment with the fundamental definition and characteristics of effective processes. These characteristics, be it adaptability, integration, scalability, or adopting a user-centric viewpoint, act as guiding principles for evaluating effective organizational transformations. They also provide the benchmark for which process-related transformations are assessed, equipping the organization with resilient, forward-looking, and efficient processes that are aligned with the organization's business objectives. So now that we have introduced the three main process analysis methodologies, let us broaden the conversation with a discussion around characteristics of effective processes.

Characteristics of Effective Processes

In organizational change management, understanding "process" is a crucial enabler for accomplishing business objectives and executing transformational change initiatives. Successful organizational change enablement is not just dependent on strategy or technology but rather it is largely influenced by the robustness and adaptability of organizational processes (Cameron & Green, 2019).

Clearly defined processes serve as the backbone that allows organizations to systematically deliver products and services with consistent and repeatable results. The delivery of these products and services relies on human-social collaboration, since processes are not only influenced by technical systems, configurations, and infrastructure, but are inextricably affected by human behaviors, emotions, decisions, and ultimately, the organization's culture. As will be expanded upon in the discussion of the fifth pillar—*people*—the human element plays a pivotal role in all aspects of process-related change, thus providing a determinative factor that influences how processes are integrated into the larger construct of organizational change. In addition to the human element, the notion of procedural interdependency and interconnectedness is also significant, since processes often represent components of larger systems and workstreams, to the degree that a change in one area invariably creates unexpected ripple effects across multiple department areas, or in some cases, the entire organization.

Given the interconnectedness and interdependencies that exist across most organizations, defining effective processes serves as a foundational building block for process optimization and represents a crucial role in optimizing complex organizational workstreams. So, while organizations often suffer from dysfunction, defining effective processes help to streamline operations, optimize workflows, and provide structure and predictability in the delivery of the organizations' products and services. On the other hand, effective process management helps to provide structure and predictability; however, formalizing them is frequently met with resistance resulting from concerns that the effort itself will impede creativity, agility, and lessen individual desires that are necessary to embrace the change initiative.

As a counterbalancing strategy, change leaders often resort to strategies that incorporate the use of empirical data to provide helpful insights aimed at reducing personal bias and resistance to the effort. In the end, organizations that expend the necessary effort to define and optimize their processes, ultimately benefit from a depth of command of their internal operations and are best suited to find opportunities in maximizing corporate profitability.

But how does one recognize an effective process? What are its salient characteristics? What considerations must be adhered to when defining effective processes? These questions are the topic of this section, so let's delve deeper.

When defining effective processes, there are several critical factors that must be taken into account. The first characteristic of an effective process is establishing a well-defined objective.

Well-Defined Objectives

George Doran (1981) provided an effective framework for defining objectives; a framework that is still in use today. Doran posits that an effective organizational process must have clearly defined objectives that align with the overarching goals of the organization, and possess the attributes of being specific, measurable, achievable, relevant, and time-bound. These attributes have become what's known today as SMART metrics when defining effective processes. Well-defined objectives bring focus and direction, directing time and effort toward the attainment of goals being undertaken. In my book Overcomers, I posited a phrase that affects human and/or organization behavior: "Where focus goes, energy flows." This mantra often focuses attention toward the attainment of desired outcomes, thereby thwarting the unnecessary expenditure of energies on activities that distract from achieving stated goals. The same is true in an organizational sense: focus compels attention and channels energy toward the attainment of organizational objectives. Therefore, a well-defined objective enables activities to be prioritized, allowing resources to be assigned based on skill alignment, departmental accountability, resource availability, consistent with the organization's process optimization goals. It's important to underscore that a well-defined objective is not merely a "nice-to-have" characteristic of an effective process, but rather a mandatory requirement when seeking to achieve effective, efficient, and successful process optimization efforts.

Adaptability

According to Nadler and Tushman (1999), effective processes must be designed to be flexible and adaptable in constantly evolving business environments. This brings us to the second characteristic of an effective process—adaptability. Process adaptability is more than just a reaction to change; it is the very core of long-term effectiveness in an ever-changing world. Whether change is inspired by technological advancements, evolving market dynamics, or is a response to an ever-changing competitive business environment, organizations must get comfortable adapting to change. Failure to adapt, as demonstrated by clinging to old rigid and inefficient processes, exposes the organization to the risk of obsolescence due to their products and services no longer being relevant in the marketplace. Conversely, organizations that embrace innovation, recognize the need to constantly evaluate underlying processes that shape the delivery of products and/or services to remain competitive. To implement new technologies and adjust to market demands, organizations must therefore learn to quickly allocate financial, technical, and human resources to ensure that products and services continue to provide value to their customers. This customer-centric view is central to achieving high degrees of customer satisfaction, a critical predicate for building customer loyalty and long-term customer retention.

Efficiency

Organizational processes must not only be defined with clear objectives and be adaptable, but processes must be optimized to utilize the least number of resources to achieve the best possible results. Hammer and Champy (1993) define this quality as efficiency: the degree to which organizational outcomes are maximized with the least amount of effort. Therefore, when defining organizational processes, efficiency ensures that resources of people, money, technology, and time are all utilized optimally so as to yield more with less. Less wastage of time; less expenditure of money, less expense of manual effort, and less consumption of materials ultimately influence profitability and service quality. While the need for "less" is also translated to mean providing cost savings in the organization's workstreams, efficient processes seek to improve quality by reducing errors, minimize wastage by finding ways to optimize service delivery processes, and saving time by ensuring the required tasks are completed in the shortest amount of time possible. Organizations that emphasize efficiency as part of their service delivery model, often achieve competitive advantage, since they are better positioned to deliver products and services faster, at lower cost, with less effort, and with less wastage. Simply stated, efficiency matters, not only because it strikes at the heart of corporate profitability, social responsibility, and corporate governance, but because ineffective processes eventually result in lost opportunities, increased expenses, and limited possibilities for organizational growth and innovation.

Visibility

In the world of audio engineering, one cannot mix what one cannot hear. While there are some caveats to that statement, a similar statement is true in the world of business process management: you can't improve a process that you cannot see! This statement goes to the heart of an important process characteristic—visibility. Process visibility is the ability to decompose a process to view all its constituent parts that include inputs, outputs, actors, etc. Visibility therefore allows for a comprehensive review of each element working individually to assess levels of efficiency, while at the same time allowing for the evaluation of the complete workstream by observing the interconnectedness of individual parts of the process. The decomposition of large processes into their constituent parts further allows for role assignment, task-level monitoring, and performance reporting/tuning—all essential elements needed for process optimization. That's why the opening statement bears relevance: you cannot improve a process you cannot see! When change leaders gain visibility into organizational processes, they can uncover bottlenecks and inefficiencies, and be able to provide accurate course-corrective measures at individual steps in the process. At the macro level, visibility provides for greater transparency between organizational units, allowing people to gain insight into disaggregated process drivers, while at the same time be able to evaluate aggregated workstream outputs. Both viewpoints are critical for accountability, fostering trust, improving communication, and ultimately, optimizing organizational process workstreams. Visibility works as a guiding light, highlighting every stage and activity by fostering an open, accountable, and continuous improvement culture, which is essential for achieving operational excellence.

User-Centric

Steve Jobs of Apple was once quoted as saying: "Design is not just what it looks like and feels like: Design is how it works." Apple's commitment to user-centric design stems from the company's commitment to making products that are both aesthetically beautiful and highly practical and intuitive for their end users. Since its early years, I have been a longstanding connoisseur of Apple's products and have served as a computer technician for most of the 1990s. It's no secret that I consumed a lot of their products over the years, and the primary reason for my overconsumption of their products is their user-centric design that results in improved productivity and efficiency across their product line. These very qualities are the drivers behind Apple's success, since the organization's design philosophy is based on the belief that technology should be easy to use in every aspect of people's lives. When you peel the layers back, it becomes quickly apparent that this very design concept lies at the core of their organizational philosophy that ultimately influences operational process excellence. Herein lies the important characteristic of a well-defined process: In order to maximize organizational processes, and by extension the assimilation and adoption the organizations' products and/or services, process design must take into account the user experience, to the degree that processes are easy to understand and follow (Garvin, 1998). In so doing, implementing a user-centric perspective guarantees that organizational processes are designed with the user's experience in mind, to improve user engagement experiences, and ultimately increase user satisfaction. In addition to increased process engagement and adoption, effective user-centric process design provides significant benefits, such as, greater feedback facilitation, increased efficiency through streamlined workflows, and greater long-term process sustainability. Therefore, when organizations put their users first, they ensure that their processes are not only efficient, but also are focused to improve the experience of those they intend to serve.

Scalability

Scalability refers to the organization's ability to adjust to changing demands while maintaining optimal levels of efficiency, quality, and profitability. This characteristic is crucial for ensuring long-term organizational sustainability and flexibility, all critical elements for effective organizational processes. As the organization evolves, so does the underlying processes that govern its operations. It is therefore imperative for organizations to ensure that their operations are calibrated and business processes optimized in order to exploit emerging prospects, address obstacles, and find creative ways to respond to market demands. Organizations that are not prepared to adjust to market demands face operational risks when growth demands capacity that the organization cannot fulfill. If scalability is not taken into consideration from the very beginning of process definition and/or optimization, future changes to accommodate unplanned growth will prove significantly costly to adapt, limiting the organization's ability to change their processes to meet rising demand. Thus, scalable processes equip organizations with the requisite tools to respond to emerging market demands while benefiting from significant cost savings over the long term. That's why business process optimization serves as a critical enabler for organizational growth and profitability since it aims to transcend the current needs of the organization to accommodate increasing demands. Scalable processes position the organization for growth by adopting efficient workflows with flexibility and adaptability. Organizations that scale quickly can capture market share more effectively, exploit cost containment opportunities, and provide a higher level of customer experience that ultimately translates to consistent product delivery and service quality. Scalability not only seeks to accommodate organizational growth, but rather seeks to ensure that as growth occurs, effectiveness, efficiency, and quality are all maintained in the delivery of the organization's products or services. In the end, designing scalable processes further ensures that processes will remain adaptable, flexible, responsive, relevant, and efficient, regardless of the external demands that are placed on the organization.

Integration

Integration is the methodical coordination and alignment of organizational systems, processes, applications, and functions that all coexist within the organization to produce cohesive workflows. Integration requires the convergence of processes across departments, applications, and workstreams so that they all work together in unison. The focus of seeking convergence points to the need to dismantle impediments and organizational silos that inhibit information sharing and intra-departmental collaboration. Integrated processes provide a "systems view" perspective that takes into account all relevant steps, processes, and components so as to enable the process to function as a collective whole, versus as a disjointed set of individual steps. The need for effective organizational process integration cannot be over-emphasized; since an integrated process not only improves operational efficiency, but also reduces inefficient workflows by removing redundancies, provides cost containment, and enables centralized data governance procedures that ultimately lead to improved decision-making.

Now that we have established the seven prominent characteristics of efficient organizational processes, it's time to go one level deeper and discuss the methods and frameworks for analyzing and enhancing them. Every characteristic, ranging from clearly defined objectives to adaptability, scalability, and operational integration, plays a crucial part in determining the overall effectiveness of the organization's processes. Nevertheless, the initial identification of these characteristics in isolation is merely the preliminary stage. So, to understand and comprehensively assess ways to enhance organizational processes, we'll now explore each of the critical frameworks (i.e., BPA, BPM, and BPR) relative to understanding how organizations analyze, comprehend, and ultimately improve their business processes.

Business Process Analysis (BPA) Defined

In today's dynamic and rapidly changing business environment, organizations must consistently pursue efficiency and effectiveness to remain competitive. As established in the previous section, organizational change management, by its very definition, facilitates organizational transformation of systems, applications, and workflows, to maximize human-social impact, and ultimately, corporate profitability. BPA is premised on the need to respond to external and/or internal pressures that require transformation of the organization's technologies, business processes, strategic imperatives/goals, and culture. Changes to one or more of these areas invariably affect people to achieve desired business outcomes. BPA is a structured approach to analyzing, identifying, and mapping an organization's existing processes to find areas that may be improved, inefficiencies that can be addressed, bottlenecks that can be resolved, and opportunities for optimization. BPA techniques map out workflows, identify key stakeholders, and develop process-related details around process inputs, outputs, actors, and actions that are required to achieve organizational outcomes.

BPA incorporates many methodologies, instruments, and techniques for analyzing, modeling, and optimizing processes. While the implementation of BPA may vary depending on the complexity of processes being analyzed, BPA's structured implementation process typically includes seven fundamental steps that include:

Step 1: Define Objectives and Scope:

The first step in BPA is to clearly determine the processes that are critical to the organization's mission, which have recurring issues, are costly, or are plagued with dysfunction and waste. This high-level qualifier helps frame the objectives and scope of the analysis and involves identifying which processes will be analyzed and listing the specific goals and expected outcomes at the conclusion of the process (e.g., cost reduction, quality improvement, faster delivery).

Step 2. Identify Key Stakeholders:

For each process identified, develop a stakeholder registry that includes all pertinent individuals who either contribute to, or consume outputs from the process. This cross-functional team is comprised of individuals intimately familiar with different facets of the process, experience and/or familiar with areas of inefficiency, and capable of prescribing solutions for achieving process optimization. The collective cross-functional team knowledge and discernment are indispensable and greatly facilitate a thorough comprehension of current and future procedures. This team of individuals may include process owners, subject matter experts, and employees who are actively engaged in daily process execution.

Step 3. Document As-Is Process:

Document the "as-is" or current state of processes being analyzed, being sure to include a supporting narrative that describes the process, inputs, outputs, consumers, steps, etc. Create supporting diagrams that provide process visualization using process mapping, flowcharts, and swim lane diagrams.

Step 4. Perform Data Collection and Analysis:

Collect pertinent process-related data and metrics as a predicate for conducting a thorough evaluation to detect recurring trends, bottlenecks, sources of inefficiency, and ultimately, opportunities for optimization. Analysis may include comparison of the organization's processes against industry standards and best practices and may also compare and contrast competitor products and/or services so as to glean competitive insights, product strengths, and variances in product and/or service quality. Often included in this step is the use of quantitative, analytical, and statistical tools and approaches for data analysis and visualization.

Step 5. Design To-Be Process Design:

Collaborate with individuals on the stakeholder registry to design improved future "To-Be" processes that address previously identified issues, while ensuring alignment with organizational goals. Catalog and proposed process improvement opportunities with accompanying process design changes, technology injection and/or expansion, workflow refinements, and workforce development and training opportunities, to operationalize new business processes. Create diagrams of future processes that provide process visualization using process mapping, flowcharts, swimlane diagrams and other modeling techniques such as Business Process Model and Notation (BPMN). Overlay legacy "as-is" processes with new future "To-Be" processes to illustrate areas where changes are being made.

Step 6. Implementation and Testing:

Conduct a pilot of the new process and document all areas requiring attention. Once issues have been remedied, implement process modifications, and conduct widespread testing to ensure that new processes yield the intended outcomes. Automate repeatable processes to improve efficiency, while taking the necessary steps to minimize errors and optimize workflows.

Step 7. Implement Continuous Improvement with Active Monitoring:

With newly implemented processes in operation, establish frequent monitoring and assessment processes to measure, assess, and report on the state of new process implementations. Track areas of prior concern to ensure that new processes have taken hold, and are meeting intended outcomes. Establish continuous improvement measures to track the performance of newly implemented processes, and actively seek opportunities for further optimization and refinement.

The above steps demonstrate that BPA is a strategic instrument that enables organizations to evaluate, restructure, and optimize their operations to achieve greater productivity and efficiency. By following a methodical implementation process, organizations are poised to achieve tangible benefits, sustaining their competitiveness in an ever-changing marketplace. Through an iterative and deliberative approach, BPA provides the requisite tools to achieve high degrees of enhanced proficiency and adaptability. Through process optimization, organizations can not only achieve cost containment opportunities, but bolster client satisfaction that ultimately leads to sustained competitive advantage in the marketplace.

BPA Element Descriptions with Examples

BPA is a strategic exploration of an organization's operations. It meticulously evaluates processes to identify inefficiencies, redundancies, and areas for improvement. By mapping out how things are done, organizations gain a clearer understanding of their workflows, enabling them to streamline operations, enhance productivity, and ensure alignment with their business objectives. In order to perform this in-depth review, BPA often requires the use of analytical tools that aid documentation and analysis. We will now outline the steps involved in BPA and provide definitions around key business-related terms that are central to BPA. While tools and templates vary across the industry, there are a few process commonalities that exist between the various data collection and analytical tools. These commonalities are best illustrated using a real-world example for an invoice approval process. In Table 3.1, each BPA element will be introduced along with a description consistent with BPA taxonomy.

By taking the time to develop thoughtful and cogent narratives for each of these identified sections, organizations will articulate rich information about their business processes,

Table 3.1   BPA Critical Elements Defined

BPA Element	BPA Element Description	Example
Process Name	"Process Name" refers to the label or designation given to the series of actions or steps being examined. It acts as an identifier throughout the analysis, ensuring clarity and concentration. This name should be concise and detailed enough so that stakeholders understand the scope and purpose of the process without needing much more information. For instance, "Invoice Approval," "Product Returns," or "Employee Onboarding."	Invoice Approval Process

(Continued)

Table 3.1 (Continued)

BPA Element	BPA Element Description	Example
Process Identification	"Process Identification" refers to the phase in which a specific workflow or sequence of tasks inside an organization is identified for investigation. This stage entails identifying the scope, boundaries, and objectives of the process, as well as ensuring that analysts and stakeholders agree on which operation is being scrutinized.	Invoice Approval
Process Scope	"Process Scope" establishes the boundaries of the specific workflow being examined. It specifies what is and is not included in the analysis, ensuring clarity and focus. Process scope helps to prevent ambiguity, ensure alignment among all stakeholders, and ensure that the analysis remains efficient and focused.	Establishes the boundaries around the invoice approval process. The process is initiated when the invoice is received from the vendor and concludes when the invoice is either approved and scheduled for payment or rejected and the vendor is informed. In-Scope items include: 1. Invoice receipt. 2. Verification against purchase contracted versus delivered work. 3. Transmittal to processing department once verified.

(Continued)

Table 3.1 (Continued)

BPA Element	BPA Element Description	Example
		4. Invoice approval or rejection. 5. Invoice approval or rejection notification. 6. Invoice disbursement. 7. Invoice recordation and archival. Out of Scope items include: 1. Invoices related to internal reimbursements or payroll. 2. Purchase order creation or modification. 3. Physical or digital payment processing. 4. Vendor communication not directly related to the specific invoice in question (e.g., negotiation of terms, dispute resolutions not tied to the approval process).
Process Description	"Process Description" gives a thorough account of the precise order in which the steps or actions in the designated process are carried out. This section provides information on the process's beginning and ending, primary	This process starts when an invoice is received from a vendor and concludes when the payment is approved or rejected. Interim details include: 1. Invoice Receipt: • Accounts Payable (AP) team receives the invoice from the vendor, either digitally or in paper format.

(Continued)

Table 3.1 (Continued)

BPA Element	BPA Element Description	Example
	tasks, key players, and overall flow. The description ensures that all parties involved have a thorough understanding of how the process functions in its current condition by acting as a fundamental reference.	• The invoice is logged into the accounting system with a unique identifier and date of receipt. 2. Preliminary Verification: • AP team validates the invoice against existing purchase orders and delivery receipts to ensure service delivery alignment. • The invoice is reviewed for accuracy and completeness. 3. Departmental Validation: • The invoice is forwarded to the department originating the purchase. • The department head or designated personnel reviews the invoice to confirm service delivery alignment. • Any discrepancies are communicated back to the AP team and, if necessary, the vendor.

(Continued)

Table 3.1   (Continued)

BPA Element	BPA Element Description	Example
		4. Budget Check: • The finance department verifies the invoice against available budget allocations to ensure funds are available for payment. • If funds are not available or there's a budgetary concern, the finance department communicates with the respective department for guidance on next steps.
		5. Final Approval: • Upon satisfactory validation, the AP team marks the invoice as approved in the accounting system. Invoices that exceed departmental thresholds may require additional approvals.
		6. Payment Scheduling: • Approved invoices are queued for payment based on the terms agreed upon with the vendor (e.g., net 30 days).

(Continued)

Table 3.1 (Continued)

BPA Element	BPA Element Description	Example
		• Payment details, including date and method, are recorded in the accounting system. 7. Vendor Communication: • The vendor is informed of the approval status and, if approved, the expected payment date. • In case of disputes or rejections, reasons are communicated to the vendor, and resolutions pursued. 8. Documentation and Archiving: • The approved invoice, along with all related communication and validation documents, is archived physically or digitally for future reference and audit compliance. End of Process: The process concludes when the payment is made to the vendor and all documentation is appropriately archived. Top of Form Bottom of Form

(Continued)

Table 3.1 (Continued)

BPA Element	BPA Element Description	Example
Input	"Input" refers to the initial resources, information, or events that originate or are required for a certain process to begin. Inputs set the stage for the subsequent sequence of activities, ensuring that the process contains all of the components required to deliver the desired result.	To ensure that the invoice approval process is thorough, accurate, and consistent with organizational financial policies and practices, the following inputs play an important role: 1. Vendor Invoice: The primary document detailing the goods or services provided, their quantities, unit prices, total amount due, invoice date, due date, and vendor's payment details. 2. Purchase Order (PO): An official document issued by the organization detailing the items ordered, agreed prices, and terms against which the invoice is validated. 3. Delivery Receipt: A signed document confirming the receipt of goods or services. 4. Contract or Agreement: A written agreement with the vendor that provides terms of service, payment terms, discounts, or special considerations.

(Continued)

Table 3.1 (Continued)

BPA Element	BPA Element Description	Example
		5. Previous Invoices and Payments: Historical data that is cross-referenced to detect anomalies or accounting issues.
		6. Budget Allocations: Approved departmental and/or project-specific budgets from which expenditures are drawn.
		7. Departmental Approval Matrix: An escalation process document that details levels of approval authority based on expenditure thresholds.
		8. Vendor Communication: Any prior written documents such as emails, memos, or other forms of communication that provide context for the invoice.
		9. Accounting System Data: Existing data about the vendor, past payments, account balances, and other related financial data to ensure consistency and correctness.

(Continued)

Table 3.1 (Continued)

BPA Element	BPA Element Description	Example
Actors	"Actors" refers to individuals, organizations, or systems that actively participate in carrying out designated tasks or actions as part of the specified process. External entities, such as vendors or customers, or internal stakeholders, including employees or divisions, may serve as actors. The identification of the actors involved in each step ensures accountability and comprehension of roles by demonstrating who is accountable for and participates in that step.	Actors play a crucial role in ensuring the invoice approval process is efficient, accurate, and compliant with organizational and regulatory standards, and may include the following roles: 1. Supplier/Vendor: The company that sells products and services and sends an invoice. 2. Procurement: The team that issues solicitations, creates purchase orders, maintains vendor relationships, and verifies invoices against orders. 3. Receiving Department: The team that validates delivery receipts of tangible items. 4. Accounts Payable Clerk: The individual that records invoice data in the accounting system. 5. Department Leaders: Management who requests goods/services and verifies receipt in accordance with quality or performance standards.

(Continued)

Table 3.1 (Continued)

BPA Element	BPA Element Description	Example
		6. Finance/Accounting Team: The team that reviews and approves invoices based on budgetary availability and spending authority. 7. Auditors: Internal or external auditors who periodically review the process to verify financial controls and requirements are met. 8. Treasury: The treasury or cash management staff ensures timely invoice payment.
Steps in the Process	"Steps" refers to the delineation and decomposition of consecutive actions or tasks that are executed from the initiation of the process to its culmination. Steps provide a detailed examination of all constituent elements that comprised the entire workflow to pinpoint areas for analysis, redesign, or optimization.	The following steps illustrate the union of inputs and actors along the service delivery continuum: 1. Invoice Receipt: Accounts Payable Clerk receives the invoice from the supplier. 2. Initial Verification: The clerk checks the invoice for completeness, ensuring it has all required details. 3. Matching Invoice with Purchase Order: The clerk matches the invoice with the corresponding purchase order to ensure they align.

(Continued)

Table 3.1   (Continued)

BPA Element	BPA Element Description	Example
		4. Invoice Approval/ Rejection: The Department Head/ Manager reviews the invoice. If goods/ services were received satisfactorily, they approve; otherwise, they may reject or query. 5. Payment Processing: If approved, the invoice is sent to the finance department for payment processing. 6. Notification to Supplier: Once payment is processed, the supplier is notified of the payment status.
Output	"Output" refers to the final outcome or product that is produced when the stated process is finished. The term "outcome" refers to the result obtained by carrying out a series of defined steps on the given inputs. Understanding the output is crucial, as it enables the assessment of the efficiency of the	Outputs that are generated based on inputs, actors, and procedural steps include: 1. Approved Invoice: Confirming accuracy and disbursement readiness. 2. Payment Authorization: Authorization that triggers the disbursement process. 3. Payment Receipt: Document that confirms amounts paid, payment method, and disbursement date.

(Continued)

Table 3.1 (Continued)

BPA Element	BPA Element Description	Example
	process and the evaluation of its alignment with the desired aims or objectives.	4. Vendor Payment History: Artifacts that include records in the vendor management that document previous payments. 5. Audit Trails: Detailed logs of the approval process that capture approval entities, transaction dates, and supporting documentation/notes collected for historical and audit compliance. 6. Performance Data: Information captured relating to accounting efficiency that takes into account time taken for approval, the number of discrepancies identified, or the number of invoices processed. 7. Feedback to Vendors: Communication sent to vendors, especially when issues and errors require corrective action.

(Continued)

Table 3.1 (Continued)

BPA Element	BPA Element Description	Example
Consumers	"Consumers" are persons, groups, or entities who use or are impacted by the results of a particular process. Internal stakeholders may include other departments that depend on the outcome of the process, whereas external parties can consist of clients or partners. Identifying the customers is crucial to ensuring that the process aligns with their requirements and expectations, ultimately enhancing the value and significance of the process.	Consumers represent a vast group of entities that are impacted by the results of the process and include, but are not limited to: 1. Vendor and/or Supplier: The primary consumer as they await payment post-invoice submission. They rely on the process's efficiency to ensure timely and accurate payment for goods or services rendered. 2. Company's Finance Department: The department that is responsible for financial reporting, cash flow management, and budgetary oversight. 3. Company's Procurement Team: Uses the results of the invoice approval process to evaluate vendor relationships and performance. Recurring issues with certain vendors might influence future procurement decisions.

(Continued)

Table 3.1 (Continued)

BPA Element	BPA Element Description	Example
		4. Company's Auditors: The dreaded team that consume the outputs of the invoice approval process as part of their auditing review activities to ensure compliance and accuracy in financial reporting. 5. Regulatory Authorities: External department that reviews process's outputs to ensure compliance with financial regulations and standards.
Tools and Technologies	"Tools and Technologies" refers to the specific software, hardware, techniques, or equipment used to carry out or assist in the process being examined. These components facilitate the optimization, automation, or improvement of the process, guaranteeing both efficiency and effectiveness.	1. Invoice Management Software: Used to track and manage invoices. 2. ERP Systems: Used for financial management, invoice processing, and matching invoices with purchase orders and inventory. 3. Communication Tools: Used for real-time communication regarding invoice inquiries, clarifications, or approval notifications.

(Continued)

Table 3.1 (Continued)

BPA Element	BPA Element Description	Example
		4. Document Management Systems (DMS): These are platforms like SharePoint or DocuWare used for storing, retrieving, and managing digital invoices. 5. Auditing and Compliance Software: Used for maintaining a record of all approved invoices, ensuring compliance with internal policies and external financial regulations. 6. Electronic Signature Platforms: Used for managing digital signatures for approved invoices, ensuring authenticity and approval traceability.
Bottlenecks and Issues	"Bottlenecks and Issues" are instances of gridlock, delays, or barriers that impede the smooth and efficient flow or performance of a process. These can arise due to limitations in resources, inefficiency, or	Bottlenecks and issues represent an unending list of possibilities, but here are a few common ones to start the ball rolling: 1. Delays in Approval: Processing delays due to internal approval issues, funding availability, or other reasons that warrant delaying invoice processing.

(Continued)

Table 3.1 (Continued)

BPA Element	BPA Element Description	Example
	inherent defects in the system. It is essential to identify bottlenecks and concerns to pinpoint areas that need intervention, thereby assuring more efficient operations and increased output.	2. Lack of Personnel: Insufficient number of staff available to reconcile invoices to make disbursement approval decisions. 3. Insufficient Funds: Insufficient funds can significantly impact the payment processing cycle, leading to various negative consequences.
Recommendations for Improvement	"Recommendations for Improvement" are suggested adjustments, strategies, or actions based on the analysis that aim to improve the process. These recommendations address observed inefficiencies, bottlenecks, or difficulties, providing solutions to improve workflow performance, decrease waste, or better match with company goals. This section represents the actionable output of the	At the culmination of the BPA exercise, recommendations often emerge to address limitations, dysfunction, and inefficiencies. As these are specific to the process under evaluation, solutions vary significantly. However, following are a few that emerge as frequent invoice approval improvement recommendations: 1. Automation: Incorporate automated software matching algorithms to align invoices with purchase orders.

(Continued)

Table 3.1 (Continued)

BPA Element	BPA Element Description	Example
	analysis, guiding future process refinement or redesign initiatives.	2. Centralized Document Management: Use a unified Document Management System (DMS) to easily store, retrieve, and track invoices. 3. Regular Training: Provide regular training sessions for staff involved in the invoice approval process to keep them updated on best practices and company policies. 4. Audit and Review: Conduct periodic reviews to identify bottlenecks and inefficiencies while exploiting opportunities for continuous improvement. 5. Implement OCR Solutions: Use Optical Character Recognition (OCR) tools to convert and transform paper invoices into digital formats. 6. Establish KPIs and Metrics: Define Key Performance Indicators (KPIs) to monitor the efficiency of the invoice process, such as "average time taken to approve" or "number of invoices processed per day."

and ultimately facilitate better communication, clearer roles, and a more structured approach to troubleshooting or optimizing their processes.

"As-Is" versus "To-Be" Business Process Analysis

No discussion around business process analysis will be complete without delving into "As-Is" versus "To-Be" processes. So, in this next section we will unpack what "As-Is" and "To-Be" processes are, their role in organizational change, how to approach both during business process analysis, and what cautions must be heeded during organizational change.

Organizational change is an unavoidable product of constantly evolving organizations. As the proverbial mantra states the only thing that is constant in the life of an organization is—

Organizational change is an unavoidable product of constantly evolving organizations!

Change! So, to successfully adapt to this ever-changing reality, organizations must get accustomed to continuously monitoring and improving their business processes to exploit opportunities for continuous improvement. As discussed in this section, one of the tools that is central to this continuous improvement is BPA, and at the heart of BPA is the methodical and intentional comparing of current processes with future processes.

"As-Is" processes refer to the existing state the organization's operations, procedures, and status quo. They provide insight into the organization's culture and ways of thinking and doing since they describe the manner in which tasks, activities, and workflows are executed. "As-Is" processes, therefore, embody the organization's customs, established techniques, protocols, and approaches that represent organizational functioning. "As-Is" process analysis therefore providing a point of origin from where improvements are prescribed, and changes measured, so as to provide a roadmap that equips the organization with the tools to remedy bottlenecks, redundancies, and inefficient processes.

Conversely, "To-Be" processes represent the anticipated future state of an organization's operations after the implementation of adjustments and enhancements discovered through business process analysis. "To-Be" processes are codifications of the organization's future workflows, procedures, and practices that align with the strategic imperatives of the organization. They seek to remedy legacy issues, inefficiencies, and areas of procedural dysfunction to bring the organization to higher levels of performance. That's why "To-Be" processes act as the guiding light toward the attainment of operational excellence, and while change management challenges the organization to journey from their present state of comfort to a desired state of the unknown, a carefully planned change management strategy provides clarity and guidance for successful transformation and process adoption. It is therefore imperative that "To-Be" process prescriptions be guided by careful planning and active involvement of all relevant stakeholders, to yield strong dedication to the future adoption of new standards of performance.

Since detailed documentation is a fundamental tenet in BPA, both organizational states (i.e., "As-Is" and "To-Be") require careful and deliberate attention in the ways in which they are documented. Data collection strategies, such as the review of Standard Operating Procedures (SOP), serve as a starting point for understanding the current organizational landscape. If formal SOPs are not available, other data collection methods are often employed, such as interviews, surveys, direct observation, or departmental workshops with all key stakeholders.

The first step in documenting "As-Is" processes includes defining the process boundary to establish where the process starts and ends. Details are then developed consistently with elements previously introduced in the earlier section (i.e., process steps determination, input, outputs, actors, consumers, etc.). The output of this data collection process produces a detailed compendium that includes descriptive process narratives, swimlane diagrams, flowcharts, BPMN diagrams, and other pertinent process maps that comprehensively describe the process under evaluation.

While documentation is central to BPA, task-level analysis is considered paramount; since analysis sets the stage to assess effectiveness, efficiency, and alignment with organizational goals. It is during this analysis phase that bottlenecks, redundancies, and dysfunction are uncovered. It is also during the analysis where process performance data is measured and analyzed against key performance indicators to assess the success or failure of existing processes. Processes that are deemed underperforming, inefficient, or dysfunctional undergo root-cause analysis to uncover the foundational reasons for poor performance as the predicate for detailed review, revision, and optimization. Throughout the entire process, stakeholder involvement is central to achieving meaningful and successful outcomes, since involving stakeholders ensures:

a. the comprehensive assessment of legacy systems, tools, and processes.
b. that the review takes into account real-world process execution along with related challenges.
c. that helpful feedback, and historical insights that guided process-related decisions are adequately documented.
d. the sharing of valuable recommendations necessary for process optimization.

These critical insights and recommendations that emerge from the analysis of "As-Is" processes serve as the impetus for designing "To-Be" processes, and are foundational for driving positive organizational change, achieving greater levels of organizational efficiency and effectiveness, and mobilizing buy-in across the organization.

Now that we have established the importance of "As-Is" processes, let's go one step deeper to discuss the future state of the organization. Simply put, "To-Be" processes represent the organization's vision for improved operational performance. They represent future processes that are aimed at achieving higher standards of performance by addressing and resolving legacy process inefficiencies and provide the roadmap for strategic organizational improvement and transformation. Just as "As-Is" process analysis is central to cataloging existing organizational procedures, "To-Be" process analysis plays a pivotal role for process enhancement by streamlining business processes so as to achieve improved service and product delivery with increased efficiency and effectiveness.

> "To-Be" processes represent the organization's vision for improved operational performance!

The steps in "To-Be" process analysis closely resemble those performed for "As-Is" analysis, to the extent that the first order of business is establishing a comprehensive understanding of how the organization currently functions. This level of detail was developed in the earlier, "As-Is" analysis where stakeholders and critical process participants engaged in the review and documentation of existing processes. However, "To-Be" analysis extends this work by developing a clear strategic view of where optimization is needed, along with formalizing points of engagement with expected outcomes for each actor and consumer of the process. This alignment is important since, the process' output influences the degree to which consumers measure service and/or product delivery completeness.

"To-Be" process documentation requirements are also identical to "As-Is" process documentation to the extent that both forms utilize a blend of flow diagrams, input and output process definition, definition of actors and consumers roles and responsibilities, and identification of technology systems and tools that can aid in process optimization.

"To-Be" process analysis is premised on the notion of continuous improvement of legacy processes. BPA, therefore, explores areas where technology systems and applications can be leveraged to improve organizational performance through process automation, workflow optimization, and strategic technology utilization.

The process of designing "To-Be" processes requires taking a creative as well as a strategic approach, that includes three main phases:

> *Phase 1: Process Redesign* This phase starts with defining and identifying process optimization targets that offer opportunities to streamline and optimize existing processes. This streamlining process focuses on eliminating organizational inefficiencies, reducing bottlenecks, and removing impediments for increased performance.
>
> *Phase 2: Industry Standards Alignment and Best Practices* This phase leverages industry practices and knowledge that guides the adoption of best practices, standards, and tested solutions to attain better levels of efficiency and effectiveness. The principle is grounded in the fact that "someone before us encountered this issue, and we, as an organization, must learn from others who implemented solutions that solves our current problem." This principle embodies the construct of the learning organization that is described as an organization that actively promotes and

facilitates learning among its members to continuously adapt, innovate, and improve its operations.

Phase 3: Organizational Goal Alignment This phase emphasizes the need to be consistent in pursuing alignment with organizational objectives since "To-Be" processes must be aligned with the organization's strategic goals, purpose, and vision. This validation process is done in collaboration with stakeholders, as proposed process-related changes must also meet the organization's core business objectives and stakeholder needs. As was established for "As-Is" process analysis, stakeholder alignment is pivotal, as it aspires to attain a future state through the articulation of future process enhancement benefits, which in turn facilitates buy-in and alignment from employees, managers, and other relevant stakeholder groups. Gaining buy-in, acceptance, and ultimately the adoption of the "To-Be" process is a critical component of effective organizational change, as it entails engaging and influencing stakeholders to accept and embrace process improvements. When proposed "To-Be" processes are aligned with the organization's strategic objectives, management credibility increases and further provides the catalyst for stakeholders to support and adopt proposed changes. Gaining buy-in also helps preempt or reduce resistance to change adoption, as resistance can serve as a degenerative corrosive agent that undermines and ultimately jeopardizes adoption of new processes. As will be discussed in an upcoming chapter, resistance is a naturally occurring artifact of change. While it cannot be completely eliminated, steps can be taken to ensure that it is carefully managed.

Given that "To-Be" processes are somewhat ethereal constructs, to the extent that no one in the organization has seen them in action, implementation of new processes must include additional steps to inspire confidence for their adoption. It is, therefore essential that "To-Be" processes undergo significant testing and validation to model new workflows, assess process outcomes, validate process assumptions and business rules, and allow for the flexibility to take corrective action wherever process deviations exist. For this reason, the adoption of new processes is often aided using process simulation or pilot programs to identify and rectify unforeseen issues before full-scale process implementation is undertaken.

Through thoughtful design, documentation, feasibility assessment, stakeholder alignment, and a focus on goal achievement, "To-Be" processes serve as a guide for achieving positive organizational change, increased efficiency, and enhanced competitiveness. While obtaining buy-in for the acceptance and adoption of "To-Be" processes is often considered a complex and multi-faceted undertaking, the adoption of enhanced processes demands clear and efficient communication, active stakeholder engagement, just-in-time education and training, and a resolute determination of management to address stakeholders' interests and concerns. Active stakeholder engagement, along with the thoughtful assimilation of the benefits of forthcoming changes, significantly increases the likelihood of adopting new business processes and, by extension, the overall success of the organizational change initiative.

Now that we have provided a foundation that establishes the importance for conducting business process analysis (including both "As-Is" and "To-Be" process analysis), let's go one step further and include another important tool in the business process management toolset: Business Process Management (BPM). BPM is a crucial enabler for organizations looking to optimize their operations, enhance efficiency, and drive continuous improvement. While BPA includes detailed examination and documentation of an organization's processes to comprehend how tasks are performed, who performs them, and who consumes process driven outputs, BPM focuses on optimizing, automating, and continuously improving organizational processes. As will be elaborated upon in the next section, BPM is premised on the need to review the entire process lifecycle of business processes, starting from the first steps of process design, to modeling, and ultimately the execution, monitoring, and refinement of future processes. Against that backdrop, let's now jump in.

Business Process Management (BPM) Defined

Business Process Management, often known as BPM, refers to an integrated approach to creating, managing, and optimizing business processes with the goal of improving organizational performance, agility, and service value. According to Dumas, La Rosa, Mendling, and Reijers (2013), BPM entails aligning processes with the organization's strategic goals to achieve effective, efficient, and adaptable processes in an ever-changing business environment. The fundamental goal, which is to harmonize the organization's strategic objectives with its processes, is facilitated through the identification, modeling, analysis, optimization, and management of business processes with the purpose of achieving high degrees of agility.

BPM conceptualizes processes as a lifecycle that encompasses stages of design, modeling, execution, monitoring, and optimization. This process-centric philosophy views the organization as a set of interrelated processes, with each activity contributing to the overall value provided to its consumers. To maximize service value, BPM provides the tools to perform comprehensive analysis of the organization's workstreams in order to glean useful insights about when, where, and how improvements can be made. At the heart of making these improvements is a core philosophical belief in the principles of continuous improvement that draws inspiration from the disciplines of Total Quality Management (TQM) and Lean Six Sigma. It is this belief system that allows change leaders to employ strategies to optimize the organization's processes to maximize efficiency, eliminate waste, and ultimately enhance the delivery quality of its products and services.

At the heart of BPM strategy is the ability to decompose complex workflows and processes by evaluating the constituent parts that make the whole system. This process of decomposition is often achieved through cross-functional collaboration between individuals overseeing the various units, parts, subprocess, and departments; an effort that requires dismantling siloed thinking and overcoming organizational barriers that obstruct process improvement. This human-social collaboration is essential

> **Effective Business Process Management requires the dismantling of siloed thinking, and overcoming organizational barriers that obstruct organizational process improvement.**

for brokering effective collaborative relationships where people work together to design, manage, and find creative ways to optimize the organization's systems and processes.

The Role of Technology in BPM

While workflow enhancement is a goal of BPM, system optimization is a central enabler for success, since BPM tightly integrates with information technology, leveraging systems and software to automate, monitor, and improve processes (van der Aalst, 2013). Why? Technology provides the foundation upon which all organizational systems reside. Therefore, and especially in service- oriented organizations, the intertwining role of technology and process is inseparable, since technology plays a pivotal role in the design, execution, management, and optimization of business processes.

Technology integration with BPM offers numerous advantages that significantly enhance an organization's ability to align its processes with its strategic imperatives. Table 3.2 provides a summary of the role that technology plays across the BPM landscape.

As summarized in the table, technology plays a crucial role in empowering organizations to fully harness the capabilities

Table 3.2   The Role of Technology in BPM

Area	Focus	IT Enablement
Process Automation	Task Automation	Technology allows for the automation of repetitive and routine processes, decreasing manual interventions, improving accuracy, and increasing efficiency.
	Workflow management	Workflow management solutions aid in the automation and optimization of processes, allowing for seamless data integration across the organization.
Process Modeling and Design	Modeling Tools	Technology offers modeling tools such as Business Process Model and Notation (BPMN), which facilitates the graphical representation of business processes.
	Simulation	Technology provides the ability to simulate process outcomes by evaluating scenarios and predicting outcomes without disrupting live operations.

(Continued)

Table 3.2   (Continued)

Area	Focus	IT Enablement
Process Execution	BPM Suites	Technology enables the use of BPM suites that facilitate the implementation of processes modeled after the organization's applications and business process flows.
	Integration	Technology provides the seamless flow of data across organizational applications, departments, and silos.
Monitoring and Optimization	Analytics and Reporting	Technology facilitates the collection and examination of process data, allowing stakeholders to glean helpful information that ultimately contributes to effective decision-making.
	Real-Time Monitoring	Technology equips the organization with continuous monitoring capabilities that provide real-time views into the organization's processes, and the ability to respond quickly as issues arise.
	Performance Dashboards	Technology enables dashboard performance monitoring by providing visualization tools to enable stakeholders to view process performance relative to predefined metrics.

(Continued)

Table 3.2 (Continued)

Area	Focus	IT Enablement
Collaboration and Communication	Collaboration Platforms	Technology provides collaboration capabilities that enable team members to collaborate through unified communication platforms, document sharing, and authoring tools.
	Notification Systems	Technology systems provide notification and alerting capabilities to keep stakeholders informed about various aspects of the organizations, and to make them aware when deviations occur.
Data Management	Data Storage and Retrieval	Technology systems offer secure storage and rapid data retrieval methods.
	Data Accuracy	Technology enables data precision and reporting capabilities using effective data management and validation tools.
Compliance and Security	Audit Trails	Technology provides that ability to record operational and transactional details that equip the organization with audit trail monitoring capabilities.
	Security	Security enforces safeguards for controlling and monitoring access to data to avert data breaches and unauthorized access to sensitive data.

(Continued)

Table 3.2   (Continued)

Area	Focus	IT Enablement
Scalability and Flexibility	Scalability	Technology enables businesses to adjust their processes in response to varying business demands with minimal disruption to existing workflows.
	Agility	Technology provides the ability to quickly accommodate process changes in response to internal and/or external demands.

of BPM through the provision of tools and technologies that streamline the processes of business process design, control, execution, and optimization. Therefore, the use of technology in BPM not only facilitates operational efficiency, but also lays the groundwork for the organization to innovate and remain competitive in an ever-changing market environment.

BPM Value Creation

The ability of an organization to effectively manage and improve its business processes is inextricably linked to the level of value creation that the company generates for its customers and is an essential component of organizational change philosophy. Thus far, we discussed the pillars of organizational change in the previous chapters relating to "Purpose" and "Planning"; however, as was introduced earlier in this chapter relating to Process, the organization's processes serve as the foundation for product and service delivery.

First and foremost, BPM is an important tool for aligning an organization's operational procedures with its overarching strategic goals. By ensuring that each process is firmly linked with the organization's strategic imperatives, BPM ensures that activities at all levels of the organization are directed toward unified objectives, thus establishing its relevance to achieving value creation for the organization. Optimizing the organization's processes is therefore a central tenet for value creation. Value creation is an essential aspect of BPM philosophy, since it is inextricably linked to the organization's ability to efficiently manage and improve its business operations. BPM leverages both strategic management and operational analysis to uncover areas of dysfunction, thereby assisting the organization to generate and deliver value to its stakeholders.

BPM value creation is garnered through this methodical approach to comprehending, examining, managing, and improving business processes with a strong emphasis on process enhancement and organizational adaptability. BPM also facilitates the synchronization of processes with the organization's strategic goals, ensuring that business operations are not only efficient, but also are successful in achieving organizational change results. When organizations have robust processes in place, they are better able to quickly react to changes, encourage innovation, and, as a result, develop new value propositions for their stakeholders. Further, by identifying sources of dysfunction, process-related bottlenecks, eliminating redundancies, and automating repetitive tasks, BPM aids in sculpting processes that are lean and efficient. The effective use of resources ensures that procedures are executed with the highest levels of efficiency, resulting in the least amount of waste, and ultimately providing improved service quality to stakeholders. As a result of these enhancements, corporate profitability is positively impacted, and the resultant cost savings achieved through process optimization further provides another source of value creation for the organization.

> Organizations with robust processes are better equipped to react to market changes.

As discussed in the previous section, technology also plays a critical enabling role in BPM execution, to the degree that when technology is combined with BPM principles, a balanced and structured methodology unfolds in a way that enables successful organizational change. As further noted, technology plays a crucial role in BPM by providing assistance for all stages of process management, and its integration into BPM strategy offers a strong foundation for automating, monitoring, and optimizing processes that result in increased efficiency, effectiveness, and agility (van der Aalst, 2013).

Although technology does offer tools and platforms, exhaustive process analysis is the foundation of BPM and the catalyst for making revolutionary improvements to organizational processes and workstreams. Technology tools, coupled with sound BPM techniques, aid the organization to uncover inefficiencies, redundancies, impediments, and process-related dysfunctions that impede service and product delivery. This is where BPM value proposition is best realized, since value creation is brokered through in-depth analysis of the organization's procedures, practices, and workflows, and the subsequent realignment opportunities within the organization's operations by adopting new methods, systems, tools, and techniques. Value creation is further realized when tangible improvement, enhancement, and optimization is achieved through restructuring, process redesign, or as will be described in the next section, a complete reengineering of the organization's modus operandi. According to Harmon (2014), this radical reengineering approach sometimes require a total revision of thinking and doing, and equips the organization with strategies and procedures that when carefully employed, facilitates the attainment of organizational objectives, further contributing to extending value creation for the organization.

BPM's symbiotic relationship between process analysis and technology utilization provides the requisite tools to empower organizations to achieve value-driven and methodical process-related transformations. Using technology, an organization's BPM adoption leads to enhanced implementations, real-time system surveillance, and the enhancement of organizational procedures and workflows. When aided with technology tools and platforms, BPM goes one step further and ensures that procedures are precisely engineered to correspond with emerging market conditions and the organization's long-term strategic goals. Therefore, by integrating technology and process analysis, BPM value creation provides the operational efficiencies and the greatest possible value throughout and after organizational change initiatives. In the end, organizations that can navigate the complexities of change in a methodical and well-balanced fashion utilizing BPM, often achieve their strategic objectives, prioritize value to their stakeholders, and ultimately, provide the capacity for the organization to maximize value in the face of evolving operational and changing market paradigms.

BPM is not merely a theoretical concept, but rather, an enormous value creation engine for organizations seeking to integrate, optimize, and execute new processes that align with the strategic objectives of the organization. In so doing, the BPM value creation construct provides the organization with the requisite tools necessary to meet the various needs of its stakeholders. By employing these tools, BPM enables organizations to adapt, evolve, and survive in today's dynamic marketplace by creating a culture of continuous improvement and delivering a methodical approach to business process optimization. As we go deeper into the fundamental principles of BPM, one tool, known as BPMN, emerges as particularly useful for modeling and optimizing business processes, while employing standard nomenclature familiar to the organization's stakeholders. In the next section, we will introduce this tool, its implementation steps, advantages, disadvantages, and how it should be strategically employed in the context of organizational change management.

Business Process Model and Notation (BPMN)

The Business Process Model and Notation (BPMN), is a graphical representation and diagramming technique that was developed to illustrate end-to-end organizational process flows. BPMN, developed by the Object Management Group (OMG), offers change management practitioners a standardized approach to map a variety of process flows consistently and uniformly. The graphical representation of organizational processes assists business analysts, process designers, and IT experts in communicating more effectively through a set of standardized diagraming vernacular that ensures that the documentation of organizational processes is both clear and consistent.

In the context of organizational change management, BPMN can be used to not only document current states but can also be used to illustrate future-state processes. This provides stakeholders with the ability to visualize and understand the impact of proposed changes and equips the requisite information to make informed business decisions. By effectively employing BPMN in organizational change management, organizations are also better equipped to (a) align their processes with the organization's strategic objectives, (b) improve collaboration between their departments, (c) increase stakeholder engagement, and (d) ultimately provide a clear plan for implementing change across the organization.

BPMN's standardized approach to illustrating organizational processes facilitates a consistent documentation method that ensures clarity, transparency, and accountability. This is essential when process optimization requires intra-organizational collaboration between technical and non-technical units. In doing so, BMPN bridges the critical gaps between business and technology units to ensure a richer understanding of the scope of process-related changes, their potential impacts, and areas where departmental synergies are required to overcome dysfunction, bottlenecks, and inefficiencies.

While BPMN provides several advantages, its implementation can be somewhat complex, and thus its adoption not suited for the faint of heart. Simple processes pose little challenge; however, complex processes often result in very intricate and interconnected diagrams are not only difficult to develop, but often challenging for readers to comprehend. Notwithstanding, training in its use provides immense opportunities for its adoption. This is why the OMG provides certification courses to empower practitioners with the requisite skills necessary to implement BPMN as part of an organizational change management strategy.

As described on the OMG website:

> *The OMG-Certified Expert in BPM 2 (OCEB 2)*
> *exams validate an individual's knowledge and*
> *skills in the way BPM is used in today's complex*
> *distributed business environments. The BPM exams*
> *test not only a candidate's knowledge of domain*
> *standards (e.g., Business Process Model & Notation*
> *(BPMN), Business Motivation Model (BMM) and*
> *Business Process Maturity Model (BPMM)), but*
> *also the application of specific aspects in the field*
> *and of industry best practices over a wide range*
> *of business process-related topics. The BPM exams*
> *were designed by the BPMN specification authors*
> *who understand what BPM practitioners need*
> *to be successful in the industry today. Peers and*
> *employers alike will be confident about a certified*
> *candidate's ability to participate in and lead real-*
> *world BPM enterprise initiatives.*

(Group, 2023)

While exploring the breadth and depth of BPMN's body of knowledge exceeds the scope of this chapter, a grasp of BPMN's core principles and implementation strategy can be summarized by the following steps:

Step 1: **Define the Scope of Process Changes:** Clearly identify the specific process that is to be modeled and/or optimized, paying keen attention to the goals, expected outcomes, current process limitations, and boundaries around what aspects of the process will be optimized.

Step 2: **Gather Stakeholder Input:** Develop a list of all relevant stakeholders that are involved in the process being reviewed. Once compiled, begin by collecting detailed information about the process under review, being sure to include details around the current state, existing pain points, areas of dysfunction, and desired areas for improvements, as well as future target areas that are outside the scope of the process review.

Step 3: **Create a BPMN Diagram:** Develop a high-level swimlane diagram that illustrates interactions between departments, business units, and/or essential roles. Translate these interactions using BPMN symbols that describe the core elements of the process. The core elements are described in a *flow sequence*, and include activities, events, and gateways that are collectively summarized as a *flow object.*

Step 4: **Standardize Symbols and Notation:** Review the draft diagram and ensure that BPMN symbols and notation are consistently used to define the flow sequence and flow objects.

Step 5: **Annotate the Diagram:** Provide contextual information and clarifications for every component within the BPMN diagram to facilitate a rich understanding of the process, provide clarity around process optimization requirements, and exhaust opportunities for making process refinements.

Step 6: **Validate and Review:** Conduct a comprehensive review of the BPMN diagram to validate accuracy with all pertinent stakeholders and take corrective actions as necessary to ensure modeled processes are accurately documented.

Step 7: **Simulation and Analysis:** Depending on the availability of technology tools, initiate process simulation and analysis to identify bottlenecks, inefficiencies, areas for improvement, and/or areas requiring continued review and modeling in order to achieve desired process enhancements.

BPMN taxonomy includes some important definitions introduced earlier. Let's take a closer look at each of these terms. At the macro level, processes can be summarized as flow objects.

Flow Object: A "flow object" provides a unitary representation of a singular container that is composed of activities, events, and gateways, which together represent the business process. Flow objects are important since they aid in defining the order in which actions, choices, and interactions occur during process execution.

Activity: An activity refers to a specific action or task that is implemented within the process flow. Within BPMN notation, activities are denoted as a rectangular box with rounded corners. As a related concept, activities are often decomposed into subprocesses to allow for decomposition of complex processes into smaller and more manageable activities to see the essential elements of the larger process. Similar to an activity, a subprocess is denoted as a rectangular box with thick rounded corners.

Events: An "event" refers to a significant occurrence that has the potential to impact the progression of a process or activity. Events are visually represented in BPMN diagrams using distinctive symbols and are classified according to their sequential occurrence in the process flow and their relative impact on it. For example:

Start Event: A start event represents the initial point of origin for a specific process and is often considered the main driver, reason, or catalyst for the process in the first place.
Intermediate Event: On the other hand, an intermediate event occurs between the process origination and its conclusion. By virtue of their location in BPMN

diagramming, intermediate events can receive inputs from a prior event, or can output and/or trigger another event. Thus, intermediate events either capture or propagate an earlier event, signifying its ability to either await an event, or trigger an event once the task has been completed.

End Event: An "end event" represents the culmination of a specific flow in the process. An end event may also signify the ultimate conclusion, outcome, or result of the process.

In defining events, the word "trigger" was introduced. Each event type can have one or more of the following types of triggers:

Message: Refers to a condition in which the process is either listening to receive a message or is actively sending a message.

Timer: Represents a precise point in time or a defined recurring interval when the event is activated.

Error: Represents the condition in which an error is detected during process execution.

Escalation: Refers to the methods and steps taken to address and resolve issues and/or exceptions occurring within the process flow.

Link: Used to connect areas of a BPMN diagram without using sequence flows.

Terminate: Used in an "end event" to signify the final completion of all flows and activities within the process.

Signal: Represents an event that has been transmitted to one or more processes.

Compensation: Signifies occurrences where compensating activities are needed.

Regardless of the state of the above-listed triggers, events are commonly depicted as circular shapes. The nature of the event is determined by the interior of the circle, such as a clock for timer events or an envelope for message events, while the circumference of the circle offers supplementary information about the event.

Business Process Management (BPM) techniques have long been instrumental in visualizing, understanding, and optimizing an organization's operations. These techniques, which employ tools such as flowcharts, swim lane diagrams, and BPMN diagrams, provide a detailed representation of current processes, equipping organizations with the requisite competencies needed to identify inefficiencies and areas of improvement. However, there are times when mere adjustments or modifications to existing business processes proves to be insufficient to meet evolving market demands, or to overcome entrenched organizational dysfunction and procedural inefficiencies. In these cases, a more radical overhaul to the organization's procedures sometimes becomes necessary. This is where Business Process Reengineering (BPR) comes into play, and the final methodology we will focus on in this chapter.

Business Process Reengineering (BPR) Defined

The term "Business Process Reengineering" refers to a process management technique that gained popularity in the 1990s as businesses sought ways to become more productive and competitive. Developed by Michael Hammer and James Champy in their 1993 book, *Reengineering the Corporation: A Manifesto for Business Revolution*, BPR represented a fundamental rethinking and radical redesign of organizational processes with the aim of achieving dramatic performance improvements. Central to this process was an assessment of key performance indicators benchmarked against cost, quality, service, and delivery metrics. BPR intervention strategies would then be applied to areas that showed poor performance, dysfunction, or procedural inefficiencies. Poorly performing areas would receive scrutiny and become targets for process optimization, and ultimately require radical process redesign to achieve significant performance improvements.

In some ways, BPR shares some similarities with BPA and BPM in terms of its initial analysis phases; however, each methodology differs by virtue of their respective goals, scope, and intended outcomes. Each methodology also has their own distinctive set of characteristics, benefits, and risks, as tabulated in Table 3.3.

Table 3.3   Business Process Analysis, Management, and Reengineering Comparison

Category	*Business Process Analysis*	*Business Process Management*	*Business Process Reengineering*
Similarity	• Rigorous analysis and documenting of organizational processes • Involves data collection, defining process flows, and locating bottlenecks, inefficiencies & dysfunction. • Often makes use of a variety of tools, including flowcharts, process maps, and data analysis, BPMN diagrams.	• Involves rigorous analysis and documentation of organizational processes • Primarily focused on optimizing and managing processes through their entire lifecycle to achieve organizational and strategic improvements	• Similar to Business Process Analysis and Business Process Management, phase Business Process Reengineering first begins with process analysis.

(Continued)

Table 3.3 (Continued)

Category	Business Process Analysis	Business Process Management	Business Process Reengineering
Differences	• Primary objective is to analyze, document, and make incremental enhancements • Prioritizes assessment and comprehension of existing processes rather than radical or future transformative changes. • Offers valuable insights to both BPM and BPR initiatives.	• Encompasses not just the analysis but also the continuous monitoring, optimization, and automation of processes. • Focuses on establishing a well-organized framework continuous improvement and organizational agility. • Often utilizes technology to optimize business processes.	• Primarily focused on the complete reimagining, redesign, and implementation of business processes. • Fundamentally challenges the status quo and existing process-related assumptions • Implementation often discard legacy processes entirely in favor of new processes, often untested within the organization.
Benefits	• Provides 360 view of current procedures. • Facilitates identification of enhancement opportunities. • Facilitates data-driven decision-making. • Brokers effective communication and fosters collaboration among team members.	• Increases process efficiency by optimizing and automating tasks. • Encourages flexibility and agility in reaction to shifting market situations. • Enables improved adherence to business rules and guidelines.	• Can provide significant process improvement and efficiency. • May offer cost containment while providing increased organizational agility. • Enables organizations to adjust to changing market conditions by reimaging operational procedures.

(Continued)

Table 3.3 (Continued)

Category	Business Process Analysis	Business Process Management	Business Process Reengineering
	• Viewed as less disruptive in comparison to BPM and BPR techniques.	• Increases stakeholder engagement and satisfaction by using streamlined and effective procedures.	• Eliminates unnecessary steps and processes, streamlining operations. • Enhances organizational competitiveness through innovation.
Risks	• May fail to address underlying issues resulting in marginal sustainable enhancements. • Requires a significant commitment of time and resources, particularly for documenting intricate procedures. • Process participants entrenched in legacy procedures and thinking may exhibit reluctance to embrace change.	• BPM systems are often costly and complex to configure and implement. • Promises of increased automation and widespread process change threaten process adoption due to employee resistance and fears of job displacement. • Ineffective implementation can lead to additional organizational bureaucracy and unnecessary process change.	• Implementation fraught with risk often resulting from high stakeholder resistance. • Expensive and often time-consuming exercise, particularly if not implemented efficiently. • Risks threat of low workforce morale due to staff reductions and layoffs due to promises of automation.

To summarize, BPA, and by extension, BPM, focus on methods and tools that aid in performing detailed process analysis of the organization's processes through their lifecycle. Business Process Reengineering extends this analysis, identifies metrics where performance is misaligned with strategic goals, and prescribes new operational procedures to radically overhaul existing procedures so as to achieve significant performance improvements within shorter timeframes. Therefore, BPA is premised on achieving incremental process improvements, while BPM's goals are to achieve life-cycle process optimization. On the other hand, BPR decisions are guided by the need to achieve immediate process improvement through radical process transformation. Regardless of the method used to optimize the organization's processes, the selected methodology must be informed by organizational change requirements, strategic imperatives, organizational objectives, and the preparedness of the organization to implement either of these methodologies given that each approach bears its own set of its risks.

The lure of shorter cadences and immediate results, often touted by BPR practitioners, could be deceptively misleading; since, in reality, BPR initiatives require adept planning, effective change management strategy, and a willingness to challenge and disrupt the status quo. The reader is cautioned to use BPR strategy taking into account these risks so as to minimize disruptions to the organization's procedures, while carefully seeking methods to maximize change adoption.

How to Implement Business Process Reengineering

From the outset, while a full exposition on BPR exceeds the scope of this chapter, the reader is advised to consult the original text, *Reengineering the Corporation: A Manifesto for Business Revolution* (Hammer & Champy, 1993), to learn more about this pioneering work. However, to provide a framework when considering a BPR initiative, the summary provides helpful insights into the implementation steps necessary for effective BPR execution.

Step 1: Prepare for BPR

i. The first aspect in preparing for BPR is engaging the organization's leadership and securing their commitment toward the undertaking. Given the disruptive nature of BPR, securing commitment from the organization's leaders ensures that the effort has the requisite level of sponsorship, empower managers to make decisions, take corrective action to overcome impediments and stakeholder resistance, and allocate resources as necessary to perform duties as assigned.

ii. The second aspect relates to assembling a cross-functional team of representatives from various departments and divisions to ensure stakeholders needs and interests are accounted for, and to ensure visibility of all decision-making activities.

iii. The third aspect relates to defining clear BPR goals with expected outcomes for the BPR initiative, ensuring that they align with the organization's strategic goals.

iv. The final aspect centers around stakeholder engagement. This includes individuals beyond the cross-functional team previously described, including employees, customers, and other key stakeholders. Taking the necessary steps to involve them in the process to collect valuable perspectives, gain insights, and strategize around probable solutions will ensure that their voice is heard, understood, and valued a part of this challenging process.

Step 2: Perform "As-Is" Business Process Analysis

i. As explained earlier, one of the most important steps in BPA, BPM, and BPR is the formal review and documentation of current business processes. This current state analysis is critical for framing issues and challenges, and articulating desired outcomes at the conclusion of the effort. This process is undertaken by comprehensively documenting all existing processes, being sure to provide visualizations through workflows, flowcharts, and other visualizations, in addition to carefully delineating inputs, outputs, and performance metrics for future reviews and assessments.

ii. An important output of business process analysis is the collection of quantifiable data that describes the actual performance from current process. This includes data such as customer hold times, production cycle times, error rates, etc., data from which objective assessments can be made.

iii. Data from the previous step provides critical insights for making process improvements, since this data will be immensely valuable in identifying bottlenecks, inefficiencies, redundancies, and in some cases, organizational dysfunction.

iv. The final step in this process analysis is the evaluative assessment against established metrics and benchmarks to evaluate how the organization is performing in relation to established performance standards, and ultimately, how performance compares to industry best practices. At the conclusion of this step, it will become quickly evident where performance gaps exist and trigger the next step in the process—process redesign.

Step 3: Initiate Process Redesign

i. The first step in the process redesign phase requires collaboration among all stakeholders, as this phase confronts departments and leaders with quantifiable areas of deficiency requiring honest assessment and creative solutioning. During this phase stakeholders take the first step toward reimagining the process(es) requiring corrective action. They do this through joint effort and collaboration with the hopes of creatively defining new processes that overcome bottlenecks, impediments, and areas of dysfunction.

ii. The next step in this process redesign phase seeks to align product and service delivery with clear objective statements to ensure that core service offerings are being produced and delivered consistently. Part of this evaluation includes workflow assessments to inform stakeholders of all steps that do not add value to the end product or service offering, followed by taking decisive action to eliminate all redundancies and non-value-added processes from future workflows.

iii. The outcome from the prior step will lead to new and streamlined processes, and thus the first and most important next step is to model the new process using software tools for analytics, find potential workflow issues, identify additional areas for optimization, and to model the process to uncover possible prospects for automation.

iv. The conclusion of the modeling process results in a tested workflow redesign. At this point, stakeholders will ensure roles, responsibilities, and resource assignments all align with new workflows, and ultimately, new business processes.

Step 4: Develop a BPR Plan

i. This is where the "rubber meets the road" as this next phase details all the necessary tasks, phases, and milestones necessary for implementing the BPR. The BPR represents a detailed project plan that outlines specific tasks, responsibilities, timelines, and milestones, and serves as the central management tool for the BPR implementation. During this phase, decisions are made relative to timing, sequencing, scope, and process-centric change methods. For example, decisions about phasing in new processes, or implementing a "big bang" approach are critical, as these decisions carry significant impact on the organization. Input into this, and other pertinent decisions, is based on resource availability, available budget, risk mitigation plans, technology readiness, and ultimately, human-social readiness to adopt and embrace the change.

ii. Once BPR planning has been completed, the necessary cost/benefit analysis performed, and critical risks mitigated, it's now time to implement the plan.

Step 5: Implement Redesigned Processes

i. While BPR advocates for making quick and sweeping changes to inefficient processes, responsible BPR execution requires a more reasoned approach that includes risk mitigation strategies through pilot testing. During pilot testing, new processes will be implemented on a small scale so as to perform real-world testing of new processes, uncover areas of concern, and take the necessary steps to implement course-corrective measures with minimal impact to the organization.

ii. The outcome of the pilot process is a more refined and tested process that has the benefit of real-world testing, actual and verifiable outcomes. This inspires confidence for larger process adoption and sets the stage for workforce development, training, and change management activities.

iii. Once the pilot is deemed a success, the next and obvious step is to initiate process expansion efforts across the entire organization, subject to the next step—adoption readiness.

iv. One of the most important aspects for user adoption is the notion of adoption readiness. Even though systems, tools, and procedures can be configured for use, if the human aspect is ignored and ill-prepared, organizations will invariably encounter avoidable failures. That's why this next step is critical for BPR adoption. During this next phase, training is provided to employees on all new processes, and proactive steps are simultaneously implemented to effectively manage resistance through a variety of communication channels.

Step 6: Evaluate New Processes

i. Now that new processes have been implemented, and employees are now equipped to begin their adoption, the final step in this phase requires active and continuous monitoring of newly implemented processes. This provides the opportunity to constantly evaluate issues, challenges, and areas where remediation is required. It also sets the stage for a formal reevaluation of processes that once were assessed as being inefficient and provides a point of contrast to assess how new processes are performing in accordance with established key performance indicators.

ii. Another important step involves formally documenting all processes implemented, along with changes, enhancements, and decisions made during the implementation. This ensures that the organization's process library is accurately maintained, and facilitates knowledge transfer across the organization, during the project's implementation, and after the project would have been completed.

iii. Finally, take the time to celebrate the major BPR milestone. Remember BPR is not for the faint of heart, so to get to this point in the process evolution is a tremendous feat! So, take the time to acknowledge and celebrate achievements and improvements resulting from the BPR initiative to boost morale, maintain momentum, and set in motion a culture of continuous improvement and innovation to ensure that BPR becomes an ongoing practice.

Implementing BPR is a significant undertaking that requires careful planning, continuous monitoring, and a commitment to change. It demands meticulous preparation, ongoing supervision, and dedication to transformation from stakeholders involved in the process. While not for the faint of heart, BPR can deliver immense value to the organization through process and strategic goal alignment—a predicate for maximizing customer value and positioning the organization for success in an ever-evolving competitive marketplace.

Implementing BPR requires careful planning, continuous monitoring, and a firm commitment to the change.

As we transition to the next chapter, we will delve into a comprehensive exploration of all aspects of organizational performance. This includes not only the impact of BPR but also other critical factors such as strategic management, leadership, employee engagement, and continuous improvement methodologies—all of which play a pivotal role in shaping the overall performance and success of modern organizations. Through a holistic examination of these facets, we will gain a deeper understanding of how organizations can thrive in today's dynamic and competitive business environment.

Chapter 4

Performance

Introduction

Performance, a crucial element in the realm of organizational change, serves as the benchmark for assessing the efficiency and effectiveness of the organization's ability to deliver its products and services. Continuous performance assessment is therefore essential to ascertain the degree to which the organization is meeting expectations, and ultimately, its ability to respond to market conditions in an ever-evolving business landscape. This perspective is supported by Cameron & Green, who agreed that as organizations shift and grow, continuous performance measurement is crucial to ensure that change processes that are adopted directs the organization toward the achievement of its strategic objectives (2015). While performance assessment reflects the periodic evaluation the organization's performance against predefined objectives or standards, performance monitoring goes a step further and provides continuous tracking of performance indicators to ensure that objectives are being met and to detect any deviations from the planned performance. It is for this reason why performance

DOI: 10.4324/9781003544883-5

monitoring is seen as an essential enabler for the successful delivery of the organization's products and services, as it illuminates the degree to which the organization conforms to internal standards of quality, and by extension, provides a reflection on how the organization is performing relative to its stated objectives.

While periodic assessment of the organization is important for assessing the degree to which its objectives are being met, continuous monitoring of performance metrics is important to track and review how these objectives are being met over time. Monitoring an organization's performance, therefore, no longer can be considered a "nice-to-have" but rather a "must have." This is due to the need to equip decision-makers with fact-based

> **Performance Monitoring is the ongoing process of tracking and reviewing performance indicators to ensure that objectives are being met.**

information to execute decisions in fast-paced and ever-changing business environments. As organizations embrace performance monitoring, they not only evaluate the efficacy of their strategic initiatives, but also able to forecast future trends, adjust to market conditions, and foster a culture of continuous improvement by consistently tracking and analyzing critical indicators. That's why embracing performance monitoring is a vital pillar in the organizational change continuum. It helps organizations pursue longevity, increase competitiveness, and ultimately achieve success in a market that is always changing.

Before we delve deeper into the topic of organizational performance, there are a few areas that are central to establishing a foundational understanding relative to the change pillars (i.e., purpose, planning, process, performance, and people) covered thus far in this book. These areas serve as broad frameworks for establishing the need for performance monitoring in accordance with the organization's strategic goals, vision, and mission. This chapter will therefore seek to provide clarity around, and define relationships between, Critical Success Factors (CSFs), Key Performance Indicators (KPIs), and organizational assessment metrics, as they pertain to performance monitoring and process optimization. So as an entry into this discussion, let's define each of these key terms:

CSFs: Fundamental elements or conditions that are essential for an organization to successfully achieve its mission and objectives. They represent tangible, measurable, and specific process areas where the organization must prioritize its activities to achieve its strategic objectives.

KPIs: Quantifiable metrics relied upon to evaluate the efficiency and effectiveness of organizational processes in relation to the attainment of its strategic imperatives. While CSFs focus on defining the fundamental areas or conditions that are essential for an organization's success, KPIs go one level deeper to define and measure organizational performance in relation to defined CSFs.

Assessment Metrics: Precise metrics that are relied upon to evaluate and determine the efficacy of an organization's operation, process, or aspect in relation to the organization meeting its strategic goals. In contrast to CSFs and KPIs, assessment metrics are designed to examine organizational performance at a more granular level. While CSFs offer a qualitative orientation that highlights the critical areas for organizational success, and KPIs provide quantifiable units of measure that provide insights into the efficacy of these strategic areas, assessment metrics provide a more detailed orientation to analyze organizational effectiveness and efficiency.

Triangulating the Big Three (CSFs, KPIs, and Assessment Metrics)

Now that we have laid the groundwork, let's look at 12 examples in Tables 4.1–4.12 to help solidify the relationships between CSF, KPIs, and assessment metrics before delving deeper into a more detailed analysis.

Table 4.1 Financial Stability Example

1. Financial Stability	
CSF: Financial stability refers to an organization's capacity to efficiently handle its finances, guaranteeing that its income continually surpasses or at least equals its costs. It demonstrates the organization's ability to fund operational expenses, allocate resources for expansion, and withstand financial difficulties.	**KPI**: Operating surplus versus deficit
	Metric: Measure income versus expenses at the desired interval (i.e., weekly, monthly, quarterly, or annually), aiming to achieve a surplus at the end of each cadence.

Table 4.2 Member/Client Satisfaction Example

2. Member/Client Satisfaction	
CSF: Member or client satisfaction is a measure of how well an organization fulfills the requirements and expectations of its customers. High levels of member or client satisfaction signify that the organization consistently delivers value to its customers and holds a favorable experience rating based on the service delivery, product quality, or overall experience.	**KPI**: Positive satisfaction surveys
	Metric: Regularly scheduled surveys to capture stakeholder feedback and areas for improvement.

Table 4.3 Fundraising Effectiveness Example

3. Fundraising Effectiveness	
CSF: Fundraising effectiveness evaluates the organization's capacity to obtain financial contributions from donors, contributors, sponsors, or grants. The process entails tracking the amounts and progress of contributions, along with maintaining financial relationships, and retaining long-term commitments and donor loyalty.	**KPI**: Donation growth rate
	Metric: Analyze year-over-year growth in donations and donor retention.

Table 4.4 Educational Excellence Example

4. Educational Excellence	
CSF: Educational excellence in higher education pertains to the quality and effectiveness of educational programs, as determined by graduation rates, academic accomplishment, and the students' performance relative to completing their academic programs.	**KPI**: Graduation rates
	Metric: Monitor the percentage of students completing their programs on time.

Table 4.5 Leadership Development Example

5. Leadership Development	
CSF: The capacity of an organization to foster, train, and promote leaders from within its existing workforce by assessing their respective levels of leadership capacity, the effectiveness of leadership training, as well as the organization's ability to identify leadership opportunities from within the organization.	**KPI**: Leadership promotions from within
	Metric: Track the number of employees who demonstrate interest, pursue leadership training, and ultimately advance into leadership roles.

Table 4.6   Transparency and Accountability Example

6. *Transparency and Accountability*	
CSF: Transparency and accountability refer to one's ability to communicate honestly, candidly, and forthrightly to the organization's stakeholders, both inside and outside of the organization. The process may include the disclosure of financial data, garnering compliance with moral principles, and submit to performance reviews, periodic audits, and other methods of disclosure that requires honesty and trustworthiness.	**KPI:** Audit compliance
	Metric: Ensure all financial and operational activities are subject to regular audits.

Table 4.7   Community Engagement Example

7. *Community Engagement*	
CSF: Community engagement evaluates the extent to which the organization actively participates in and influences its local or target business community. Community engagement is measured by the degree of participation in community activities, organizational initiatives with a focus on providing benefits to target groups in the community, or the general disposition toward social responsibility and accountability.	**KPI:** Community event participation
	Metric: Measure attendance and participation in community events and initiatives.

As illustrated above, the triangulating approach that unifies CSF, KPI, and assessment metrics provides an effective framework to assess and improve organizational performance across diverse organizational sectors. While each organization may prioritize these factors based on

Table 4.8   Ethical Compliance Example

8. Ethical Compliance	
CSF: Ethical compliance refers to an organization's dedication to ethical conduct as well as its adherence to predetermined ethical norms and standards. It entails continuous monitoring and reporting of ethical infractions and providing appropriate responses to remedy and mitigate the infraction.	**KPI**: Ethical violations reported
	Metric: Record and investigate any reported ethical violations.

Table 4.9   Staff Retention Example

9. Staff Retention	
CSF: The capacity of an organization to retain its workers, thereby minimizing hiring costs and minimizing the threat of disruption to the organization's business operations.	**KPI**: Employee turnover rate
	Metric: Calculate the percentage of staff leaving annually and take steps to reduce it.

Table 4.10   Risk Mitigation Example

10. Risk Mitigation	
CSF: Risk mitigation entails the process of identifying, evaluating, and mitigating risks that may have an influence on the organization's operations, reputation, or financial stability.	**KPI**: Risk assessment completion
	Metric: Ensure all major risks are identified and assessed regularly.

its specific mission and goals, each example highlights the importance of accurately framing CSFs, together with their corresponding KPIs and assessment metrics, utilizing qualitative and quantitatively measures to evaluate organizational progress. This carefully intertwined process

Table 4.11   Partnership Development Example

11. Partnership Development	
CSF: Partnership development is centered around forming strategic alliances and partnerships with other organizations, institutions, or entities, with the primary objective being to enhance resources, knowledge, and capabilities.	**KPI**: New partnership acquisitions
	Metric: Measure the number of new strategic partnerships formed.

Table 4.12   Academic Achievement Example

12. Academic Achievement	
CSF: Academic achievement pertains to the educational outcomes of students that encompass performance in academic courses, standardized assessments, and their capacity to successfully complete academic requirements for pursued degree programs.	**KPI**: Academic performance metrics
	Metric: Assess student performance through GPA, standardized test scores, and course completion rates.

effectively provides the requisite information to empower leaders to make data-driven decisions and to ultimately ensure long-term organizational success.

CSF: Defines "What" and its Desired Outcomes
KPI: Quantifies the Desired Outcome
Metric: The quantifiable measure's dataset

Now that we have established the relationships between CSF, KPIs, and assessment metrics, let's unpack each foundational element individually to better understand its role in effectively moderating organizational performance.

What Are Critical Success Factors (CSF)?

As introduced in the earlier section, CSFs are foundational elements or circumstances that must exist for an organization to properly accomplish its goals and objectives. They are a representation of real, quantifiable, and specific process areas in which the organization must prioritize its efforts to fulfill its strategic objectives. CSFs are essential in assessing organizational performance, as they prescribe areas where the organization must focus and prioritize its resources (i.e., financial, personnel, technological, etc.) in order to meet its strategic goals. In so doing, CSFs offer management a clear perspective to frame what truly matters to the organization, and therefore aids in effectively guiding decision-making activities. Effective decision-making ensures that organizational imperatives receive the attention that is required to ensure that the organization focuses, actively pursues, and successfully achieves its business objectives. By focusing on what truly matters, CSFs aid decision-makers with a unique assessment perspective to evaluate the degree to which organizational objectives are defined and achieved and are also instructive in highlighting areas where improvements are urgently required.

Why Are CSFs Crucial in Performance Management?

In context of organizational change management, CSFs play a crucial role in three specific areas:

a. *Strategic Goal Alignment*: Providing clarity and aiding in strategic alignment of organizational goals. I once heard Kirk Franklin, a multi-Grammy award winning singer and songwriter, recount an experience on his recent tour.

"... I noticed yesterday in sound check that the band sounded horrible because each individual player was listening to their own music in their own mind. They were going through each of the individual things that they each needed to do, so it sounded like chaotic noise! Until a creator of music (i.e., one of the original composers for whom the band was accompanying), someone who originally composed the song stepped on stage and brought a collective unity to what was before chaos. It is amazing that in our lives sometimes, there can be a lot of noise and chaos because we are all trying to figure out life on our own. But when the Creator walks on stage, and we let Him do his thing, it's amazing how the 'writer of our songs' can make chaos sound like a beautiful melody."

Similarly, imagine an orchestra without a conductor, a cruise vessel without a captain, an aircraft without a pilot? As Kirk Franklyn surmised, even if each musician is skilled on their own instrument, and exhibited prowess, command, and dexterity, the orchestra/band will be utterly discordant and chaotic without effective collaboration and careful performance coordination. The same is true for a captain or an aircraft pilot who requires careful synchronicity of instrument controls to ensure that the vessel safely and successfully arrives at its intended destination. This is why CSFs play such a crucial role in organizational performance, since much like the composer, conductor, captain, or pilot, CSFs ensure harmony of musicians, crew, and flight attendants in the execution of their duties. In parallel, clearly articulated CSFs foster a shared sense of purpose, vision, and direction in the pursuit of mutually beneficial goals, to the degree that everyone expends the necessary effort toward achieving the group's collective objective. In the end, efficiency and effectiveness are increased when strategic alignment of the organization's goals is achieved, and the overall mission of the organization is attained.

b. *Identify Key Drivers for Success*: When organizations are afflicted with competing priorities, there needs to be a stabilizing force that reminds decision-makers of the key drivers of success. CSFs act as this stabilizing force that provides direction, filters the noise created by ambivalence, removes ambiguity around the "end-game," and ensures that nonessential activities do not distract from the organization achieving its purpose. Without CSFs, organizations risk wasting time, money, and effort on non-consequential activities to the peril of other critical activities that require focus, attention, and resources. By articulating CSFs, key success drivers come into view, providing helpful insights into where resources are needed, and ultimately informing the prioritization of time, effort, money, and personnel in the pursuit of the organization's goals.

c. *Instills Accountability and Enhances Monitoring*: Finally, CSFs not only highlight what needs to be done, but they also specify who (e.g., individual, team, or department) that is responsible for executing it. In turn, this creates accountability and empowers people or groups to take responsibility for the execution of tasks that are aligned with CSFs. Encouraging individuals and teams to take charge of activities or processes that are essential to meeting CSFs further instills ownership, which in turn creates a culture of responsibility, accountability, and commitment in meeting organizational goals.

In meeting organizational goals, it's important to remember that CSFs are not fixed targets, but rather, they serve as dynamic metrics of progress. Organizations may make strategic adjustments in response to insights gleaned from continuous performance monitoring to meet market conditions while remaining aligned with the organization's stated objectives. Organizations that take the effort to routinely assess their performance are better able to stay on track and adapt to shifting market conditions.

Effective performance management relies heavily on identifying and focusing on CSFs. They integrate organizational actions with strategic objectives, highlight the critical factors for success, and provide the essential framework for defining responsibility, instilling accountability, and facilitating effective performance monitoring.

Without CSFs, organizations risk wandering aimlessly, losing sight of their goals, and squandering important resources.

> **Without CSFs, organizations risk wandering aimlessly, losing sight of their goals, and squandering important resources.**

Now that we have exhausted the need for and importance of defining CSFs, let's now focus on the arduous task of defining them.

How to Define Critical Success Factors (CSFs)

The process of determining CSFs is a determinative and carefully executed process to define the primary factors that influence the organization's ability to meet its mission and objectives. This structured endeavor is comprised of several steps, each being pivotal in ensuring clarity, precision, and alignment with the organization's strategic objectives and stakeholder expectations. This process is comprised of the following seven steps:

Step 1: Define Organizational Goals and Objectives
Step 2: Identify KPIs
Step 3: Conduct Stakeholder Analysis

Step 4: Analyze Industry and Market Trends
Step 5: Prioritize CSFs
Step 6: Validate CSFs with Leadership
Step 7: Communicate and Monitor CSFs

Step 1: Establish Organizational Goals and Objectives

Why do we exist? What are our core products and services? What does success for our customers look like? These questions represent the heart of the organization and embody the organization's mission and strategic imperatives. To answer these questions in quantifiable ways, CSFs provide the utility in not only establishing a comprehensive understanding of the organization's strategic objectives, but aids in defining the broad aspirations of what and how the company hopes to accomplish its objectives. The process of defining CSFs starts with the organization's key leaders and top executives to align their "vision of the future" with the organization's fundamental goals and objectives. Since vaguely written objectives invariably lead to equally vague CSFs, it's imperative that executives carefully focus and articulate what truly matters to the organization. This top-down approach promotes clarity of purpose, precise CSF definition, and ultimately, provides specificity needed to eliminate ambiguity in pursuit of CSF attainment.

Step 2: Identify Key Performance Indicators (KPIs)

As defined earlier, KPIs are quantifiable metrics used to evaluate the efficiency and effectiveness of organizational processes in relation to the attainment of its strategic goals. These metrics are closely intertwined with CSF definition, providing the ability to not only define, but also measure organizational performance in relation to CSFs. For each strategic objective identified, organizations must identify KPIs that are both quantifiable and measurable so that CSF development can be monitored. Focus on quantifiable metrics is a hallmark of effective KPIs; thus, choosing metrics that can be objectively measured, organizations avoid ambiguity and subjective assessments. This not only enhances the accuracy of performance tracking but also makes it easier to determine the impact of CSFs on strategic objectives. While KPI identification will be elaborated on in a subsequent section, its reference in this sequence of steps is intended to contextualize its role relative to CSFs process identification and evaluation.

Step 3: Conduct Stakeholder Analysis

Chapter 1 provided an exhaustive list of stakeholders that are central to organizational change success. This list of stakeholders must be consulted when defining CSFs, since understanding who has a vested interest in the organization's success is crucial for aligning CSFs with stakeholder expectations. During this stakeholder analysis step, organizations identify their key stakeholders, including internal groups like employees and management, as well as external entities such as customers, suppliers, and regulatory agencies. Stakeholder expectations are managed by carefully listening, documenting, and prioritizing interests and concerns, and ensuring that these reflections are captured in CSF definition. By actively involving stakeholders in the process, organizations will enlist the support of its stakeholders while cataloging critical perspectives on factors that are deemed crucial for achieving success. These insights are collected via surveys, interviews, focus groups, and other collaborative approaches, outputs of which further lend to CSF credibility, monitoring, and attainment.

Step 4: Analyze Industry and Market Trends

As industry, market, and customer trends evolve, so should CSFs. That's why one of the most important attributes of effective process monitoring is adaptability. Since organizations exist within environments that are influenced by ever-changing market demands, industry changes, and external influences, evaluation and comprehensive assessment of these changes is crucial to identify potential threats and opportunities for the organization. CSFs must be similarly flexible to these changing conditions and be able to accommodate new requirements, customer expectations, and stakeholder demands. This adaptability ensures that the organization remains relevant to its target market, while at the same time ensuring alignment to the organization's mission and strategic imperatives. In the end, CSF flexibility ensures their continued relevance and ability to propel organizational success amidst dynamic environment changes.

Step 5: Prioritize CSFs

CSFs vary in their level of importance to the organization— they are not all ranked critical. The reason being that certain factors and conditions may dictate and influence the attainment of strategic objectives to a greater extent than others. For this reason, organizations must evaluate and assess each CSF to determine the level of significance relative to organizational objective alignment, and their capacity to achieve strategic results. During this evaluation process, CSFs are ranked according to this strategic significance, the outputs of which then informs resource allocation decisions to ensure that the most urgent factors, with the greatest impact on organizational success, receive resource allocation priority.

Step 6: Validate CSFs with Leadership

In this step, CSFs are scrutinized based on accuracy, priority, and relevance to meeting organizational objectives. Thus, this step requires that CSFs are demonstrably aligned with stated organizational objectives to receive requisite levels of endorsement from the organization's senior leadership. The input and approval of senior leadership are critical for CSFs to garner significance within the organization, and by extension, represents an important step that demonstrates senior leadership's dedication and adherence to the strategic direction of the organization.

Step 7: Communicate and Monitor CSFs

Once senior leadership has signed-off on CSFs for alignment, prioritization, and relevance to meeting the organization's core strategic imperatives, CSFs are then ready to be disseminated across the organization. Team members working together in business groups, verticals, and departments must become intimately acquainted with approved CSFs, regardless of their divisional associations. Effective sponsorship and communication from senior leaders help to articulate the urgency of CSF attainment relative to organizational performance. This in turn aids in creating a unified workforce where all key personnel are aligned and collaborating toward the attainment of shared organizational objectives.

While effective communication is mandatory for CSF attainment, the final step in this process requires tracking and monitoring to ensure "actual" outcomes align with "planned" outcomes. In this regard, organizations must employ capable performance monitoring tools to effectively monitor progress of CSF goal attainment. This entails the ongoing gathering of data pertaining to KPIs, periodic reporting, and ongoing analysis While these activities will be elaborated upon in the next section, these techniques offer important insight into the organization's performance, enabling timely, relevant, and environment-adjusted modifications to ensure that CSFs remain a top priority for the organization.

As outlined in the seven steps above, the process of establishing CSFs is a deliberate and repetitive process that ensures alignment of organizational objectives, involves relevant stakeholders, adjusts to evolving market conditions, and eventually facilitates organizational goal attainment. By diligently adhering to each phase, organizations will be able to develop a roadmap that not only directs their operations, but also enables them to accomplish their strategic objectives with accuracy and intentionality. However, for organizations to properly traverse the route to success, they need a set of precise instruments that measure progress and ensure that CSFs are being addressed adequately. That's where KPIs come into play: KPIs take the conceptually vague ideas of CSFs and translate them into a set of concrete, quantifiable measurements that allow businesses to track their progress on the path toward attaining their strategic objectives. In their most basic form, KPIs serve to bridge the gap that exists between strategic planning and operational execution by turning CSFs into data points that can be put into action. The outcome of which then informs decision-makers and gives teams the ability to optimize organizational performance. Against that backdrop, let's take a deep dive into the world of KPIs.

What Are Key Performance Indicators (KPIs)?

KPIs are elements of a strategic plan that provide quantifiable measures for assessing organizational performance. They represent metrics or indicators that can be used to measure, evaluate, and track progress toward specific strategic goals and objectives (Neely, Adams, & Kennerley, 2002). KPIs therefore provide a holistic view of how the organization is performing in relation to its stated goals and objectives by providing specific and time-bound outcomes in relation to meeting CSF performance. They are carefully selected to provide a clear and measurable representation of an organization's performance in critical areas, enabling informed decision-making and targeted improvements, (Neely, Adams, & Kennerley, 2002).

According to Heyden Enochson of OnStratey (2023), KPIs should minimally accomplish the following objectives:

■ Outline and measure the organization's most significant set of outputs.
■ Provide a data-centric focus for the organization's performance management process.
■ Provide progress assessments to confirm if performance is being made against strategy.
■ Articulate time-bound future goals that express what is to be achieved, and by when.
■ Measure quantifiable components of the organization's goals and objectives.
■ Assess the most significant leading and lagging measures in the organization.

In describing KPIs, Enochson differentiates the characteristics between indicators and KPIs, with the primary differences being:

Indicators: Are metrics used to evaluate various aspects of organizational performance. Organizations employ and monitor these metrics based on departmental monitoring requirements, leadership interests, reporting requirements, etc. However, while many of these metrics provide data, useful insights, and ultimately information for management, these metrics are not connected in any way to the organization's overarching strategic objectives, and this is the key difference between indicators and KPIs.

Key Performing Indicators: are specific indicators that monitor organizational progress toward the attainment of its strategic objectives (i.e., specific goal, target, or outcomes). As described earlier, while indicators provide data, useful insights, and ultimately information for management, KPIs focus on providing information relating to the greatest and most reliable measures that are connected to the long-term strategic plan of the organization and the attainment of its stated objectives.

He further posits that for KPIs to be actionable and credible, they must facilitate the attainment of CSFs and include the following five critical attributes:

- **A Measure:** Every KPI must have a measure. A measure is a verbal expression of what is being evaluated (e.g., number of new customers in 2023).
- **A Target:** Every KPI needs to have a numeric target that matches your measure, and include a timeframe in which the goal is to be achieved (e.g., onboard 1000 new customers by the end of 2024).
- **A Data Source:** Every KPI must have a clearly defined data source to minimize erroneous reporting and analysis. The data source will be provisioned from a central location where data is queried, measured, and analyzed. During this process, its critically important to use consistent metrics across attributes, such as numeric assessment, percentages, and/or variance assessments to monitor relative changes between KPIs.
- **Reporting Frequency:** While different measures may have different reporting requirements and cadences, it's generally considered good practice to monitor, analyze,

and report KPIs at least monthly. The organization will evaluate KPI alignment with its CSFs and establish the data collection frequency.

■ **Owner:** While not a mandatory requirement for KPI management, it is also considered good practice to define roles and set expectations for KPI management. This includes delineating who will perform monitoring, reporting, and refining of KPIs in accordance with meeting CSFs.

Why Are KPIs Important in Performance Management?

KPIs play a pivotal role in performance management since they provide organizations with a structured and quantitative approach that helps them accomplish their long-term strategic goals. At a high level, KPIs enable organizations to make informed decisions, promote an environment of continuous learning, foster progress, and ultimately enhances organizational competitiveness by measuring performance in accordance with the organization's most important goals.

The use of data further allows for quantifiable metrics to be frequently evaluated against organizational performance. This fosters an environment of performance optimization where performance measurement informs leadership's decision-making, strategic goal alignment, and ultimately, organizational process optimization. Through the use of periodic data analysis, benchmarking, and target setting, decision-makers are able to fine-tune performance management strategies using data-driven insights to guide strategic and operational decisions. This data-driven, evidence-based, and decision-making methodology is critically important in organizational performance management, as it affords organizations the opportunity to make informed choices that are aligned with their strategic objectives, while actively taking requisite steps to mitigate risks, allocate resources judiciously, and ultimately foster ongoing organizational process improvement.

Now that we have introduced a few of the key benefits associated with the use of KPIs in performance management, let's take a deeper dive into some of these areas given their significance in creating tangible benefits to the organization.

Strategic Alignment

Strategic alignment is a critical function of organizational performance management to ensure that all levels within the organization are committed to and working toward the accomplishment of the organization's strategic objectives. Thus, KPIs facilitate strategic alignment by:

Linking to Strategic Objectives: KPIs are chosen to directly mirror and evaluate progress toward meeting organizational strategic goals and objectives. KPIs therefore must link to distinct strategic goals to precisely assess the impact that an individual, team, or department's performance has on the attainment of the overall organizational mission.

Providing Clarity of Purpose: Providing individuals and teams with a defined set of KPIs enables them to understand their respective duties and responsibilities relative to how their work impacts the attainment of the organization's strategic goals.

Prioritizing Action: KPIs focus attention on what matters most to the organization. This insight then helps the organization prioritize activities and allocate critical resources to maximize impact and ultimately the attainment of the organization's strategic goals.

Providing Assessment Consistency: KPIs ensure that goals and priorities are consistent across different levels of the organization, including both top-level executives and frontline staff. Aligning everyone's efforts toward attaining the same set of KPIs reduces the likelihood of conflicting or misaligned activities.

Enabling Performance Decomposition: Higher-order KPIs can be decomposed into smaller and more focused KPIs in order to ensure specificity, uniformity, and familiarity of organizational goals across every department, team, and individual.

Instilling Accountability and Responsibility: KPIs enable ownership and responsibility to individuals and/or teams by ensuring that they are accountable for attaining specific KPI goals, while maintaining a vested interest in achieving the overarching strategic goals of the organization.

Facilitating an Adaptive Strategy: KPIs must be adaptable to respond to changing organizational needs and requirements. Adaptability is important to accommodate shifts in market conditions, client preferences, or realignment of internal needs while maintaining alignment with the organization's long-term strategy and objectives.

Enabling Performance evaluations and feedback: Consistent performance evaluations centered around KPI performance provide an opportunity for managers and staff to evaluate progress, monitor and mitigate risks, take course-corrective action, and ultimately align team-level activities with the organization's strategic imperatives.

Providing Effective Decision-Making: KPI data offers decision-makers timely and periodic insights into the organization's progress toward the attainment of its strategic objectives. This information facilitates executive decision-making by ensuring that decisions are in line with the organization's strategic goals.

Providing Continuous Improvement: Organizations rely on KPI performance data as an input toward implementing course-corrective actions when organizational performance deviates from required performance standards. This allows organizations to adjust, align, and optimize their processes to meet their strategic objectives.

Progress Monitoring

KPIs play a crucial role in monitoring organizational performance by providing a methodical and data-driven approach for observing and evaluating the extent to which organizations meet their strategic objectives and goals. KPIs facilitate progress monitoring in the following ways:

Providing Quantifiable Measurements: One of the benefits of KPIs is the ability to quantify organizational performance. KPIs facilitate progress monitoring by detailing clear and quantifiable numerical measures of performance in relation to predefined performance baselines. When performance is measured against these baselines, leaders can achieve objective, efficient, and reliable assessments of the organization's performance while reducing subjective human-interpretation errors.

Frequent Performance Assessments: With baseline targets defined and performance measures established, organizations are equipped to begin the process of collecting performance data. Since KPIs provide insights into organizational performance in real-time or nearly real-time, organizations are positioned to quickly respond when observed performance deviates from established thresholds. Data collection frequency is dependent upon the metric being assessed; however, once a consistent cadence is determined (i.e., daily, weekly, monthly, quarterly, or annual intervals), the organization is then equipped to collect and analyze performance data, review data patterns, and respond to triggers and alerts when performance falls outside of predefined thresholds. Frequent performance assessments ultimately enable stakeholders to make data-driven decisions and provide targeted course-corrective adjustments based on quantifiable performance data and trends.

Visual Representation: KPI data collection and analysis, which was performed in the previous step is aided using graphs, dashboards, scorecards, or other forms of data visualizations. This visualization capability enables stakeholders to glean helpful insights, monitor performance trends, and take corrective action to bring about compliance with established CSFs. Data visualization aids data-driven decisions through use of comparative analysis between past and current organizational performance or when the organization's performance is compared against industry benchmarks, competitor performance, or other sources of historical performance data.

Provide Objective Analysis: KPIs provide the ability to offer objective feedback to individuals, teams, and departments regarding their performance. Whether analyzed through departmental reports, or via electronic dashboards, the primary goal of KPI progress monitoring is to provide objective feedback and organizational performance analysis. In so doing, decision-makers will be able to (a) quantify progress in relation to achieving the organization's strategic objectives, (b) identify performance trends, issues, and problems requiring course-corrective action, and (c) enable the transparent communication of organizational performance with objectivity, reliability, and accuracy.

Continuous Improvement

Thus far, we have established that KPIs provide strategic alignment with organizational goals that ultimately form the basis for effective performance monitoring. These two outcomes are essential for ensuring that the organization's objectives are achieved. However, at the heart of KPI monitoring is another important and critical outcome—continuous improvement. Continuous improvement is one of the most important outcomes of performance monitoring, as it ensures that the organization continually seeks ways to improve its operations, and in so doing, continually improve the delivery of its product and services to its customers.

KPIs are, therefore essential elements needed for effective continuous improvement processes since they provide quantifiable data, helpful feedback, and insights that are necessary to identify areas for improvement, facilitate data-driven decisions, and to foster a culture of product/service delivery excellence and innovation. In this regard, KPIs provides the necessary framework and tools necessary to make organizational improvements through the following methods and techniques:

> **KPIs facilitate data-driven decisions, and to foster a culture of service delivery excellence and innovation.**

Performance Analysis: As established earlier, ongoing analysis is central to performance monitoring, and by extension, continuous improvement. Performance analysis therefore provides the ability to measure the organization's performance against performance targets and provide reliable conclusions about performance deviations. It is this frequent analysis that enables organizations to pinpoint areas of performance concerns, and identify areas where improvements are required.

Root Cause Analysis: Pinpointing areas of performance concerns, and identifying areas where improvements are required is an important outcome of performance analysis; however, what are the underlining causes that led poor performance in the first place? This is where Root Cause Analysis comes into focus. KPIs reveal areas of poor performance, or deviations from required objectives, giving organizations the ability to undertake detailed analysis to uncover underlying causes. These fundamental reasons are referred to as root causes and thus the analysis is referred to as Root Cause Analysis. The results of this analysis ultimately and precisely identify why problems occurred, and enables leaders to prescribe course-corrective actions to avert reoccurrence of undesirable performance. While many books have been written on Root Cause Analysis, and a detailed exposition is beyond the scope of this section, this abbreviated description is intended to provide context on how Root Cause Analysis is used in relation to continuous improvement and performance monitoring activities.

Continuous Monitoring: As described earlier, continuous, or periodic monitoring of KPIs enables organizations to monitor progress over time. In so doing, organizations can spot performance issues and identify areas needed for improvement. Continuous monitoring is aided through effective feedback mechanisms and self-reflection processes that provide insight into individual, team, or departmental performance. As improvement opportunities are identified and exploited, organizations are then enabled to make data-driven and performance optimization decisions. This enables leaders to compare the organization's performance against established benchmarks, industry best practices, and competitor service offerings and/or product catalogs.

Data-Driven Decisions: Continuous monitoring, that is aided through effective comparative analysis, provide the organization with critical insights about its own performance in relation to its competitors, and provides the vehicle for the adoption and implementation of optimized performance strategies. These improvements are facilitated by insights and quantifiable performance measures aimed at providing a view into performance trends, process related bottlenecks, organizational dysfunction, and critical areas where course-corrective actions are needed. Decision-makers therefore rely on this data to make informed decisions about process related changes, resource assignments, or the need to allocate additional financial resources in pursuit of achieving optimized organizational processes and performance.

Performance Review: Continuous improvement requires the constant review and analysis of organizational activities, and implied in this process is the need to "push the envelope" for even higher levels of performance. This is done through target setting in which current targets are evaluated, performance assessed against those targets, and set even higher targets for areas where targets are exceeded, to encourage greater levels of performance. When targets are frequently exceeded, individuals, teams, and/or departments are recognized and rewarded as high-performing units. This intentional recognition process is central to establishing a culture that celebrates high-performance achievements. KPIs enable all facets of this process, from review and analysis, to target setting decisions, and ultimately, performance monitoring with tangible and desirable rewards. In the end, KPIs demonstrate their value in organizational performance monitoring.

Accountability and Transparency

The final area that we will discuss that explains why KPIs play an important role in performance management focuses on the need for accountability and transparency. KPIs provide a structured framework for defining performance standards, evaluating outcomes, assigning accountability, and promoting transparency and openness. This framework is utilized to assist organizations establish a culture of ownership` and prioritizes the adherence to organizational performance standards. Individuals, teams, and departments who espouse these values assume responsibility for their performance that contributes to the organization accomplishing its strategic objectives.

In this regard, KPIs facilitate accountability and transparency using effective human-social collaborative techniques that starts with expectation setting. From the outset, KPIs set explicit and measurable performance standards for individuals, teams, and departments by providing criteria for determining success and expected outcomes. Expectation setting is fundamental to reducing ambiguity and establishing ownership. When individuals, teams, and departments take ownership of KPIs that are aligned to their respective areas of specialization, accountability is instilled. These units of performance (i.e., individuals, teams, departments) therefore become responsible to provide outcomes that are consistent with, and aligned to, the attainment of established organizational objectives. Conversely, performance deviations often result in implementing corrective measures to hold poorly performing units accountable, while high-performing units are recognized—further galvanizing a culture of continuous improvement.

Performance deviations can only be monitored when KPIs are evaluated against clearly defined objective performance measures. This is yet another reason why KPIs play such a pivotal role in performance management, since they provide standardized objective performance measures, along with an evaluative strategy that ensures that organizational performance is reliably analyzed and tracked across the organization. As established earlier, KPI tracking and monitoring is performed at predetermined cadences so that data can be collected, analyzed, and reported on with regularity. This data collection and analysis process provide data transparency that empowers stakeholders to access and assess performance related information that ultimately informs their decision-making.

KPIs facilitate effective decision-making, as they provide the ability to map performance data with performance targets. This mapping provides real-time access to information that allows stakeholders to process performance deviations, broker discussions with affected individuals, teams, or departments, and utilize feedback strategies to reinforce the importance of meeting KPI targets. This ultimately instills performance accountability, since KPIs are direct reflective measures of the organization's strategic imperatives. The attainment of the organization's strategic imperatives represents an important milestone in performance monitoring. Leaders then codify KPIs into performance agreements and contracts, and find ways to incentivize desirable behaviors. Performance incentives, whether at the individual, team, or department level, provide compelling justification for units to adhere to performance standards since reward systems help to provide high-performance reinforcement strategies. In the end, KPIs foster data transparency, clearly articulated performance standards, and reinforcement systems that incentivize high-performing organizational units. But how are KPIs measured? What is the relation to performance metrics? That's the topic of the next and final segment in the pillar performance management.

What Are Organizational Performance Metrics?

Now that we have established the importance of critical success factors and key performance indicators, we will now delve into the elements, steps, and phases of defining performance metrics.

The first and most important aspect of performance monitoring starts with knowing what to measure! While this may be obvious to many, articulating specific organizational metrics that provide insight into CSF attainment can sometimes be daunting. Despite the challenges, defining assessment metrics serve as the bedrock for performance monitoring as it aids in distinguishing the relevant operational and strategic metrics that align with the organization's strategic imperatives, goals, and objectives.

Assessment metrics are measures of quantitative assessment used for evaluating, comparing, and tracking organizational performance, business processes, technology projects, or prescribed goals set by the organization. Metrics can take a variety of forms and are aimed at providing insight into specific organizational performance areas. For example, financial metrics may provide insight into the organization's profit margins, return on investment, inventory turnover, cash conversion cycle, budget variance, earnings per share, sales growth rates, etc.

Metrics can also take the form of qualitative assessment measures that offer descriptive insight into performance data, and hence the term "descriptive data." Descriptive data refers to qualitative measures that aren't always based on numerical values, but rather on human observations, sentiments, and/or interpretations. Qualitative data can also be garnered from customer feedback, product reviews, and answers to interview questions with examples such as: rates of customer satisfaction, staff turnover, and operational efficiency.

Improvado, a data analytics organization that specializes in AI data integration, offers a concise and contrasting summation of quantitative versus qualitative metrics in Table 4.13 (Linker, 2023):

Table 4.13 Quantitative versus Qualitative Metrics

Feature	*Quantitative Metrics*	*Qualitative Metrics*
Definition	Metrics that can be measured and expressed numerically.	Metrics that provide insights based on non-numerical data.
Nature	Objective	Subjective
Data Source	Surveys with closed-ended questions, web analytics, etc.	Interviews, open-ended surveys, feedback, and observations.
Examples	Revenue, website visitors, bounce rate, conversion rate.	Customer satisfaction, brand perception, and user experience.
Use Case	To measure performance, track goals, and forecast.	To understand user feelings, motivations, and preferences.
Tools & Methods	Spreadsheets, charts, statistical software.	Focus groups, one-on-one interviews, and thematic analysis.
Data Presentation	Graphs, bar charts, pie charts, and histograms.	Word clouds, affinity diagrams, and narrative summaries.
Advantages	Specific, measurable, and easily benchmarked.	Offers depth, context, and understanding of user behavior.

(Continued)

Table 4.13   (Continued)

Feature	Quantitative Metrics	Qualitative Metrics
Limitations	Lacks depth and context; can miss nuances.	Time-consuming, not easily scalable, and harder to benchmark.
Ideal for	Tracking KPIs, monitoring growth, and financial reports.	Exploratory research; understanding "why" behind data.

Now that we have established the different types of metrics, let's go a step further and establish why defining metrics is so critically important to organizational performance monitoring.

Assessment Metrics:

1. **Improves Decision-Making:** Assessment metrics facilitate effective decision-making by leveraging data to inform organizational performance improvements, and to provide valuable insights necessary for resource allocation and prioritization. Assessment metrics should be specific to the area being monitored, aligned to the organization's strategic goals, clearly defined with straightforward outcomes, and easy to understand. These attributes will ensure that metrics are widely understood, adopted, and monitored.

2. **Facilitates Trend Analysis:** Assessment metrics are invaluable for providing trend analysis across key areas of the organization that impact service quality and delivery. Organizations that monitor metrics over time are able to forecast future performance based on current data and leverage current data to anticipate potential impediments that can hinder the achievement of the organization's strategic objectives.

3. **Ensures Alignment with Organizational Goals:**
   Assessment metrics helps to galvanize departmental goals
   by ensuring adherence to the organization's overarching
   strategic goals, thereby creating synergy, cohesion, and
   alignment. It is important that assessment metrics be
   relevant to the function or process that is being assessed.
   For instance, customer service may be evaluated by
   the use of satisfaction surveys with customers, or
   manufacturing efficiency might be measured by the
   number of units produced in an hour.
4. **Instills Accountability:** In addition to galvanizing
   teams around organizational goals, assessment metrics
   ensure that stakeholders and teams are held accountable
   for performance outcomes, which ultimately ensures that
   individual responsibilities are met and the organization's
   strategic objectives are achieved. In order to adequately
   instill accountability, metrics need to be quantifiable, and
   by the same token, the organization must have the requisite
   tools and systems available to accurately measure them.
5. **Provides Continuous Improvement:** Assessment
   metrics help organizations exploit opportunities for
   advancement, development, and process optimization
   by assessing performance and providing feedback for
   improvement. Metrics must, therefore be continually
   monitored in order to assess current performance
   against specified organizational standards, industry
   standards, or competitor service offerings. This allows
   the organization to gain insights into its performance
   and relative position in the marketplace. As established
   in the earlier segment on KPI definition, continuous
   improvement is one of the most important outcomes
   of performance monitoring, as it ensures that the
   organization continually find ways to improve its
   operations, and in so doing, continually improve the
   delivery of its product and services to its customers.

6. **Build Stakeholder Confidence:** Assessment metrics that consistently reveal high degrees of organizational performance often result in increased shareholder confidence, morale boost for its stakeholders, and ultimately, increased loyalty of its customers.

The six points above describe why assessment metrics are the building blocks for effective performance measurement and monitoring of an organization, as they offer precise and evidence-based data that provide valuable insights into the organization's operations, its market position, opportunities for strategic coordination and improvement, and areas where performance accountability is required. Through the use of properly defined and accurately monitored metrics, decision-makers will be equipped with the requisite data to creatively improve organizational performance, cultivate a culture of high-performance standards, and exploit opportunities that provide ongoing service delivery enhancements for the organization. In the next section, we will expand the discussion and detail the necessary steps for defining assessment metrics within the context of organizational performance management.

> Assessment Metrics offer evidence-based data that provide valuable insights into the organization's operations.

How to Define Assessment Metrics

Within the framework of organizational performance management, establishing evaluation criteria is a crucial step in ensuring that the organization accurately measures and improves its performance. One of the most important steps in this performance optimization process is to define assessment metrics.

Earlier we established that assessment metrics are precise, quantifiable measures that are used to evaluate and determine the organizational effectiveness relative to its ability to meet its strategic goals. These quantifiable measures provide critical insights that enable analysis of the organization's performance relative to its CSF and KPIs. As a refresher, Table 4.14 illustrates scenario-based examples that illustrate the important relationship between CSF, KPIs, and assessment metrics as a predicate for defining assessment metrics.

Table 4.14   CSF, KPI, and Assessment Metric Relationships

Example	*Critical Success Factor (CSF)*	*Key Performance Indicator (KPI)*	*Assessment Metric*
New Product Launch	Market research	Number of new product sales	Customer satisfaction survey of new product
Employee Training	Employee knowledge, retention, and skills	Training completion rate	Training feedback via employee surveys
Manufacturing	Product quality	Unit defect rate	Quality control inspections
Software Development	Requirement analysis	Code defect density	User Acceptance Testing (UAT) results
Supply Chain Management	Supplier performance	On-time delivery percentage	Supplier scorecards
Educational Institution	Student satisfaction	Graduation rate	Course evaluation surveys
Renewable Energy Project	Government regulations	Renewable energy output	Environmental impact assessment

(Continued)

Table 4.14 (Continued)

Example	Critical Success Factor (CSF)	Key Performance Indicator (KPI)	Assessment Metric
Sales Team Performance	Sales training	Monthly sales revenue	Sales team performance review
IT Helpdesk	Customer support quality	Average resolution time	Customer satisfaction surveys
IT Project	Project planning	On-time project delivery	Weekly progress reports
Social Media Marketing	Content strategy	Engagement Rate	Social media analytics
Human Resources	Employee development	Employee turnover rate	Employee engagement surveys
Church Fundraising	Congregational engagement	Tithe revenue	Tithe-payer retention rate

Now that we have demonstrated the relationships between CSFs, KPIs, and assessment metrics, the steps needed to accurately and adequately define assessment metrics will depend on the organization's data collection priority relative to achieving its CSFs. This is due to the fact that assessment metrics, while they tend to be data intensive while providing rich organizational information, may not always be construed with the same level of priority as KPIs. Nevertheless, assessment metrics still require careful thought and intentionality, as data collection efforts can be resource-intensive and time-consuming.

The following steps are therefore intended to address the foundational processes that are necessary to provide meaningful assessment metric definition; however, it's important to establish from the outset that defining assessment metrics includes overlapping processes similar to those performed when defining CSFs and KPIs. This is due to their interconnectedness in establishing effective and efficient performance monitoring measures and processes that are central to the organization achieving its intended outcomes.

Step 1: Define the Context

The first step for defining assessment metrics is to understand the organizational context that warrants the metric. This is done through a review of the organization's strategic objectives, missions, and goals. Against this backdrop, critical organizational imperatives will come to light that inform the formal development of CSF and then subsequently, KPIs.

Step 2: Establish CSFs

Once the organizational foundation is established, the next step is to codify CSFs by identifying the fundamental components and/or processes that are essential for the organization to achieve its objectives. This is done through brokering executive-level discussions to ascertain the organization's strategic plan and identify the key elements needed for the organization's success. Be it customer retention, revenue maximization, fortifying brand loyalty, or any other element needed for the organization to achieve its goals, output of these discussions will result in a list of CSFs that will then be prioritized, and KPIs developed to facilitate performance monitoring and, ultimately, process improvement.

Step 3: Define KPIs

With CSFs established, defining quantifiable metrics that measure and track progress is important. This is done through KPI development, and it is during this step that KPIs are evaluated and linked to CSFs to ensure organizational goal alignment. In addition, the KPI development phase also facilitates metric refinement to ensure that performance targets are clearly established, and SMART (i.e., Specific, Measurable, Achievable, Relevant, and Time-bound) goals are developed.

Step 4: Identify Performance Metrics

With SMART goals developed, a list of key stakeholders is identified to assess organizational performance. This list of elements will inform data collection processes and systems of record to ensure that consistent and reliable sources of information are both available and accessible. While internal systems and benchmarks are useful for making performance assessments, a more holistic approach will include industry-specific assessment metrics and best practices. This data set can then be used to evaluate against historical organizational performance data to identify organizational trends and patterns, juxtaposed to other sources of external assessment performance measures.

Step 5: Prioritize Performance Metrics

The next step is the prioritization of metrics. Since the importance of each assessment metric varies considerably, a priority assessment based on their respective impact on organizational success is made, in addition to an assessment against established CSFs and KPIs. The prioritized ranking is then ordered based on the most critical metrics and those that provide valuable organizational performance insights.

Step 6: Articulate Assessment Metrics

With a prioritized list of metrics ordered on the basis of CSF importance in place, the next step is to articulate the intent of each metric by providing a detailed description of what is being captured, measured, and calculated. This articulation includes defining the relevant data sources from which elements are captured, formalizing the data capture frequency (e.g., hourly, daily, weekly, monthly, quarterly, annually, etc.), and creating a roles matrix that identifies the owner of the data element who is responsible for data collection and reporting accuracy.

Step 7: Formalize Data Collection Processes

With data elements identified, and data collection cadences established, the next step is to formalize the data collection process. The data collection process represents standardized procedures and instruments used to collect, evaluate, and transmit performance data pertaining to assessment metrics. As this process represents actual measures of organizational performance, the resultant data set, data collection procedures need to ensure that data sources are accurate, consistent, and aligned with organizational objectives.

Step 8: Monitor, Refine, and Optimize

As performance data is compiled, analyzed, and reported, the next step in the process requires ongoing monitoring and refinements. During this step, it's imperative to consistently evaluate and scrutinize performance data in order to pinpoint areas of deficiency and dysfunctional processes. This information will equip decision-makers with reliable data to make informed data-driven decisions, modify strategies, and ultimately enhance CSFs, KPIs, and assessment metrics.

Step 9: Provide Feedback

Feedback is an important output of performance monitoring, as it is in this phase where stakeholders glean insights into how the organization is performing at macro and micro levels of the organization. Therefore, the output of the data analysis phase in the previous step informs this step which requires sharing performance data results with all affected individuals, teams, and departments. Disseminating CSFs, KPIs, and assessment data with all pertinent organization stakeholders ensures that organizational units are made aware of the importance of performance metrics in attaining organizational success and provides the basis for units to assess their individual and/or collective inputs against the overall performance of the organization. This organizational awareness is important for the final step: continuous improvement.

Step 10: Implement Continuous Improvement Measures

Organizations that intentionally implement strategies for identifying, defining, and utilizing assessment metrics in accordance with CSFs and KPIs position themselves to optimize organizational performance, achieve strategic alignment with organizational imperatives, and ultimately find ways to continually improve the delivery of their products and services. This consistent evaluative process therefore enables organizations to continually modify performance targets, review areas for performance improvements, and ultimately take the requisite steps necessary to make organizational realignments, maintaining congruence with evolving organizational objectives and priorities.

In this chapter, we explored the vital role of CSFs, KPIs, and assessment metrics relative to effective organizational performance management. We explored these foundational elements by elaborating on the essential interdependent functions that influence organizational performance. We further discussed that CSFs, KPIs, and assessment metrics act as a compass that guides organizational strategic activities, enables performance evaluation monitoring, targets areas that require improvement, and ensures alignment with the organization's strategic goals.

As we now transition to the next chapter, it is vitally important to recognize that organizational change is not motivated exclusively by numerical and statistical data, but rather predicated on the central role that people play in bringing about effective and efficient organizational transformations. So, while quantitative measures are important to drawing inference from an organization's performance, it's imperative to recognize that organizational transformation is not solely driven by numbers and data but rather, it is orchestrated by the people who breathe life into these metrics and ultimately shape the narrative of change within the organization's fabric.

People, therefore, represent the next and final pillar in the change continuum and will now be the topic of the next and final chapter.

Chapter 5

People

Introduction

The dynamic role that "people" play in organizational change management is foundational for effective organizational transformation. Why? People determine the objectives of change projects, imbuing them with significance and ensuring that these objectives are realized. From the onset of change initiation, articulating the organization's vision and mission serves as the foundation upon which effective transformation strategies are devised. Whether they are individuals from the C-Suite (i.e., CEO, CAO, CIO, etc.), divisional leaders, or internal/external stakeholders, it is *people* who will serve as the architects to shape the organization's *purpose* by reimagining a new organizational reality that enables, empowers, and equips its stakeholders with the requisite competences to successfully undertake and achieve organizational transformation.

The importance of "people" extends well beyond the act of envisioning the organization's change trajectory; people are the masterminds behind the *planning* process that translates the organization's strategic goals into

DOI: 10.4324/9781003544883-6

actionable steps. In this phase of planning, people stimulate creative ideas that spark innovation, while collaboratively devising strategies to overcome obstacles, impediments, and dysfunction. Through collaboration, creative solutions are birthed through effective team engagement to remedy challenges, and to implement solutions that facilitate the attainment of the organization's strategic goals. Planning therefore ensures that people make it their responsibility to manage tasks, resources, and deadlines by adhering to a working strategy that adapts to an ever-changing organizational environment.

Effective business *processes*, the backbone of organizational efficiency, are intrinsically intertwined with the welfare of people. Streamlining workflows, automating tasks, and optimizing organizational procedures all serve the dual purpose of enhancing productivity while minimizing workforce demands. While achieving optimized workflows through workforce automation, and increasing productivity with less overhead are desirable objectives, people are intricately involved in achieving what seems like paradoxical objectives. But when organizations prioritize the well-being of its workforce in pursuit of its strategic objectives, they are able to garner commitment toward achieving the organization's strategic goals.

Performance management, another essential component in the organizational change continuum, serves as a driving force for achieving organizational objectives while fostering a sense of belonging and purpose. While processes serve as the glue that unites organizational goals and strategy, *performance* measures the degree to which these goals are achieved. It further helps cultivate a culture of continuous improvement by providing opportunities for advancement, while recognizing the impact that people have made on the organization's transformative initiatives. When people are motivated, empowered, and equipped to undertake the tasks to which they are assigned, not only do they excel, but the entire organization stands to reap copious rewards.

Correlating the 5-Ps

Now that we have recapped the role of people in relation to the pillars of purpose, planning, process, and performance, it's now time to "go under the hood" and dissect this important and often complicated relationship, recognizing that people are the intertwining thread in the complicated fabric of effective organizational transformation.

Purpose and People

In the dynamic landscape of organizational change, purpose emerges as a pivotal element, anchoring and guiding organizational change strategy. A foundational element that influences the definition of purpose is the people within the organization—their values, visions, and aspirations that collectively shape the overarching mission of the organization. This human-centric approach ensures that the purpose resonates at a personal level, fostering engagement and alignment across all levels. This strategy, therefore, guarantees that the organizational mission connects on a personal level, which in turn fosters engagement and alignment at all levels of change execution. From the outset, people are not just mere passive recipients of change; they are active influencers, driving and shaping the change process. Their unique perspectives, skills, and experiences become the catalysts for innovative solutions and sustainable change. Thus, understanding and leveraging the human element is crucial in defining a purpose that is both meaningful and effective in steering organizational change.

As a recap from the first chapter, we established that purpose refers to the underlying reason or objective that governs a change initiative. It establishes the reasons why change is needed and codifies the desired outcomes or goals that the organization must seek in order to achieve its strategic objectives. Purpose provides clarity and direction around expected outcomes for its stakeholders and serves as the "north star" that aligns the organization's efforts with the needs and interests of stakeholders, fostering a deep sense of meaning, significance, and community for all involved in the change process.

On a practical level, understanding how purpose impacts people can be better understood by answering questions that probe why change is needed in the first place. Questions such as:

- Why is change necessary?
- What are the expected outcomes?
- What benefits will be derived?
- What improvements will be achieved beyond the status quo?
- How will people respond?
- To what degree will those impacted by the change embrace or reject it?

Answers to these questions help provide strategic stakeholder alignment by defining a shared understanding of the reason behind the change, so that all stakeholders can work toward a common goal. Answers also help focus effort by prioritizing actions and resources necessary to ensure harmony towards the attainment of the most important outcomes for the organization. Purpose also provides a reference point that focuses decision-making and allows stakeholders to assess whether actions and decisions are aligned with the organizational objectives. This alignment is critical because it increases commitment and buy-in, ultimately leading to higher levels of stakeholder engagement, and ultimately attainment of organizational strategic objectives.

As illustrated, defining purpose serves as the point of entry for successfully initiating organizational change initiatives. By extension, the role that people play in the process includes articulating a vision that motivates, directs, and compels people at all areas of the organization. People including both internal and external stakeholders are then inspired with a clear sense of the future, further galvanizing enthusiasm around the pursuit of shared and mutually beneficial goals. Inspiring the pursuit of shared goals provides a sense of organizational continuity and stability amidst turbulence. This creates a unifying force for people, which ultimately provides meaning and fulfillment at the individual level. Finally, a well-defined purpose affects people when it communicates authenticity, builds trust, and fosters long-term relationships. In the end, people are prone to express commitment to and for the change by inspiring the desire to acquire new skills, learn new methods, and master new tools and techniques needed for effective change adoption. When people believe in the purpose of the change, it focuses attention and equips the organization to navigate organizational change challenges with clarity, resilience, and a sense of direction.

Planning and People

In the context of organizational change, planning is a systematic, forward-looking, and strategic alignment process that defines the framework and supporting activities to effectively execute organizational transformations. Planning involves careful and meticulous articulation of tasks, schedules, phases, and milestones all which are mapped to the organization's strategic imperatives, business requirements, and stakeholder needs so as to yield the desired organizational outcomes. Planning lays out a series of interdependent steps that are necessary to achieve the strategic goals, relative to planned phases, schedules, and milestones, along with making the necessary resource assignments to effectively steward their completion.

Effective planning is best undertaken through a collaborative approach that involves key stakeholders at all levels of the organization. Organizations often enlist the help of professional consultants to act as project managers, ensuring that project planning activities are undertaken with the breadth and depth of execution–planning required to meet all business level requirements. Organizations may also seek support from management and technical staff to ensure intra-departmental visibility and collaboration, thereby brokering an inclusive strategy that ensures that considers diverse perspectives. This collaborative approach helps to garner trust and ultimately leads to the development of comprehensive and robust implementation plans.

In this entire approach, people play a critical role in the execution of project plans, inclusive of executive, project management, and task level resource execution. For this reason, people are central to charting the course because they bring a wealth of knowledge, experience, and insights about the organization's operations, culture, and potential roadblocks. They are also instrumental in the execution of said plans since they, at various levels of the organization, are responsible to not only harness their expertise, but also to foster a sense of ownership and commitment in the execution of assigned tasks. It's through this collective input and engagement strategy that planning become more than just a theoretical framework, but rather the transformative engine that enlists, motivates, empowers, and drives task level execution through people. In this integrated and methodical process, adept project managers can "see the end from the beginning," foreseeing obstacles, defining effective risk mitigation strategies, and ensuring that the project successfully achieves its objectives. Planning further impacts people since it requires a careful and intentional coordination of personnel, resources, and schedules in order to articulate and attain short- and long-term goals. While anticipating and addressing potential obstacles, and actively mitigating risks that threaten the attainment of organizational goals, people are instrumental in devising creative strategies to maximize organizational outcomes, while strategically anticipating and mitigating risks that threaten the attainment of critical organizational goals.

The role that "people" play in the planning process becomes even more evident during the translation of organizational goals into actionable implementation steps. The transformation of intangible concepts into concrete steps and actions provides a roadmap for people to facilitate the attainment of organizational change objectives. Effective stakeholder engagement further requires that people define clear objectives, conduct resource availability assessments, evaluate implementation threats and risks, and define measures for effective stakeholder engagement throughout the lifecycle of the change initiative. That's why the planning phase in organizational change is such a critical step, involving and relying on people who can significantly influence the success and sustainability of the change efforts.

Ultimately, the role that people play in the planning process ensures that new systems, tools, techniques, and processes are effectively adopted, strategically facilitating future organizational objectives with clarity, objectivity, and adaptability.

Process and People

One of the most impactful outcomes of organizational transformation is process-related change. Understanding and optimizing organizational processes are critical steps needed to make efficient and effective improvements. As introduced earlier, "process" refers to the structured sequence of activities or tasks that are necessary to achieve a specific organizational outcome. People are vital to defining efficient and effective business processes, since they aid in equipping individuals, teams, and business units with repeatable methods for predictable and consistent outcomes.

The ability to accurately assess process efficiency and effectiveness is critical for identifying bottlenecks, dysfunction, and suboptimal organizational procedures that impede high levels of performance. Business process analysis (BPA) and business process optimization are two key methodologies that are used to help organizations improve their business operations, providing a structured way for achieving increased organizational performance.

As a quick recap, BPA conducts a thorough review of the organization's existing processes to identify inefficiencies, redundancies, bottlenecks, and areas of dysfunction, whereas business process optimization seeks to achieve refinement and improvement of these processes relying on data-driven analysis and human-social collaborative insights gained only by working through people.

Herein lies the centrality of people in relation to "process" optimization. Their involvement, particularly those who are directly engaged in process execution, enables the organization to review, codify, refine, and optimize their critical processes. People also provide invaluable and contextual knowledge about the organization's workflows, challenges, and areas where improvements can be achieved, so as to ensure that both quantifiable and qualitative data aid in meaningful analysis and thus effective process optimization. Moreover, involving people in organizational process analysis and optimization efforts deepens their sense of value to the organization and creates high levels of ownership and acceptance of proposed changes. Ownership and acceptance are critical change enablers that facilitate process adoption, and thereby increase the likelihood of successful change implementation. This intricate human-social collaboration often uncovers hidden organizational knowledge along with unique understandings and procedural nuances that may not be apparent solely through data analysis alone. That's why the role of people is so vital in the review and optimization of the organization's processes. People provide depth of understanding about the organization's process, while offering rich information that ultimately leads to practical recommendations and widespread acceptance of strategic change initiatives. When organizations leverage, value, and integrate their people in their process analysis and optimization efforts, they position themselves to developing resilient, forward-looking, and more efficient processes that are aligned with the attainment of the organization's strategic business objectives.

Performance and People

When considering organizational change, performance serves as an essential indicator to assess the effectiveness of change initiatives by providing tangible feedback about how well the organization is adapting to new changes in relation to the attainment of its strategic goals. The role that "people" play in performance monitoring is central for the interpretation and translation of quantifiable goals and Key Performance Indicators (KPI) that are implemented in accordance with specific organizational change objectives. Consistent monitoring of performance metrics, supported by periodic evaluations and feedback assessments, provide an evaluative foundation that organizations rely upon when implementing performance-monitoring systems. Effective performance monitoring is not wholly a quantitative process, but may include additional measures of performance that represent other strategic areas of the organization. For this reason, organizations employ a mix of performance assessment modalities, such as the balanced scorecard methodology, to offer a more comprehensive evaluation of performance that incorporates a cross sectional view of the organization that spans financial, customer satisfaction, internal operations, and organizational learning and development metrics.

Regardless of the assessment modality, people form the backbone of organizational performance monitoring, since they are frequently the ones implementing tasks and activities that moderate organizational performance. Thus, their valuable insights, participation, and recommendations are pivotal for achieving process improvements, and their insights can be relied upon to uncover areas of bottlenecks and dysfunction that ultimately affect the organization's performance. These valuable insights therefore illuminate areas that require improvement. More importantly, they compel action where poor performance threatens the organization's viability.

In addition to their valuable insights, people also enable human-social collaborative working environments where dialog, just-in-time feedback, and team collaboration foster a deep sense of ownership, accountability, and corporate responsibility. The results of this human-social collaborative engagement promote a culture of continuous improvement where people are able to

> People enable collaborative environments where dialog, feedback, and team collaboration foster ownership, accountability, and corporate responsibility.

identify and own their various roles in the change process, thereby feeling empowered to proactively recommend and lead process improvement efforts.

Finally, people-centric KPIs provide essential information about how the change effort is actually impacting people. KPIs may include employee feedback, assessments of employee morale, and levels of engagement; all of which are influenced by individual responses to the change initiative. This feedback is critically important and instructive, as it provides pivotal information that ultimately impacts process and/ or system adoption. For these reasons, human-social factors directly influence sustainability, and ultimately, the degree of change permanence that is achieved at the conclusion of the organizational change initiative. Prioritizing people in the organization's performance-monitoring schema, therefore, not only improves the precision and applicability of performance monitoring, but also significantly puts the organization on a path toward cultivating a workforce that is invested in the attainment of its strategic goals, by employing adaptable and effective organizational-transformation strategies.

The Role of Competencies in Organizational Change

In the ever-changing landscape of corporate life, one thing remains true: the only constant is "change." Whether prompted by technological advancements, shifting market conditions, or product-related innovations, organizations must continuously adapt to survive and thrive. While strategies, processes, and technologies play vital roles in moderating organizational change, it is "people" within an organization who are most pivotal in determining the organization's success or failure. The critical role that "people" play in organizational change cannot be overstated, as their skills, attitudes, and competencies are critical enablers of success.

The role that "people" play relative to change adoption is underscored by another important truism: "being willing is admirable, but being capable is more desirable!" This is particularly important in environments where skills and individual capabilities are essential for success. Thus, one of the fundamental questions that must be addressed from the outset is: what skills are needed to successfully enable and execute change? Further, how does competency moderate success, and what assessments must be performed to ensure alignment between organizational expectations and its resulting performance? That's where Parry's definition of competencies helps to contextualize the enigmatic term—competencies—stating:

> **Competencies are a cluster of related knowledge, attitudes, and skills.**

"Competencies are a cluster of related knowledge, attitudes, and skills that affect a major part of one's job, correlate with performance, can be measured, and can be improved" (Parry, 1996). Based on Parry's definition, competencies require individuals to gather pertinent knowledge about areas of responsibility, exude attitudes that inspire continual personal and professional development, and take the necessary steps to develop requisite skills needed to master tasks and activities that are assigned.

This collective group of knowledge, attitudes, and skills act as the genesis from where mastery originates. Competencies equip people with the capacity to tackle procedural complexity and uncertainty. Competencies enable leaders to exact decisive and effective leadership, utilize effective communication strategies, and activate problem-solving skills that are indispensable for navigating organizational challenges. Competencies are not relegated to leaders; rather, employees must also possess adept command of the areas for which they are responsible and draw on that knowledge as needed to guide and support change activities. That's why organizations that fail to emphasize ongoing professional development risk stagnation and, ultimately, the plateauing of their collective technical ability. Without the required set of relevant skills and competencies, even well-conceived organizational change initiatives will fail!

As previously established in the earlier chapter—Planning— the ADKAR (i.e., awareness, desire, knowledge, ability, and reinforcement) model prescribes a unique continuum that people undergo to achieve change permanence. This linear model includes the steps of awareness, desire, knowledge, ability, and reinforcement; however, it is the third and fourth steps (i.e., knowledge and abilities) that are required in order to build the necessary competencies to fully adopt and implement new processes, technologies, methods, and tools. In order to build knowledge and abilities, organizations often employ training and development programs to assess areas of skill deficiency, bridge skill gaps, and ultimately increase individual competencies. This assessment is pivotal to ensure that people are equipped with the capacity to perform the tasks required confidently and effectively to undertake organizational change with positive attitudes, leading to the next point.

In addition to building competencies, one of the most foundational elements required for skill development is inculcating positive attitudes. Positive attitudes direct focus, coalesce team effort, and drive individual desires toward adopting change. Positive attitudes foster a culture of openness, curiosity, and adaptability and provide resilience when confronted with obstacles. Positive attitudes inspire people to embrace change with optimism and enthusiasm, enabling them to visualize themselves participating in the organization's future. Positive attitudes enable people to ultimately embrace a shared vision in which they see themselves thriving by utilizing their competences for long term organizational success. So, while long-term change relies on building competencies in order for new processes and systems to take hold in the organization's culture, the catalyst for enabling the process of change is positive attitudes!

Change is not merely a process: it is a collective journey led by "people" who hold the power to shape the future of the organization. With positive attitudes, leaders and employees rally together to inspire and motivate the attainment of the organization's strategic objectives.

Their collective quest for seeking collaborative harmony requires effective communication skills. Through effective communication, they are able to convey the organization's vision and strategic objectives while carefully navigating, addressing, and resolving concerns as they arise. Ultimately, by recognizing the importance of, and by intentionally valuing the contributions of people in the continuum of organizational change, organizations position themselves to successfully navigate change effectively and thrive in an ever-changing business environment.

The Human Element of Change

The success or failure of organizational change initiatives is predicated on one word—*people*! People, often regarded as the human element, play a pivotal role in change adoption, since their skills, attitudes, and knowledge (i.e., competences) determine the level of effectiveness and efficiency that will be realized when pursuing transformative change. While strategies, procedures, and systems are essential for enabling transformative change, they are secondary to the importance of "people" and the role they play in human-social transactions that enable change adoption.

Transformative organizational change represents a complex process that includes a set of tightly intertwined elements, with one stage feeding another, building upon its successes or failures, until a new norm is established within the organization. This complex and multifaceted process involves reshaping the way an organization thinks and operates by leveraging human factors that influence, moderate, and enable organizational change adoption. This adoption process can be described through a series of steps:

Step 1: Understanding the human construct of the organization
Step 2: Employing effective communication

Step 3: Devising effective and decisive leadership
Step 4: Providing training and development
Step 5: Adoption and continuous improvement
Step 6: Celebrating success

Step 1: Understanding the Human Elements of the Organization

Before required change can be executed, desired change must be understood. Herein lies the first step in the multifaceted process: Understanding the human elements of the organization. The human elements are influenced by invisible forces that either enable or impede the organization's ability to bring about change; therefore, before required change is pursued, the first and most important step is to assess the organization's culture. The organization's culture is typified by its shared values, beliefs, and behavioral norms. This information is often gleaned from historical insights, lessons learned from past change initiatives, and a general understanding of what makes the organization "tick."

Armed with this preliminary set of information, the next step requires active engagement through listening, understanding, and evaluating employee sentiments—shared either directly or indirectly—to get a pulse of what people are experiencing within the organization. This process is pivotal, as it helps to contextualize underlying fears, concerns, and issues that may threaten change adoption. Data collection strategies may include focus groups, anonymous surveys, and one-on-one interviews in which a clear sense of what "people" are feeling about the organization, the change initiative, or other areas of concern are collected. As these sentiments represent real human emotion and could provide valuable insight about areas of possible sources of resistance, effective stakeholder engagement becomes paramount to inform possible solutions and/or to mitigate concerns. Stakeholder engagement therefore includes mapping out interests, desires, concerns, levels of influence of all the key individuals and/or groups that will be most affected by the change in an attempt to validate their position, standing, or concern. In so doing, change leaders will be able to qualify stakeholder fears, understand their motivations, and validate their aspirations, recognizing that these emotional factors play a pivotal role in the change process.

Stakeholder engagement relies on effective communication, and understanding the various organizational communication channels is vital to ensuring that information is disseminated accurately, frequently, and in a timely fashion. Effective communication also focuses on barriers or noise that could threaten the effective transmission of intended messages. This is why it's critically important to leverage established communication channels, processes, and tools to maintain familiarity, trust, and information access with stakeholders.

Another aspect that describes the human elements of the organization is the organization's leadership. Assessing the organization's leadership styles and management dynamics can provide helpful insights into their strategic imperatives, communication styles, priorities, decision-making process, and ultimately, their ability to influence people, and by extension, the ability to facilitate change. Assessing the organization's leadership may also offer insights into how earlier organizational decisions were made, along with associated lessons learned about prior organizational change successes and/or failures. This information gives context into leadership's resilience and their degree of adaptability when confronting obstacles. When leaders are fully committed to making lasting change, their "people" know it! It is therefore imperative to implement change management strategy that demonstrates alignment with the organization's culture; a strategy that is focused on meeting the needs of the organization's "people," while achieving the organization's strategic goals.

Step 2: Employing Effective Communication

Effective communication is the cornerstone of successful organizational change management that entails the use of methods, tools, and techniques employed to exchange information about the change initiative. Communication seeks to provide timely information about the change by articulating the vision for the change, strategic goals, and the required steps necessary to ensure two-way dialog within the organization. This two-way dialog is pivotal to ensuring alignment between leaders and stakeholders, by building support, mitigating risks, and establishing a collective understanding of change strategy relative to the organization's strategic objectives.

In addition to facilitate two-way dialog, effective communication goes a step further by cementing the vision for the change with stakeholders by articulating the need for change, and galvanizing support around anticipated benefits. Building awareness is further supported when themes and messages are articulated that are consistent with the organization's strategic goals. This provides message reinforcement, while assuaging fears caused by misinformation. Effective change strategy therefore relies on effective communication strategies to foster collective alignment with change objectives, while enlisting buy-in and support from affected stakeholders. By providing opportunities for skill development and training, soliciting employee input, and involving them in decision-making, organizations can foster a sense of ownership and participation, since engaged stakeholders are more receptive to the benefits of change and are more committed and "bought-in" to its achievement.

One of the barometers for change adoption is the degree of buy-in that stakeholders provide in support of the change. Buy-in is important, as it facilitates the support needed from stakeholders to adopt proposed changes.

Stakeholders therefore have a greater chance of feeling involved, appreciated, and valued when they are provided with communication that is both clear and consistent. Because of this involvement, a sense of ownership is fostered that ultimately increases the level of buy-in while overcoming impediments and resistance that threaten change adoption.

Resistance, a topic that we will delve deeper into the next section, is a psychological and behavioral response characterized by the reluctance or refusal of individuals or groups to accept, comply with, or support proposed organizational changes. Resistance is a natural response to perceived threats to organizational norms, practices, or personal interests. Resistance is often evidenced by tendencies that range from passive non-compliance to direct active opposition to proposed changes. People resist change for a variety of factors; however, the predominant causes for resistance are fear of the unknown, the perceived loss of control, ambiguity resulting from poor communication, and the lack of perceived benefits sufficient to overcome the discomfort associated with disruptive change. Successful change management acknowledges and addresses these emotions, offering support mechanisms such as counseling, coaching, or peer support groups to help individuals cope and adapt. Because of the threats posed to achieving the organization's goals, resistance must therefore be carefully managed in order to successfully bring people along the organizational-transformation journey.

Step 3: Devising Effective and Decisive Leadership

One of the most important enablers for organizational change success is leadership. While volumes have been written about its importance in organizational life, effective and decisive leadership remains a key success factor that hinges on five fundamental qualities. First, let's establish a definition pertinent to organizational change. According to Gary Yukl, leadership is defined as, "the process of influencing others to understand and agree about what needs to be done and how to do it, and the process of facilitating individual and collective efforts to accomplish shared objectives" (Yukl, 2013). Effective leaders therefore make well-informed decisions promptly, provide clear instructions, and effectively articulate a vision that inspires and motivates stakeholders toward attaining shared goals and ideals. Yukl's definition further highlights five key aspects that are central to leaders successfully facilitating organizational change initiatives. These qualities include:

- *Influence*: This is the ability to guide, shape, and influence attitudes, beliefs, and actions of those they are entrusted to lead. In so doing, they ensure that their message of change is consistent with meeting the needs of stakeholders by articulating the reasons for the change and the benefits it will bring.
- *Shared understanding*: This is the ability to establish a common set of beliefs, desires, and understandings that result in the collective pursuit of organizational goals. In the pursuit of shared goals, leaders facilitate change adoption by gaining stakeholder buy-in, and by ensuring public and private comments are demonstrably consistent with stated organizational goals.
- *Facilitation*: This is the ability to provide support, delegate personnel, commit financial resources, while removing impediments and preemptively confronting sources of resistance that threaten organizational goal attainment.
- *Collective effort*: The ability to enlist others to commit to, support, and harmonize efforts toward the attainment of shared objectives. In the process, effective leaders empower stakeholders to adapt and embrace change

by equipping them with requisite training, tools, and support needed to develop proficiency, capacity, and competency.

∎ *Goal-focused*: The ability to focus time, effort, and resources toward the attainment of the organization's strategic objectives, even in the face of uncertainty.

Step 4: Providing Training and Development

Effective training and development programs are crucial for fostering positive change within an organization, since they not only impart knowledge, facilitate skills development, and deepens individual competencies, but they are pivotal in cultivating attitudes and behaviors that are required for change adoption. In cultivating attitudes and behaviors, training programs must be adaptable, relevant, targeted, practical, and offer engaging learning experiences that are directly aligned with the strategic objectives of the change initiative.

Training and development programs derive their value from the transference of meaningful and transformative information aimed at improving individual competencies. These programs ensure that stakeholders develop the requisite skills and knowledge to perform assigned tasks and duties that are aligned with new process, methods, tools, and techniques. With the goal of achieving skill development, training and development programs target both the acquisition of technical and operational skills to equip stakeholders with the necessary resources to adapt to new roles, technologies, or assignments.

Equipping stakeholders with new skills also position them for new opportunities to excel and advance in the organization. Thus, effective training programs not only seek to counter misinformation, but rather provide a resource-rich menu of courses that focuses on building operational mastery. Acquisition of new skills that lead to mastery further serves as a counterbalance to resistance, since stakeholders are more likely to embrace change when they are empowered to adopt it. For these reasons, training and development programs contribute to the development of a resilient, adaptable, and flexible workforce that can adjust to ongoing organizational challenges. Ultimately, when organizations are dedicated to ongoing stakeholder development via effective training and development programs, individual success, stakeholder morale, and individual engagement levels are invariably affected for the better.

Step 5: Adoption and Continuous Improvement

Organizational change adoption, intertwined with continuous improvement strategies, is not merely a necessity but a significant moderator of organizational growth, sustainability, and long-term success. It is the barometer of any change initiative since deployment of new technologies and the implementation of enhanced workflows and business processes will ultimately fail unless people adopt them. As a program manager in the technology space, I have often said, "implementing an expensive solution that no one chooses to use, oxymoronically tantamount to successfully implementing a failed solution!" For this reason, organizations must focus on the "last mile" of the change management continuum by employing all the necessary strategies and measures needed to secure adoption.

When organizations effectively navigate the complexities surrounding change adoption by fostering an environment of adaptability, innovation, and continual growth, they significantly increase their chances that "solutions deployed are solutions employed." The key to success lies in utilizing a holistic approach that integrates strategic planning, employee involvement, and continuous evaluation measures, so as to ensure that the intended change not only gets implemented, but also that it takes root and flourishes in the new organizational paradigm.

How? Let's dig a bit deeper.

Organizational change adoption is the process through the organization systematically and intentionally implements change strategy to achieve the organization's strategic objectives. Adoption, therefore, includes embracing, implementing, and institutionalizing new behaviors, practices, or processes consistent with the achieving the organization's strategic objectives. The implementation of new processes, systems, tools, and procedures are not in themselves adequate to meet the strategic goals of the organization; rather, it's the degree to which they are operationalized that determines if transformative change has occurred.

Organizations that focus on change adoption are often adaptable to changing market conditions, technological advancements, and competitive pressures. They are also intentional in achieving increased operational efficiency and effectiveness as evidenced through streamlined workflows, processes, and workstreams. They often focus on innovation, by fostering an environment that encourages risk taking, transparency, and continuous improvement.

As discussed earlier, continuous improvement is intricately connected with organizational change since it offers a methodical framework for continuously identifying and implementing improvements to processes, systems, tools, and techniques. Continuous improvement strategy often borrows from Kaizen principles that emphasize small, continuous changes. It may also leverage principles from Lean Six Sigma, that utilizes data-driven approaches to increase value creation, improve quality, and reduce waste. Regardless of the influencing principles or strategies, blending continuous improvement methods with change adoption strategy promotes a culture of excellence that focuses on delivering improved products and services, while ensuring that people are not only equipped to utilize new ways of thinking and doing but also that they develop the requisite levels of mastery needed in their execution.

Step 6: Celebrating Success

One of the most often-overlooked aspects of change management is celebrating team success. This overlooked activity is crucial for achieving change permanence since it fosters individual motivation, facilitates reinforcement, and ensures that the desired changes become an integral part of the organization's operations and culture. One of the possible reasons why this process is often overlooked stems from the organization's need to refocus on the upcoming initiative, to the degree that they fail to correlate the strategic objectives of the prior initiative with the upcoming initiative. However, failure to intentionally reflect on the successes of the change implementation, along with its underlining processes, outcomes, and team contributions, can expose the organization to risks of repeating errors, overworking key individuals responsible for the prior success, and ultimately create an environment of declining team morale.

Recognizing and rewarding individuals and/or groups who made significant contributions to the change initiative may take the form of a simple letter of recognition, public mention of appreciation, or offering meaningful gifts and promotions that are commensurate with individual/group effort. In so doing, it encourages stakeholders to maintain their commitment to current and future change initiatives, making them more inclined to advocate for, and publicly support future change initiatives.

Celebrating success also generates a sense of forward progress by cultivating positive attitudes, reducing resistance, and providing a clarity of purpose, enabling stakeholders to actualize the benefits, advantages, and advancements of the change initiative. This ultimately helps to reinforce new behaviors and processes that the organization is seeking to cultivate, signaling to stakeholders the behaviors that are valued and required, thus guiding them toward the attainment of a new organizational culture.

Finally, celebrating success also helps to send the important message that the organization values and appreciates people over profits, providing another opportunity to reinforce the organization's desire to nurture a people-centric culture, and with values and behaviors that align with the organization's strategic objectives.

> **Celebrating success sends the important message that the organization values and appreciates people over profits.**

As we conclude this section, understanding the human element of change is certainly a critical enabler for organizational change success and long-term adoption. This understanding is grounded in the recognition that organizations are comprised of people with unique needs, motivations, and fears. As a result, effective change planning is required to take into account these individual characteristics, thereby leading to the creation of a change strategy that aligns with the organization's strategic objectives. During the change implementation process, effective communication is paramount, requiring clear, consistent, and empathetic messaging to influence behavioral outcomes consistent with the ADKAR model. Aided by effective training and development programs, stakeholders are then ably equipped to acquire the requisite skills and knowledge (i.e., competencies) through continuous learning opportunities to exploit advancement opportunities for personal and professional growth. When these human elements are instilled across the organization, then and only then will organizations be able to achieve successful change adoption, increased competitiveness in the marketplace, and the instantiation of a culture that is centered on people.

While acknowledging organizational success and encouraging people to embrace change are both essential drivers for change adoption, the predicate for organizational change success hinges on strategies that identify, mitigate, and resolve resistance that threatens organizational success. That is the topic of the next section.

How to Manage Resistance to Organizational Change

Organizations exist in rapidly changing environments where the only "constant" is change. To successfully adapt and thrive in these environments, organizations must possess the requisite capacity and competency to effectively execute organizational change initiatives. While striving to adapt and excel in ever-changing environments, organizations are often confronted with resistance. In response to this threat, organizations employ strategies to carefully manage the associated risks, since resistance often threatens to derail even the most well-intentioned endeavors. Understanding the nature of resistance, its diverse forms, and effective strategies to overcome it is crucial for successfully implementing change and ultimately achieving successful organizational transformation. But what is resistance, and how does it significantly influence organizational change success?

Resistance is a natural and inherent response to organizational events that threaten to disrupt, displace, impact, or inhibit one's sense of wellbeing afforded by the status quo. It encompasses psychological, emotional, and behavioral responses to changes that threaten established routines, working practices, or power dynamics (Burnes, 2004);

> Resistance is the natural response to organizational events that threaten to disrupt, displace, impact, or inhibit one's sense of wellbeing or belonging.

responses that are triggered by one's perceived threat to security, control, or group associations (Lewin, 1947). In response to these perceived threats, people may react overtly or covertly. An overt response may include direct expressions of opposition to the change initiative typified by aggressive postures, verbal objections, open defiance, or intentional acts sought to compromise and derail the initiative (Kotter, 1996). Conversely, covert forms are more subtle and aimed at inflicting harm in less direct ways. Covert forms of resistance are exemplified by withdrawal or significant reduction of interest, effort, and participation in the initiative. Covert forms may also be revealed by a reduction in productivity, increase in absenteeism, passive–aggressive postures aimed at challenging forward progress of the initiative, or verbal behaviors that insight cynicism, skepticism, or doubt.

Regardless of whether resistance adopts overt or covert forms, resistance often can be categorized in one of the following categories:

a. Cognitive resistance
b. Emotional resistance
c. Behavioral resistance
d. Cultural resistance
e. Political resistance

Cognitive Resistance

What Is It?

Cognitive resistance refers to the mental or psychological resistance that people or groups construct when presented with new concepts and ideas, methods, or procedures. Cognitive resistance emanates from one's unfavorable view of the change initiative, usually in response to misinterpretations, insufficient or inaccurate information, pre-existing biases, or any other perceived impediment that threatens their adoption of proposed solutions. Once these pre-existing biases are established, people then demonstrate their opposition to the change through expressions of negative sentiments, pessimistic ideas, false assumptions, personal convictions, and other debilitating attitudes toward the change that ultimately impede its effective execution.

At the heart of cognitive resistance is fear: fear of the unknown; fear of uncertainty around possible impacts; fear of change to one's organizational standing, role, responsibility, or relevance; fear of the loss of personal security; fear of disruption to one's comfort. In addition to fear, the concept of "a bird in the hand is better than two in the bushel" influences what is regarded as loss aversion. People often avoid pursuing the "promise" over reality and thus tend to value what is known and possessed, over the promise of achieving personal and sometimes life-altering gains. This cognitive response results in a natural guarded response if they perceive any loss of familiar routines, group memberships, personal benefits, or reduction in organizational standing/responsibilities. This is especially true if they seek, and subsequently receive confirmation that reenforces their belief systems or perceptions. This—often defined as confirmation bias—often results in their overlooking of proposed benefits (i.e., personal and/or organizational) by focusing on the perceived risks, their negative belief constructs, and perceived downsides if the change is adopted.

> **The heart of cognitive resistance is fear!**

This downward cognitive spiral does hit a bottom when people begin desiring something new, different, and beholden to something greater even in the face of conflicting information. This is where another factor of cognitive resistance comes to light—cognitive dissonance. Cognitive dissonance is the mental discomfort and inconsistency that results from holding two conflicting beliefs, values, or attitudes. While a detailed exposition on cognitive dissonance exceeds the scope of this section, within the context of organizational change, cognitive dissonance exists when individuals oppose change in an effort to alleviate the discomfort caused by the incongruity between their worldview and the introduction of new concepts or methods. This incongruity, often a direct response to their emotional attachment to normative behaviors, is often entrenched in longstanding personal routines, business processes, and group practices that create a deep-bonding emotional attachment to the status quo. The strength of this emotional attachment often results in cognitive resistance, fueled by their personal fears.

Why Does It Happen?

First and foremost, cognitive resistance is a response. This response, when triggered by perceived negative impacts to one's well-being, could severely undermine the success of the change initiative as a result of a number of factors, some of which include:

- Misinterpretation or insufficient knowledge: When people are uncertain about the purpose, impacted process(es), scope, planned activities, and intended outcomes, and how it affects their wellbeing, they tend to be more likely to form negative perceptions and unfavorable belief systems that ultimately undermine the execution of the change effort.
- Fear of the unknown: Organizational change for many is perceived with consternation, particularly when it threatens to disturb established norms and the status quo. Thus, fear of the unknown, emanating from the possible loss of job, position, social standing, or organizational authority, invariably results in resistance.

- Failure to understand benefits: One of the enablers for change adoption is effective communication. Communication is central to highlighting the WIIFM (what's in it for me?) to the degree that ambiguous or poorly worded statements about the benefits of the change do more harm than good. Thus, when people are unable to recognize the personal or organizational value of the change in response to these poorly worded statements, they are less inclined to believe in the change, or worst, adopt it.

- History of bad experiences: It has been said, "nothing succeeds like success." The converse is also true: nothing hardens failure more than failure! That's why previously failed change initiatives are so detrimental. They act like acidic elements that eat away at trust, belief, hope, and desire. When these elements are destroyed, it provides fodder for skepticism and pessimism, making it more difficult to pursue new initiatives, particularly when they lack confidence in leadership to carefully execute the change.

- Personal uniqueness: Change is achieved one person at a time! Not only is this statement true, but it underscores the fact that each person brings to the change initiative their unique blend of personality traits, idiosyncrasies, tendencies, cognitive approaches, and personal values, all working in harmony to influence how they think, act, and respond to change.

How to Overcome It?

Having established that cognitive resistance is a natural emotional and psychological response, the following strategies can be employed to effectively manage and mitigate its impact:

- Effective communication: Clear, effective communication, with timely, targeted, and relevant messages, helps to send clear, unambiguous and consistent information about the change, its objectives, and its associated benefits. Communication that is transmitted using familiar channels and platforms, such as company meetings, town halls, and other forms of electronic transmission, help to widen the message's reach, thus utilizing a comprehensive information dissemination strategy. This helps to not only ensure that various audiences are effectively reached, but it helps to maintain messaging accuracy while proactively confronting misinformation and mitigating its impact.

■ Build trust: In order for followers to follow, leaders must lead! This is true in organizational change, and particularly true when confronting cognitive resistance. Confidence is an attribute that must be demonstrated through technical proficiency, emotional awareness, and human-social competencies. This suite of skills aids in inspiring followers to believe in, and commit to, the strategic goals pursued by the change initiative. Leaders must therefore understand the need for building confidence while exhibiting high levels of proficiency that demonstrates their own comprehension, dedication, and assurance in leading the change process.

■ Broker dialog: Change will never be successful without effective user engagement. That's why, in order to overcome cognitive resistance, leaders must intentionally engage stakeholders in the process. Effective engagement is critical for change adoption since it facilitates dialog through transparent communications in order to confront misconceptions and individual concerns directly. Through dialog, leaders are also able to facilitate input and make strategic improvement to processes necessary for achieving change success. Dialog not only entails receiving information, but also is essential in reinforcing behaviors by providing commendation, acknowledgment, and rewards for significant milestones attainment, which ultimately aids in generating forward progress toward change adoption.

■ Provide support: When learning to ride a bicycle, kids often use training wheels. Training wheels provide a counterbalancing support system that enables the rider to stay on the bike. Similarly, support strategies are essential when implementing change initiatives, as they too keep users aligned to new processes, methods, tools, and techniques necessary for change adoption. Support systems aid in equipping and developing requisite skills needed to effectively perform duties that enable successful change. Support is not limited to skill refinement, but it is also essential to overcome cognitive resistance by utilizing effective counseling, coaching, or other emotional support methods necessary for people to navigate, embrace, and fully adopt the change. This two-part focus (i.e., skill development and emotional bracketing) ultimately helps to foster a symbiotic organizational environment where people trust their leaders, and leaders build their people, using mutually-beneficial people-centric strategies.

■ Actively listen: Listening and hearing are both auditory processes, but listening goes a step further beyond simply "hearing" by incorporating a thoughtful and reflective component needed to enlist and gain the support of people. While listening requires actively taking into account the words, emotion, and desires of people, input is not limited to words only. Effective emotional awareness requires consistent monitoring of emotional states, as evidenced by levels of understanding, apprehensions, and levels of resistance exhibited in opposition to the change initiative. Leaders who are emotionally mature will receive input, process it, and be willing to modify plans in response to valid concerns, thereby reducing and mitigating cognitive resistance.

Organizational change cognitive resistance is a multifaceted problem impacted by a range of psychological and emotional elements. Overcoming cognitive resistance requires an intentional, deliberative, and multifaceted approach that tackles the underlying factors threatening organizational change adoption. To effectively address and eliminate cognitive resistance, it is imperative that leaders prioritize transparent communication, employee engagement, training, and support. By cultivating a constructive and encouraging atmosphere conducive to long-term organizational transformation, leaders will effectively combat cognitive resistance and ultimately receive the support that is needed to successfully achieve the organization's strategic objectives.

Emotional Resistance

What Is It?

Emotional resistance refers to adverse emotional states and psychological barriers that people may experience when in the midst of organizational change. This resistance is often not governed by logical reasoning, but rather reflects the state of personal feelings, perceptions, or the perceived sense of impending personal discomfort. According to Ford, Ford, and D'Amelio, emotional resistance may also include fear, uncertainty, anxiety, anger, frustration, and sadness (Ford, Ford, & D'Amelio, 2008), and can be triggered by several factors, including fear of the unknown, loss of control, and disruption to routines (Kotter, 2007). The genesis of emotional resistance bears similarity with cognitive resistance, as they both may originate from personal anxieties about job security, the loss of status, and the ability to cope with new demands (Weick & Quinn, 1999). When these triggers exist, emotional resistance may then be visible through symptoms such as personal withdrawal, workplace absenteeism, direct or indirect attempts at sabotage, and ultimately decreased productivity (Armenakis, Harris, & Mossholder, 1993).

Why Does It Happen?

Emotional resistance can occur for a variety of reasons, some of which were alluded to in the previous section. However, at the core of emotional resistance is the fear of the unknown, since change often disrupts established routines and introduces uncertainty regarding individual roles, responsibilities, and their sense of job security. This uncertainty often triggers fear and anxiety, causing people to question their place within the organization following the change initiative. Compounding this fear is a sense of loss of control that creates a sense of powerlessness that further exacerbates this anxiety. This anxiety is further deepened when organizational changes are executed without effective communication strategies or provide adequate channels for people to give input into the change. The result: people ultimately feel disconnected from the initiative, and frustration, resentment, and emotional resistance hardens.

In addition to feeling frustrated and resentful, feelings of inadequacy sometimes compound emotional resistance. This happens when one's identity and self-esteem are undermined; or long-held beliefs, values, skills, and competence are questioned; or one's perceived place within the organization is devalued. This is where empathetic leadership is critical, since the extent to which people have faith and trust in the leadership, and by extension the transformation process, is a significant determinant for overcoming emotional resistance. Emotional resistance to new initiatives will more likely occur when people have had prior negative experiences with change initiatives, experience inadequate communication, or perceive a sense of secrecy that clouds or undermines trust. Effective, empathetic leadership aids in quelling this skepticism before mal-behaviors and ill-constructed opinions of the change become entrenched, making lasting change challenging to surmount.

Finally, another reason that explains why emotional resistance occurs is due to what's called "emotional contagion." Emotional contagion is the phenomenon where emotions are transferred from one person to another, either consciously or unconsciously. This process can occur through various forms of communication, including verbal cues, body language, facial expressions, and even tone of voice. Emotional contagion therefore plays a role in the spread of emotional resistance, since negative emotions like fear or anger can rapidly permeate an organization, especially when amplified by the collective mood amongst people. When people observe their colleagues expressing negative emotions, they are more likely to experience and express these emotions themselves, leading to a collective movement of resistance against the change initiative.

Similar to cognitive resistance, emotional resistance is a complex multifaceted issue that is deeply intertwined with psychological factors and emotional responses. Stemming from a fear of the unknown, a loss of control, threats to identity and self-esteem, lack of trust in leadership, and the contagious nature of negative emotion, overcoming it is critical in order to successfully achieve organizational change goals.

How to Overcome It?

Now that we have unpacked what emotional resistance is, let's take a look at a few strategies that can be employed in overcoming it, starting with open and transparent communication.

■ Transparent communication: Emphasize the importance of clear and open communication during change. This involves providing detailed information about the rationale and goals of the change, encouraging dialogue to address concerns, and keeping everyone updated about progress and any emerging issues.

■ Participation and involvement: Actively involve employees in the change process by seeking their input and feedback. Empower them by delegating tasks and responsibilities related to the change, and foster teamwork and collaboration to create a sense of community and shared purpose.

■ Empathy and support: Acknowledge and validate employees' emotions and concerns about the change. Provide necessary resources such as training and mental health support, and maintain an open-door policy to create a comfortable environment for expressing emotions and concerns.

■ Addressing fear and uncertainty: Communicate clearly and realistically about potential challenges and positive aspects of change. Address specific worries and anxieties with clear solutions, and anticipate potential issues with proactive problem-solving.

■ Building trust and confidence: Demonstrate strong leadership and commitment to the change process. Maintain transparency and accountability in decision-making, and encourage two-way communication to actively listen to employee feedback.

■ Celebrating successes: Recognize individual and team achievements throughout the change process. Use positive reinforcement to boost morale and showcase the benefits and positive outcomes of the change to demonstrate its value and impact.

■ Managing expectations: Set realistic goals and timelines to avoid creating unrealistic expectations. Communicate clearly about implementation timeframes, and be flexible and adaptable based on feedback and unforeseen circumstances.

- Continuous improvement: Monitor the effectiveness of the change regularly and measure its impact. Seek ongoing feedback to identify areas for improvement, and be open to learning from mistakes and adapting the approach.
- Foster a culture of change: Frame change positively as an opportunity for growth and development. Encourage risk-taking and innovation in a supportive environment, and promote collaboration and knowledge sharing to support learning and adaptation.
- Emotional intelligence Training: Equip managers with emotional intelligence skills to understand and manage both their own and their employees' emotions. Develop communication skills that foster trust and empathy, and train managers in effective conflict resolution to address issues arising from emotional resistance.

Given the similarities between emotional and cognitive resistance, let's quickly compare and contrast three important takeaways between emotional and cognitive resistance before moving on to the next section on behavioral resistance.

Origins

- Emotional resistance is a direct response that reflects individual emotions such as fear, uncertainty, and their unique frustrations. It is frequently associated with perceived risks to job security, personal identity, and self-worth, and is often influenced by previous adverse encounters resulting in the lack of confidence in leadership.
- Cognitive resistance, on the other hand, refers to the rational evaluation and examination of the change initiative, taking into account individual concerns, and those shared by the group regarding the practicality,

logic, and potential negative repercussions following the change initiative. The moderating factors behind cognitive resistance include uncertainty regarding the advantages of the change initiative, along with reservations held about the ability of leadership to effectively carry out the change.

Symptoms

■ Emotional resistance is exhibited through negative emotions and behaviors like withdrawal, dissatisfaction, and decreased productivity. While often experienced at an individual level, emotional resistance can metastasize into a collective response of shared opposition, due to its negative propensity on organizational group dynamics.

■ Cognitive resistance, on the other hand, is exhibited through acts of questioning, criticizing, or planting seeds of doubt and skepticism. While it may entail suggesting alternatives, identifying issues with the current strategy— actions that may be construed as productive—at the heart of cognitive resistance is the tendency to oppose the attainment of strategic objectives by providing input that raises questions about strategy and implementation.

Management Implications

■ Emotional resistance requires the implementation of strategies that focus on building trust, addressing emotional needs, while providing avenues for offering support through the change continuum. Strategies must include transparent communication, leadership compassion, and providing safe and secure environments for voicing concerns.

■ Cognitive resistance requires sound logic, rationale, and supporting arguments in order to instill confidence in the change initiative. This strategy therefore requires well-articulated data-driven communications that use clear, factual, logical arguments to effectively address concerns. A key enabler for successfully mitigating cognitive resistance is readiness to provide fact-based reasoning and responses to inquiries to build trust, while being willing to modify strategies in accordance with feedback provided.

After discussing cognitive and emotional resistance, let's take a step further and discuss the third form of organizational change resistance: behavioral resistance. While cognitive resistance arises from logical reasoning and emotional resistance from personal emotion associated with the change, behavioral resistance reveals itself through direct acts and conduct of people in the midst of change. Let's unpack this topic now.

Behavioral Resistance

What Is It?

Behavioral resistance is concerned not only with what people believe or feel, but rather with how these ideas and feelings manifest themselves in actual behaviors. It is therefore the outward manifestation of cognitive and emotional states and is distinguished by observable actions that ultimately impact organizational change.

> Behavioral resistance focuses on how ideas and feelings manifest themselves in actual behaviors.

Behavioral resistance is defined as the visible and tangible conduct exhibited by individuals or groups to obstruct organizational change. This conduct may result in decreased productivity, absenteeism, or direct sabotage of the change effort, and its supporting procedures and processes (Burke & Litwin, 1991). Behavioral resistance may also include subtle actions of intentional procrastination and decreased effort, to more deliberative actions such as vocal opposition, belligerence, or blatant refusal to embrace new techniques.

One of the more blatant approaches is openly opposing the change, in which people actively express dissatisfaction and raise concerns in meetings. This is supplemented by more subtle activities such as concealing information, delaying duties, undermining attempts, and displaying negative body language. Another prominent example is the purposeful decline in productivity and output, in which people deliberately slow down their work speed, provide mediocre products, or ignore their work obligations. As introduced in the emotional resistance section, emotional contagion may result in the creation of alliances that propagate negativity; deliberately urging others to reject change and thereby fostering a toxic work environment. Others may employ more subtle and passive approaches, such as ignoring the change completely, refusing to comply with new regulations, or refusing to acquire the skills and knowledge needed to perform new duties.

Invariably, these deliberate attempts to oppose the change process stem from the desire to maintain the status quo and avoid perceived threats posed by the change (Armenakis & Harris, 2002). Behavioral resistance is an essential component of the change management process that connects people's internal thoughts and feelings with their outward expressions and conduct. Understanding behavioral resistance is critical because it represents actual obstacles that management must confront and overcome in order to effectively implement change.

Why Does It Happen?

Behavioral resistance to organizational change can be attributed to a variety of factors, each of which contributes to people's unwillingness to accept new initiatives. One major concern is the lack of communication and openness. Employee resistance increases when they are not fully educated on the nature of the change, its rationale, and the anticipated consequences (Kotter, 1996). For example, if a corporation decides to introduce a new technology without fully explaining its advantages and benefits, employees may object out of fear and uncertainty. Because of the lack of transparency, employees may question if the change is in their best interests.

Another important aspect is fear of the unknown, which can be very unpleasant (Kübler-Ross, 1969). People who are afraid of losing their jobs, position, or influence over their work might remain attached to the status quo. For example, people may reject a company reorganization effort if they fear losing their job, or fear experiencing undesirable changes in their duties.

In addition, a lack of trust in leadership is critical (Mayer, Davis, & Schoorman, 1995). Employees are more likely to reject change if they lack trust in their leaders' ability to manage it successfully, especially if they have a history of previously failed experiences with poorly implemented changes and inadequate stakeholder involvement. As a result, people invariably grow skeptical of a new strategic direction because of this historical reference of unsuccessful attempts at organizational change, further undermining their confidence in the change initiative.

Employee inflexibility and lack of adaptation provide additional difficulty (Oreg, 2003), as some people often find it difficult to adapt to new technology, systems, tools, and approaches, or develop new abilities needed for successful change adoption. As an example, people who are comfortable with old procedures often find it difficult to adjust to digital transitions.

Finally, and building on the emotional and cognitive resistance models previously described, feeling devalued or disregarded greatly contributes to behavioral resistance (Kotter & Schlesinger, 1979). This is due to the fact that people will resist change as a means of expressing dissatisfaction if they believe their issues and viewpoints are being ignored. People who experience this form of disregard to their viewpoints often exist within organizations that embrace top-down decision making without regard to the respective inputs and contributions of their people. When this occurs, organizations unknowing convey to their people that their inputs, efforts, and contributions are not needed, valued, nor appreciated.

When taken together, these factors highlight the complexity of managing behavioral resistance, and further underscores the importance for leaders to implement intelligent and inclusive change management strategies.

How to Overcome It?

To effectively confront and eliminate behavioral resistance, leaders must carefully employ a variety of strategies that are tailored to address and remedy sources and causes of the resistance. These strategies may include a delicate blend of the following approaches:

- Effective communication and transparency: Similar to cognitive and emotional resistance discussed previously, the central tenet for effectively managing resistance is clear, honest, and transparent communication. Managers must clearly articulate the rationale and goals of the change, provide regular updates on progress, and address concerns openly to enlist and receive the trust of their people. Transparency in communication builds trust and understanding, thus helping people to feel more secure and informed about adopting the change.
- Open and inclusive dialogue: Creating platforms for open dialogue, such as focus groups, knowledge sharing forums, town hall meetings, or one-on-one conversations,

allow people the opportunity to voice their concerns and offer feedback (Armenakis & Harris, 2009). This approach not only aids in identifying potential issues early but also fosters a people-centric culture where trust and inclusivity form the bedrock of the organization.

■ Participation and ownership: Involving employees in the planning, implementation, and decision-making processes related to change encourages a sense of ownership and commitment, that significantly reduces resistance to the change (Kotter, 1996). This participation can take various forms, ranging from facilitating input in planning stages to making roles assignment on implementation teams to help guide the change initiative and oversee the attainment of the organizational change objectives.

■ Training and support: Providing necessary training and support helps people acquire requisite skills and knowledge needed in the new environment, while addressing fears and boosting confidence (Lewin, 1947). Effective training and support programs, the topic of an upcoming section, are especially effective in easing anxieties about the unknown and building the necessary competencies (i.e., knowledge, attitudes, and skills that affect a major part of one's job) in order to ensure a successful change initiative.

■ Positive reinforcement: Acknowledging and rewarding people who positively embrace change can be a powerful motivator for others. According to Skinner, positive reinforcement creates a culture of acceptance and encourages adoption of new behaviors (1953).

■ Addressing individual needs: Recognizing that resistance varies among individuals is key. Tailoring approaches to meet different needs and offering extra support where necessary can be highly effective in mitigating resistance (Herzberg, 1968).

- Measuring progress and celebrating success: Regularly tracking progress and celebrating small wins keeps employees motivated and engaged (Kotter, 2012). This not only maintains momentum but also provides tangible evidence of the benefits of the change.

Behavioral resistance to organizational change is a natural phenomenon, but with thoughtful strategies focusing on communication, transparency, participation, and support, managers can significantly reduce its impact. These strategies, rooted in foundational change management theories, are crucial for the successful implementation of change and the long-term health of the organization. However, having now delved into the complexities of behavioral resistance, let's pivot our focus toward cultural resistance. While behavioral resistance is rooted in individual actions and attitudes, cultural resistance encompasses the collective norms, values, and beliefs that define an organization's identity. This type of resistance emerges when proposed changes challenge the ingrained ways of thinking and operating within an organization. Transitioning from individual to collective sources of resistance highlights the layered complexity around managing organizational change resistance. It further underscores the need for and importance of implementing holistic change strategies that span the entire human-social construct when implementing organizational change.

Cultural Resistance

What Is It?

According to Smith and Lewis (2011), cultural resistance is the opposition to organizational change that arises from deeply embedded values, attitudes, assumptions, and behaviors shared by a group of people within the organization. This resistance is evidenced through negative attitudes, decreased motivation, and actions that undermine the implementation of the change initiative (Ford & Ford, 2009).

Cultural resistance represents deep-seated, pervasive, and tightly interwoven belief constructs that are deeply embedded in the social fabric of the organization. Given its pervasiveness that stems from entrenched cultural norms, values, and belief systems, cultural resistance often represents a collective response that is manifested through the subtle undermining of the change initiative. It is often characterized by a reluctance to accept new ways of working, attitudes, or values that are incongruent with the established organizational culture.

As cultural resistance often involves opposition from people who are deeply attached to the existing organizational culture, it is significantly more challenging to detect, address, and fully mitigate. Passive resistance (i.e., ignoring or avoiding change), active resistance (i.e., openly opposing the change), or covert strategies that intentionally sabotage the change, are all examples of cultural resistance. Given the tightly interwoven behaviors that form the basis for its opposition, cultural resistance therefore requires an approach that not only addresses individual behaviors but also seeks to understand and reshape cultural dynamics that drive resistance at an organizational level. It is therefore imperative for leaders to acknowledge the emotional and psychological elements that contribute to cultural resistance and decide to engage in open and transparent communication by actively engaging stakeholders, while providing a supportive environment to facilitate effective organizational change.

Why Does It Happen?

Cultural resistance is an inherently natural reaction that results from deeply entrenched human emotion and perspectives. Similar to previously discussed forms of resistance, cultural resistance is often motivated by uncertainty related to the fear of the unknown. Deeply established organizational routines and cultural norms are often difficult to upend, resulting in apprehension and uncertainty toward embracing new organizational norms. Apprehension towards adopting a new cultural paradigm is moderated by the belief that the current culture offers stability and predictability, making people anxious about embracing new paradigms that may be difficult to adjust to.

Implicit in cultural resistance is the tendency for people to maintain attachment to the existing culture. The need to maintain attachment is a powerful and influential factor that affects cultural resistance due to the emotional attachments people experience, that often resulting from their shared values, feelings of stability, and their general sense of belonging. People will therefore resist changes that threaten or challenge this sense of belonging, perceiving such changes as an assault on their fundamental values, convictions, and identity.

Cultural resistance is also manifested by the "loss of control" people sometimes experience when confronted with change. This sense of relinquishing grip on established processes, systems, and norms creates real feelings of loss, threatens their sense of security, and challenges them to learn new daily routines in order to function within the new organizational paradigm. Further, the fear of being rendered redundant or obsolete can evoke a primal instinct to protect one's interests when job security, status, or expertise is threatened. Fear-induced resistance serves as a defensive mechanism in response to perceived threats, regardless of their veracity. As a result, people must confront the reality of having to navigate uncharted waters that invariably results in resistance to change. Therefore, as people embark on the journey of change, they must strive to create their sense of purpose, relevance, autonomy, and a sense of belonging in the new and emerging organizational culture.

How to Overcome It?

Overcoming cultural resistance requires a multi-faceted and systematic approach that takes into account a variety of engagement, communication, and professional development strategies. Implementing strategies requires a dedication and deep appreciation for cultural norms, organizational dynamics, and the needs people have to create a sense of belonging with the organization. Leaders must therefore aim to create an environment that is conducive to effective change that leverages the following methods of engagement:

■ Build trust and transparency: Transparent communications help to build trust, while frequent communication instills confidence. Both trust and confidence are essential ingredients for overcoming resistance. Effectively communicating the reasons for a change, while recognizing and immediately mitigating risks and concerns, promotes an environment built on trust, and helps people embrace and ultimately adopt the change.
■ Craft a shared vision: Creating a shared vision where people can see themselves participating and thriving is crucial for overcoming cultural resistance. It is therefore essential for leaders to involve people early in the process to understand their interests, needs, and desires, and ultimately secure their involvement in shaping the organization's future. This helps to create a sense of ownership and commitment, making the vision a collective endeavor, rather than a top-down directive.
■ Identify and address cultural issues: Before cultural change can be undertaken, it must be understood. That's why it's imperative to decode the specific cultural elements that act as the root cause for resistance within the organization. Whether it's issues such as value incongruency, or distrust in leadership, recognizing the

sources of resistance allows for the effective targeting and tailoring of strategic interventions.

■ Invest in training and support: Providing comprehensive training and ongoing support equips people with the necessary tools, skills, and knowledge necessary to enhance confidence and reducing adoption anxiety. Providing effective training and support programs help to facilitate the seamless adoption of new systems, processes, workflows, and procedures, thereby aiding in overcoming resistance and ultimately the implementation of the organization's strategic objectives.

■ Empower and engage: Empowering and delegating decision-making authority is an important change strategy, and when done correctly, it instills a sense of ownership and commitment that is needed in creating lasting change. Therefore, encouraging active participation, valuing people's unique perspectives and expertise, and enlisting their collective support and commitment ultimately to act as a catalyst for overcoming resistance.

■ Celebrate achievements: Acknowledging and commemorating significant milestones, helps to strengthen and reinforce favorable behaviors. When people receive commendations for notable contributions, it helps to motivate, incentivize, and promote forward progress, while minimizing resistance.

■ Cultivate patience and persistence: Cultural change, by its very nature, is a gradual and enduring endeavor that requires significant patience and adaptability. Exhibiting dedication, unwavering patience, and dogged persistence help to inspire trust and confidence, even when confronted with impediments that threaten change adoption.

■ Leverage change champions: A change champion is someone who actively demonstrates enthusiasm and excitement about the change and is able to influence others in its adoption. Change champions therefore work as ambassadors to communicate positive sentiments, influence behavior, and exude enthusiasm about the benefits of the change to their peers.

■ Gather feedback and adapt: "All things" related to organizational change invariably require ongoing feedback, frequent revision, and situational adaptation. By facilitating feedback and situational adaptation, people begin to feel valued, heard, and appreciated. As a result, the change initiative stays relevant, enjoys increased stakeholder buy-in, and ultimately experiences decreased levels of resistance.

■ Foster a culture of learning: In addition to facilitating feedback and allowing for situational adaptation, creating an environment that values continuous learning is essential for overcoming resistance. Therefore, providing opportunities for skill development, knowledge acquisition, and workforce support helps to foster a workforce that is characterized by innovation, adaptability, and enhanced capacity to successfully navigate and adopt change.

■ Track progress and measure success: Consistent with strategies outlined in the "Process" and "Performance" pillars, the intentional evaluation of organizational change results that utilize quantifiable measures of performance, data, and metrics, leads to the identification of improvement areas, and subsequently the implementation of effective change strategies. Therefore, implementing change strategies with dedication and a deep understanding of cultural dynamics, leaders are equipped to create an environment that is conducive to successful and lasting change, and in the process, mitigating the negative impacts of cultural resistance.

As we transition from cultural resistance to the next and final form of organizational change resistance—political resistance—it is crucial to recognize the similarities and interdependencies within the context of organizational change. While cultural resistance often originates from deeply rooted beliefs and organizational customs, political resistance arises from the power dynamics and interests within an organization. Understanding the underpinnings of political resistance, specific to forging a path that reconciles the interests of individuals, leadership authority, and internal politics, are all essential ingredients for maneuvering change effectively. Overcoming political resistance therefore requires a careful and nuanced approach that aligns organizational objectives with the diverse, and sometimes competing, interests of organizational stakeholders.

Political Resistance

What Is It?

Political resistance is a complex and multifaceted phenomenon that refers to behaviors, attitudes, and mindsets of people within an organization who utilize their authority and influence to oppose efforts aimed at effecting organizational change. Political resistance frequently originates from fear of relinquishing power, reduced status, loss of influence or personal gain, or the reassignment of resources (i.e., human and/or fiscal) that were once under one's purview. Political resistance invariably manifests itself in direct opposition to these fears, often evidenced by subtle forms of non-cooperation, or overt forms of resistance that explicitly rejects the premise of the change initiative and its subsequent actions. For this reason, understanding the contours of political resistance is important, not only because of the power dynamics that can affect the organization's culture, but also because of the causative effects it has on eroding organizational efficiency.

Why Does It Happen?

At the heart of political resistance is self-preservation and the strategic use of power to influence organizational change outcomes. Ironically, the strategic use of power is often a result of the perceived loss of power or influence that diminishes one's authority, span-of-control, or decision-making responsibilities. Political resistance is further exacerbated when change threatens established networks and relationships, disrupting the existing alliances and power dynamics within the organization. When power dynamics is disrupted, or one's sense of influence is diminished, the response is often one that includes the formation of coalitions. Coalitions are groups of people who share common interests, needs, and views, and who strategize to maintain control, or more directly, take steps that directly oppose the change so that their desires can be achieved. Coalitions may also mobilize people to engage in lobbying efforts to utilize their influence to sway decision-makers toward abandoning or altering the proposed changes in keeping with their self-reservation objectives.

Political resistance also often involves the spread of misinformation, where negative rumors and distorted facts are deliberately disseminated to weaken support for the change, or when direct forms of sabotage are carried out to thwart change adoption. Some of these acts of sabotage may include withholding support, erecting departmental/organizational barriers, or displaying a lack of cooperation that ultimately hinders or negatively affects the change process. This lack of cooperation, at its core, is often a representation of a lack of trust in leadership where people doubt leadership's ability to manage change effectively. While this could be due to ineffective communication and the sense of inadequate participation in the change process, people who feel uninformed or excluded are more likely to become suspicious, disengaged, and take steps toward self-preservation as mentioned earlier. Collectively understanding how these complex negative strategies can derail organizational change is central devising strategies to quell the impact of political resistance, which is the focus of the next section.

How to Overcome It?

Effectively managing political resistance is a nuanced task that requires a comprehensive, multi-pronged strategy. At the core of this strategy is the need to build trust and transparency with people who perceive the loss of influence, personal gain, or a diminished sense of one's authority, span-of-control, or decision-making responsibilities. Abridging this psychological chasm requires engaging in open communication and dialog about apprehensions, fears, and rationale behind the change, while ensuring that concerns and questions raised are addressed with honesty and clarity. As a mitigating step, it is critical to enlist those resisting the change in both planning and implementation activities, thereby fostering a sense of ownership and commitment to the change initiative. Taking this first step will better enable success for the following activities aimed at overcoming political resistance, starting with addressing power dynamics:

- ▪ Confront power dynamics: Addressing power dynamics first begins with identifying and understanding the motivations of key stakeholders, recognizing that each one plays a unique role in the organization, and therefore the change process. Once this understanding is established, galvanizing people around interests, needs, and desires—as it pertains to the organization's strategic objectives—help to create coalition alignment with people who can influence others toward pursuing change goals. Further, involving key stakeholders in planning and implementation activities, and entrusting them with decision-making authority where appropriate, can further alleviate concerns about loss of power or influence, thus promoting a more cooperative organizational change environment that transforms opponents into partners.

■ Employ effective communication: Similar to all the other forms of resistance previously discussed, effective communication is paramount in mitigating political resistance. Providing timely and accurate information to all stakeholders and using a diverse array of communication channels ensures that messaging reaches and resonates with all intended audiences. Effective communication not only requires effective transmission of intended messages, but also requires proactively confronting false narratives, rumors, and misinformation. Effective communication also requires promoting open and honest dialogue about the change, which ultimately helps to maintain a transparent, inclusive, and a trusting environment where stakeholders perceive goodwill, and the sense that their concerns and suggestions are received and valued.

■ Provide continuous monitoring: Regularly assessing the political landscape of the organization allows for early identification of potential sources of resistance, enabling timely intervention strategies as discussed in this section. Being prepared to adapt the change strategy in response to new challenges is essential for being flexible, adaptable, relevant, and ultimately effective. Providing continuous monitoring of positive behaviors is also central in mitigating political resistance, as these behaviors often lead to successes along the way. When these successes occur, it's important to not only celebrate these "wins" but to acknowledge the efforts of those involved so as to promote a people-centric organizational culture while maintaining change innovation, momentum, and adoption.

■ Provide support and training: Providing adequate support and training is another vital component in overcoming political resistance. This involves equipping employees with the necessary competencies required for change adoption. As organizational change often requires structural adjustments in various areas, equipping people with the necessary knowledge and skills through comprehensive training programs helps reduce skill deficiencies, build resource capacity, and alleviate concerns of inadequacy people feel when tackling new systems and processes. In addition to technical support, providing emotional support is equally important. Recognizing and addressing the emotional impact of change can mitigate declining morale and help stakeholders better cope with the change. Specifically, as it pertains to political resistance, providing training in conflict resolution and negotiation skills is important in empowering stakeholders to manage disagreements constructively, promoting a healthier and more resilient organizational culture.

In this section, we unpacked how resistance to organizational change is multifaceted and how it encompasses cognitive, emotional, behavioral, cultural, and political dimensions. Cognitive resistance stems from individuals' thoughts and beliefs, where change contradicts their existing knowledge or perceptions. Emotional resistance arises from feelings of fear, loss, or uncertainty, often leading to a visceral reaction against change. Behavioral resistance is observed through actions, or lack thereof, demonstrating reluctance or non-compliance with new initiatives. Cultural resistance is embedded in the shared values and practices of an organization that may conflict with proposed changes.

Political resistance involves power plays and strategic actions to maintain status quo or control.

Transitioning from understanding these forms of resistance to developing effective training and development programs requires recognizing that each form of resistance must be addressed distinctly within the learning environment. Training and development programs can be designed to acknowledge and mitigate these resistances, providing knowledge to alleviate cognitive concerns, emotional support to ease fears, behavioral interventions to encourage engagement, cultural considerations to align with organizational values, and the political acumen to navigate power structures. In the next section, we will discuss effective training programs and how they can be crafted to transform resistance into a force for positive change and organizational growth.

Training and Development—A Strategic Perspective

Thus far, we have established that the only constant that confronts today's evolving organization is change. Organizations must constantly strive to adapt in an environment where innovation and change are crucial for achieving success. Amidst this dynamic backdrop of continuous change, effective training and development programs serve as a critical enabler for organizational success, and the cornerstone for building human competency, capacity, and resilience. Effective training and development programs are not only a requirement for achieving change permanence but serve as the catalyst for achieving sustainable growth and organizational competitiveness. These programs are intended to provide a comprehensive strategy to enhance people's knowledge, skills, abilities, and behaviors within an organization. These programs are therefore focused on equipping people with the requisite competencies needed to perform their current roles optimally while also preparing them for future responsibilities emerging along the change continuum.

In the context of organizational change, the mistake has often been made to relegate change management strategy to this singular process, much to the demise of achieving lasting and sustainable change. Thus, and consistent with the precepts of the 5-Ps of change presented thus far in this book, building effective training programs must include (a) realignment and rearticulation of the organization's *purpose* relative to its strategic imperatives, (b) an intentional *plan* that focuses on building competency, capacity and resilience within the workforce, (c) a *process* assessment that juxtaposes legacy processes against optimized and enhanced workflows, (d) assessment measures that quantify *performance* relative to change adoption, and finally (e) a skills-based curriculum that emphasizes the development of human-social capital in order to achieve long-lasting and effective change adoption through *people*. This comprehensive approach therefore spans each of the pillars previously discussed (i.e., purpose, planning, process, performance, and people) and provides continuity across the entire change management process. That's why effective training and development programs are never to be construed as a one-time event, but rather a multifaceted process that aligns with the organization's strategic objectives.

Organizations that invest in effective training and development programs often experience continuity between executive visioning all the way through to employee adoption. Adoption is evidenced by improved performance and productivity that often translate to stronger organizations. In order to achieve improved performance, however, training programs must be tailored to meet the specific needs of the organizations. As will be expanded upon in the next section—Benefits of Effective Training and Development Programs—skills assessment is one of the building blocks for designing effective programs, aiding in identifying areas where skills gaps and/or other deficiencies may exist. Effective training and development programs not only help to build top talent, but they also help to foster innovation, adaptability, and resilience—ingredients needed to provide a competitive edge for the organization. While these are compelling reasons for organizations to pursue and undertake effective training and development programs, let's go a step deeper and describe how these benefits translate to increased organizational agility.

Five Tenets of Effective Training and Development Programs

Training and development programs play a critical role in facilitating organizational change by fostering growth, promoting adaptability, and creating an environment conducive for organizational innovation. Organizations that are innovative and forward looking are therefore required to develop a proficient workforce by utilizing a variety of strategies, methods, tools, and assessment techniques to ensure long-term organizational change success. At its core, effective training and development programs provide a roadmap that helps organizations achieve high levels of proficiency by focusing on five foundational tenets.

Effective training and development programs:

- *Provide opportunities for enhanced performance*: Well-designed training programs empower people to perform to their full potential, thereby increasing productivity and efficiency.
- *Encourage adaptability*: A skilled and well-trained team of individuals is the most important asset needed in an ever-changing market.

■ *Promote talent development and retention*: People often admire organizations that take the time to invest in their growth by aligning their skills, interests, and competencies with the organization's strategic imperatives. When this alignment occurs, the organization is then able to not only attract top talent, but also retain outstanding personnel.

■ *Fosters innovation*: Effective training and development programs promote creative thinking and innovation, providing organizations with a competitive advantage in an ever-changing and evolving market.

■ *Ensures safety and compliance*: Effective training is crucial for preventing accidents and limiting legal exposure in organizations where safety and compliance are critical.

In accordance with these core tenets, effective training programs:

Provide Opportunities for Enhanced Performance

In order to achieve enhanced performance across all areas of the organization, it is important to underscore the importance of specificity, active learning, and continuous learning when developing effective training programs. By prioritizing targeted, interactive, and continuous learning approaches, organizations can implement efficient training programs that enhance individual performances, while providing improved organizational agility and competitiveness in a dynamic business environment. This enhanced performance mandate is facilitated by three core strategies:

■ *Employing specificity in training program design:* The conventional approach of implementing a uniform training program to meet a homogeneous organizational need is progressively becoming outdated. Rather, effective training programs require thoughtful, targeted, and focused attention to address skill deficiency, role alignment, and targeted development of competency-enhancing strategies. This empowers, equips, and actualizes areas of expertise needed for long-term organizational viability. It entails progressing beyond generic training modules, to implementing programs that are specifically tailored to the responsibilities, tasks, duties, and assignments of the workforce. Utilizing a customized training approach guarantees that the required training aligns with the acquired skills, resulting in accelerated and substantial enhancements in organizational performance.

■ *Employing active learning techniques*: Enhanced workforce performance can also be achieved through active learning techniques that employ simulations, role-playing, and hands-on training modalities to cultivate a deeper level of learning. Compared to conventional lecture-based techniques, active learning methods not only focus on maintaining attention, but aims at building and retaining experiential knowledge in the long term. By facilitating knowledge retention and skills development, active learning strategies foster creativity and innovation, requiring people to think and act beyond their typical boundaries.

■ *Cultivating a culture of continuous learning:* Finally, enhanced performance requires the cultivation of a culture that prioritizes continuous learning by intentionally incorporating coaching, efficient feedback systems, and providing access to easily available instructional resources. Cultivating a culture of continuous learning further enables people to stay current in their respective disciplines, provides opportunities for advancement, and creates opportunities to improve technical abilities. Ultimately, a continuous learning culture leads to sustained performance, growth, and increased readiness to respond to market changes, thereby providing increased organizational agility and resilience.

Encourage Adaptability

A skilled and well-trained team of individuals is the most important asset an organization can possess and one of the most important attributes needed for survival in an ever-changing market. Effective training and development programs must, therefore, focus on developing a strategic training framework that addresses not only current skill requirements, but also anticipates the future

> A skilled and well-trained team is the most important organizational asset.

needs of the organization. By cultivating a workforce that is not just skilled for today's challenges but is also equipped to handle future developments, organizations can ensure sustained growth and resilience in a world where change is the only constant. They do this by embracing three foundational enablers:

- *Future-proofing skills:* The foundation of a resilient workforce lies in its ability to not only perform current duties effectively, but also to adapt to future challenges. Adaptability is, therefore, one of the foundational drivers for organizational resilience, requiring organizations to build upon current and future workforce competencies that ultimately equip people to perform their functions efficiently and effectively. In future-proofing skills, effective training and development programs must encompass not only technical or job-specific abilities, but also expand to include the development of transferable skills such as critical thinking, effective communication, and strategic team-collaboration. These transferrable skills, when pursued in tandem to developing current and future competencies, prove to be essential enablers to overcome the complexities of an evolving marketplace.

■ *Cross-training and upskilling:* In addition to future-proofing workforce skills, another essential driver for effective training and development programs resides in the ability to cross-train and upskill the organization's workforce. Implementing cross-functional training and upskilling initiatives have often proven to be an effective strategy in developing a workforce with diverse skills and abilities. This diversity provides organizations with the flexibility to make dynamic resource allocation by leveraging a broader pool of resources that possess the relevant skills needed to perform assigned duties. In addition to providing a broader pool of resources, cross-training facilitates collaboration and information exchange among teams, departments, and divisions, promoting a more unified and harmonious corporate culture.

■ *Embracing innovation and technology:* Finally, keeping pace with new technologies and industry trends is essential, especially in an age characterized by constant technological advancement. Effective training and development programs must integrate emerging technologies and innovations, empowering people to comprehend not only their intended benefits, but also their effective use and applications. This proactive approach to technology adoption positions the organization at the forefront of innovation, enabling it to capitalize on new opportunities, maintain a competitive edge in the marketplace, and position itself for sustainable long-term growth in an ever-changing business environment.

Promotes Talent Development and Retention

Effective training and development programs provide a
unique opportunity for strategic development that focuses
on creating and maintaining a work environment prioritizing
workforce development. By providing comprehensive training,
personalized career paths, and a culture of mentorship and
skill sharing, organizations demonstrate genuine value for their
people. In turn, people admire organizations that invest in their
growth by aligning their skills, interests, and competencies with
the organization's strategic imperatives. When this alignment
occurs, they can attract top talent and retain outstanding
personnel. Organizations promoting talent development and
retention therefore employ the following strategies that promote
a culture of mentorship and skill development:

■ *Prioritize investment in people*: Future-oriented
organizations that value their workforce often implement
effective training and development programs as catalysts
for boosting employee morale, loyalty, longevity. By
implementing robust training programs, organizations
clearly demonstrate its commitment to invest in, and
prioritize the needs of its people. By prioritizing
investments in people, organizations demonstrate that they
are serious in not only attracting but ultimately retaining
top talent within the organization, ultimately contributing
to a more motivated and productive workforce.

■ *Provide career development pathways*: In addition
to investing in people, providing customized career
development plans aligned with effective training and
development programs demonstrates a holistic and
people-centric approach focused on the well-being
and personal advancement of the workforce. In so
doing, people will be able to visualize themselves on a
well-defined career advancement trajectory within the

organization, thereby promoting a sense of purpose, direction, and renewed engagement.

■ *Establish mentorship programs*: Establishing mentorship programs, or peer-to-peer learning initiatives is an effective way to encourage knowledge sharing within the organization. When aligned with the organization's training and development strategy, this approach not only enhances the learning experience but also creates a collaborative environment that builds strong team bonds and ultimately encourages a culture of continuous learning and development.

Fosters Innovation

Effective training and development programs are essential catalysts for fostering organizational innovation. By focusing on creative problem-solving, encouraging experimentation and risk-taking, and promoting collaboration and diversity of thought, organizations can create a fertile ground for innovative ideas and practices. Effective training and development programs can therefore provide value and facilitate:

■ *Creative problem-solving*: Effective training and development programs aimed at improving critical thinking and creative approaches to problem-solving are essential for fostering organizational creativity. These programs not only prioritize traditional problem-solving methods but also actively promote brainstorming and innovative thinking, enabling people to go beyond conventional methods by finding new and creative ways to perform daily routines. In order to better facilitate innovation, organizations must cultivate a culture that values and encourages creative thinking. This involves motivating people to propose and implement new ideas, which greatly enhances the organization's capacity for innovation.

- *Experimentation and risk-taking:* In addition to facilitating creative problem-solving, experimentation and risk-taking are also essential enablers for innovation since they often require venturing beyond traditional norms and questioning the status quo. Effective training programs that promote a culture of experimentation and strategic risk-taking are invaluable; they help establish a safe environment for experimentation, where people can engage in trial-and-error without fearing the consequence of failure. Ultimately, encouraging experimentation and risk taking not only fosters a mindset that promotes creative thinking, but also cultivates an attitude that regards failures as valuable learning experiences.
- *Collaboration and diversity of thought:* Building on creative problem-solving, experimentation, and risk-taking, the richness of innovative ideas often stems from diverse perspectives and collaborative efforts. Effective training and development programs, which bring people together from different functions, backgrounds, and areas of expertise, can lead to a cross-pollination of ideas. This diversity of thought is a powerful driver for innovation, as it combines varied insights and experiences, leading to more comprehensive and creative solutions. Promoting such collaboration not only improves the learning experience but also reflects the type of collaborative, multidisciplinary teamwork that is crucial for encouraging creativity in real-world situations.

Ensures Safety and Compliance

The importance of meeting safety and compliance requirements cannot be overstated within an organizational context. For this reason, effective training and development programs are pivotal in mitigating threats to the organization by preventing accidents and restricting legal exposure, especially for organizations where safety and compliance are critical. It is imperative, therefore, for organizations to adopt a cohesive strategy that provides comprehensive training, continuous awareness, frequent analysis, and proactive error-reporting to minimize organizational risks while upholding safety and compliance standards. Effective training and development programs that focus on safety and compliance often employ the following strategies:

- *Adopting comprehensive safeguards*: Effective safety and compliance strategies rely on the development and implementation of intensive instructional programs covering all pertinent safety legislation and compliance requirements unique to the organization's industry and practice. Thorough training not only equips staff with the essential information and abilities necessary to function securely, but also showcases the organization's dedication to upholding a secure and compliant work environment. Therefore, by ensuring that all employees possess a thorough understanding in all relevant domains, the likelihood of accidents, incidents, and adverse legal exposure will be greatly reduced.
- *Fostering continuous awareness*: Adherence to safety and compliance standards requires careful and continuous effort rather than being limited to singular training occurrences. In order to meet the standard of continuous awareness, organizations must leverage ongoing awareness campaigns and frequent refresher trainings so as to maintain focus, awareness, and acuity on safety standards. In so doing, organizations ensure that safety practices are not merely a theoretical exercise, but rather a requirement to embed safety values and principles deeply into organizational life.
- *Near-miss reporting and analysis*: While adopting comprehensive safeguards and fostering continuous awareness are critical steps in ensuring safety and

compliance, a holistic strategy will be incomplete without feedback and analysis reporting. Adopting a proactive stance toward safety therefore entails not just responding to occurrences, but also taking measures to prevent them. Encouraging the reporting and thorough investigation of near-miss accidents is an essential element of this analysis process. Near-misses, defined as incidents that had the potential to cause an accident but ultimately did not, provide vital insights on possible risks that may not be immediately obvious. Through the analysis of these instances, organizations may be able to extract valuable insights to alleviate future hazards. This strategy not only improves workplace safety but also fosters a culture of continuous improvement, where helpful insights are utilized to improve the organization's overall safety posture.

Training and Development—The Soft Side of Change, the Hard Facts to Learn!

Organizational success in today's complex and dynamic business environment is predicated on building a robust foundation, the core of which is anchored in human-social capital development. Human-social capital is an organizational construct that describes the pivotal role that people play within the organization. So, let's unpack this term and contextualize it within the training and development universe.

Understanding Human-Social Capital

The term "human-social capital" engenders the collective knowledge, skills, relationships, and social networks of people to the extent that the sum of their parts is greater than their unitary influence on affecting organizational productivity, innovation, and growth. Human-social capital also highlights the idea that people, through their interactions, collaborations, and shared experiences, create a powerfully valuable resource that can be leveraged to enhance organizational performance. Therefore, when organizations invest in the competency development, well-being, and collaborative relationships of their people, to the degree that this investment results in increased productivity, innovation, and growth, they invariably position themselves to reap the benefits of a more resilient, adaptive, and thriving enterprise.

Simply stated, people are the architects and custodians of human-social capital, and their individual and collective contributions serve as the foundation upon which thriving organizations are built. This reality, further underscored throughout this book, reveal the fact that people are the heart of the organization, since:

- The organization's vision, strategy, and operations impact people.
- The organization's services, programs, and initiatives impact people.
- The organization's projects, programs, and portfolios impact people.
- The organization's mission, processes, and strategic outcomes impact people.
- The organization's technology, systems, and collaboration platforms, impact people.
- The organization's culture, attitudes, and pervasive behaviors are shaped by people.

Effective training and development programs are therefore essential in equipping people with the requisite competencies necessary for change adoption. This creates an environment that focuses on improving organizational performance and implementing meaningful change. Investing in effective training and development programs also enhances the organization's capacity to effectively and efficiently perform the requisite tasks needed for daily operations, leading to sustained organizational competitiveness. For these reasons, investing in effective training and development programs is no longer a luxury. It is a strategic imperative that requires organizations to explore and align its resource pool with the technologies, systems, processes, and tools that are needed for its long-term viability and sustainability.

Another aspect of understanding the importance of human-social capital centers on diversity. Encouraging human-social capital diversity is an important enabler for organizational change success since it positions the organization to adopt a range of skills and experiences that foster a culture of innovation and creativity. The strength of the organization's diversity—the colorfully interwoven fabric of differing backgrounds and perspectives—enables the organization to leverage its collective creative strengths to generate new and unique solutions to recurring problems. This creativity is strengthened by the organization's social networks and relationships that facilitate communication, collaboration, teamwork, and knowledge sharing between its people. That's probably why organizations with rich human-social capital are often more adaptable and flexible. The strength of their diversity, enhanced collective competencies, and strong social networks harmoniously work together to enable long-term change adoption across the organization.

As described in the earlier segment, organizations that value and invest in their human-social capital are also more attractive to top talent. They are more successful in retaining this talent by prioritizing skill development, effective working relationships, and building strong collaborative work units. This inter-organizational collaboration supported by effective training and development programs further bolsters organizational success. It reinforces shared values, norms, and behaviors thereby influencing and/or improving how people identify their role and place within the organization. For example, people who feel valued and have growth opportunities within the organization tend to be more satisfied and engaged with their work. This leads to lower attrition, higher productivity, and better overall satisfaction with the organization.

Finally, the benefits of investing in effective training and development programs extend beyond the organization to external relationships with customers, suppliers, and partners. As discussed in an earlier chapter, the influence of these critical stakeholder groups (i.e., customers, suppliers, and partners) is pivotal for business growth, innovation, and exploiting new market opportunities. Thus, when organizations invest in effective training and development programs, they invariably entertain diverse perspectives within a rich human-social capital framework. This often results in more informed, balanced, and optimized decision-making outcomes due to the collective benefit of having multiple perspectives.

Understanding human-social capital and its role in effective training and development programs is paramount for organizations seeking to optimize their human resources. Human-social capital recognizes that people are not just individual contributors but a collective force possessing a wealth of knowledge, skills, and relationships that can drive organizational growth and innovation. Acknowledging this fundamental concept is crucial. It underscores the need to harness and nurture this resource through well-defined and carefully executed training and development programs. Against this backdrop, let's now delve into the first critical step when planning effective training and development programs—*Setting Clear Objectives*. Setting clear objectives is a foundational requirement. It ensures that training efforts are purposeful, aligned with the organization's strategic imperatives, and leverage human-social capital to its fullest potential.

Training and Development—A Practical Guide

Step 1: Set Clear Objectives

In the chapter devoted to the planning pillar, I established the need for "planning" in the design and implementation phases for the *Icon of the Seas* cruise liner. In the planning phase, designers and architects carefully mapped out every intricate detail, identified design challenges, and took corrective actions that were necessary to optimize the construction process. Similarly in organizational change management, and by extension, the delivery of effective training and development programs, effective planning provides the opportunity in "seeing the end from the beginning," foreseeing obstacles, defining effective risk mitigation strategies, and ensuring that the initiative meets the organization's strategic imperatives.

One of the most critical steps when planning training and development programs is setting clear objectives. Imagine the opulent *Icon of the Seas*, headed out with crew and passengers with no designated destination or plan? Its journey would be devoid of purpose, inefficient, and misdirected. The same holds true for training and development programs that lack well-defined objectives; they encounter hurdles, participants feel frustrated and disoriented, and ultimately, they lose interest simply because the objectives were not clear. That's why setting clear objectives at the outset is such an essential component of delivering effective training and development programs, because it:

■ *Provides focus and direction:* Clear objectives serve as a road map directing all areas of the training effort from the evaluation of participants' needs, the development of the curriculum, and ultimately the achievement of the intended goals of the program. By providing focus and direction, everyone involved is intimately aware of "why" the program is being implemented, which then focuses attention on the attainment of the training goals.

■ *Provides motivation and engagement*: Clear objectives help motivate participants by illustrating the desired outcome and encompassing the skills and information they will attain. This promotes active involvement and motivates people to actively participate in the process of learning.

■ *Provides improved performance*: Clear objectives provide organizational goal alignment and aids in targeting specific areas where performance improvements are needed. Setting clear objectives facilitates defining methods and strategies to aid in goal attainment, and ultimately, organizational change success.

■ *Provides the effective use of resources:* Clear objectives help to ensure that the organization's resources are prioritized and allocated toward meeting the most critical needs of the organization. This helps to minimize wastage of time, money, and human capital, and redirects the use of resources toward efforts that help the organization achieve its strategic goals.

■ *Provides a basis for evaluation*: Clear objectives finally serve as the benchmarks against which training and development program effectiveness can be assessed and evaluated. Progress evaluation, in relation to predetermined program objectives, enables effective data-driven decisions, continuous improvement, and provides the basis for return-on-investment assessments.

As described in the five bullets above, setting clear objectives is a fundamental step in designing effective training and development programs. It allows organizations to comprehensively analyze gaps relative to competencies needed to effectively adopt change. By understanding the organizational context, identifying challenges, strategic goals, and desired competencies, organizations are equipped to tailor training programs to address specific needs and issues. Supportive of this effort, needs assessments further help to pinpoint individual and team skill gaps, knowledge deficiencies, and behavioral needs while performance reviews, customer feedback, and other forms of historical data provide valuable insights for improvement.

Consistent with methods defined in the Process and Performance charters, defining clear objectives can be achieved using the specific, measurable, attainable, relevant, and time-bound (SMART) objectives. As a reminder, SMART objectives possess specific, measurable, achievable, relevant, and time-bound attributes that help to define, refine, and enable the attainment of organizational goals. Using this approach, SMART objectives provide a clear vision of what needs to be achieved, provide the avenue for measuring and tracking progress, and inform recurring organizational needs relative to the attainment of the organization's strategic objectives.

Thirdly, prioritizing and refining objectives based on importance and stakeholder feedback helps streamline efforts and ensures alignment with broader organizational goals. Clear and concise objectives that everyone can understand foster engagement and commitment toward desired training program goals. Developing assessment measures that further align with the objectives enables organizations to evaluate the program's effectiveness. Assessment measures can be operationalized using methods and processes such as pre- and post-training evaluations, performance appraisals, and skill demonstrations. These allow for a comprehensive analysis of individual progress relative to required competencies needed for change permanence to occur.

As described in this section, in order to establish effective training and development programs, it is paramount to have a clear grasp of the organization's objectives and goals. Setting clear objectives serves as the cornerstone for the delivery of effective training programs. They ensure the organization's strategic objectives are not only understood, but also achieved. However, in order to fully implement effective training and development programs, it's also critical to evaluate and prioritize training needs. The next section will delve into this next crucial step that allows for the personalization of training efforts so as to target the most pressing needs that are required for lasting change.

Step 2: Identify and Prioritize Training Needs

Organizations that invest and undertake change initiatives often confront the reality that their success not only hinges on the skills, agility, and knowledge of one individual, but rather on the collective competence of their workforce. In order to equip the organization with the collective ability to effect lasting change, it is essential to build training and development programs that understand the various needs critical for establishing competence.

Identifying and prioritizing training needs is analogous to building a sturdy rope bridge that spans a rocky chasm of transformation. Confronting the dangers that lie below, teams must be equipped with the tools needed to overcome obstacles, adapt to the new landscape, and ultimately construct a bridge that provides safe passage for its travelers. Analogously, without a clear understanding of what training is needed, and a strategic plan for its deployment and execution, change initiatives will fail, leaving organizations stranded in the valley of missed opportunities. Therefore, organizations must invest in effective and targeted training initiatives that empower their workforce to bridge skills gaps and develop the requisite competencies that are needed for effecting lasting change within the organization.

Identifying and prioritizing training needs is therefore the next critical step in the execution of effective training and development programs. They lay the groundwork for understanding core requirements and workforce development needs. The first question that governs the identification and prioritization of training needs is, *why?* Why is the training being conducted, and why is it important? Answering these questions establish the broad vision, and helps to articulate the strategic objectives being pursued. Understanding the "why" further aids in defining desired behaviors and competencies that are essential to support the execution of tasks and duties in the new organizational paradigm. Aligning the needs of the new organizational paradigm with the existing needs of the workforce provides helpful insights for identifying where skill-gaps exist, providing important clues and strategies on how to remedy. Strategies may range from developing skills inventories for the organization, holding workshops, polling through surveys, holding one-on-one or group interviews, or performing job skill evaluations; all of which are aimed at providing insight into assessing and closing skills gaps.

Skills assessments provide helpful insight into understanding current organizational competencies; however, additional steps may be needed to formally assess the training needs of the workforce. These steps may include referencing performance evaluations that propose areas for improvement; undergoing formal skills assessment to gauge individual skill levels; and defining competency frameworks that define a set of attributes, skills and knowledge that are needed for each role within the new organizational paradigm. In addition to these strategies, informal stakeholder engagement methods, and workforce skill assessment strategies may also be employed that include discussions with team leaders, mentors, and subject matter experts within the organization to (a) provide qualitative insights about potential workforce limitations and skills gaps, and (b) to understand leadership's perspectives and needs, thereby ensuring that provided training is relevant and addresses the actual needs of the organization.

These insights, gathered through formal and informal strategies provide valuable information that will now be used to prioritize training needs. The prioritization process is foundational; as it helps to define where valuable resources to time, money, and effort will be spent to achieve the maximum training impact. The process, therefore, must be data driven and include a mapping of immediate versus long-term needs, associating assessment of high versus low impact. This assessment is often tabulated in an "urgency matrix' that plots the most urgent and impactful objectives of the organization and provides a structured framework to make informed decisions about where to focus training efforts. The urgency matrix is divided into four distinct quadrants that allow tabulation of high-priority and time-sensitive activities while deferring or eliminating less critical activities given available resources. While an urgency matrix may prove to be an invaluable tool, another strategy that offers a more simplified approach includes the 80/20 rule. Based on the Pareto principle, the 80/20 strategy aims to prioritize training that benefits the largest group or address the most critical needs that provide the greatest return to the organization. Both strategies, when informed by an understanding of the various training needs of the organization, enable it to make informed decisions about learning styles, delivery modalities, and nuances that offer clues to design impactful effective training and development programs.

After completing the identification and prioritization of training requirements, the next important phase is the actual design and development of the training program. This transition represents a pivotal change from analysis to implementation where identified training needs serve as critical inputs directing focus and ultimately moderating the execution of the training program.

Step 3: Initiate Training and Development Program Design

In the earlier sections, we established the need for setting clear objectives and provided strategic recommendations relative to identifying and prioritizing training needs. These two activities serve as input into this next step, and transitions the initiative from analysis to execution.

Initiating effective training and development programs is a multifaceted effort that takes into account a variety of considerations ranging from defining the learning objectives, instructional modalities, and delivery approaches to determining other training logistics needed for effective execution. Let's unpack each of these critical activities, starting with learning objectives.

Develop Learning Objectives

Learning objectives are the foundation of any successful training program. They serve as guideposts that align individual development needs with mandated organizational goals and provide the pathway for instructing what participants should be able to accomplish by the end of the training endeavor. Well-defined learning objectives also help to focus both instructors and participants on core instructional goals, while engaging, motivating, and facilitating active learning postures. While developing learning objectives can facilitate improved assessment and evaluation following training programs, the effort required for their development is sometimes considered time-consuming. For this reason, opponents conclude that defining learning objectives often result in inflexible instructional processes from which it is difficult to deviate. While there may be validity in the required effort needed, the return on investment provides a pathway that focuses time, effort, money, and human capital toward the attainment of measurable outcomes; outcomes that serve in the attainment of training goals, and ultimately the strategic objectives of the organization.

Developing effective learning objectives requires four essential checkpoints to ensure that instructional goals are met. These checkpoints include the following:

■ *Determine specific outcomes*: Develop SMART objectives that precisely delineate what participants should know, understand, or be able to do after completing the training. Learning objectives will therefore focus on knowledge, skills, and capabilities to be gained, thereby leading to building the requisite competencies needed to sustain the change long after the initiative would have completed.

■ *Ensure organizational goal alignment*: Once specific outcomes have been established, its critical to ensure that they align with long-term organizational goals. This ensures that the broader objectives that lead to the organization achieving its vision and mission are central to designing and implementing efforts aimed at equipping its workforce. In so doing, this aids in maximizing the efficacy and impact of the training program. Further, in ensuring organizational goal alignment, it's important to analyze the organization's needs, skill gaps, and desired outcomes. One does this by taking into account how the learning objectives not only aligns with the organization's goals, but how they align with individual career aspirations. This provides a holistic, 360-degree perspective that encourages the union between the organization and its workforce—a concept highlighted as pivotal when creating people-centric cultures earlier in this chapter.

■ *Utilize measurable criteria*: In defining learning objectives, use action verbs to define observable behaviors that enable clear articulation and assessment of learning outcomes. Words such as analyze, create, evaluate, define, develop, etc. lead to activities that produce observable results thereby making it easier to measure and assess progress.

■ *Define attainable goals*: Ensure that the learning objectives are attainable, given the availability of resources and time that has been allotted for the training initiative. Achieving prescribed goals at the end of the initiative significantly aids in building confidence needed to repeat and master behaviors that lead to change permanence.

Determine Learning Modalities

Now that learning objectives have been established, the next step in the training implementation process requires deciding on the most effective training modality. Training modalities refer to the diverse methods and approaches used to impart knowledge, skills, and expertise with the aim of enhancing individual competencies. Training modalities include formal educational sessions, workshops, e-learning, microlearning, on-the-job training, etc. Each modality provides unique benefits depending on learning preferences and delivery considerations. For example, visual, auditory, and kinesthetic approaches provide unique advantages to aid in the assimilation of information. Visual learners thrive when presented with images, diagrams, and videos, which not only improve their comprehension but also enhance memory retention and spatial reasoning. Auditory learners excel in settings involving lectures, discussions, and audiobooks, as they develop strong listening skills and foster effective communication and teamwork abilities. On the other hand, kinesthetic learners flourish when engaged in hands-on activities, role-playing, and simulations, as this approach strengthens muscle memory, boosts engagement, and enhances practical skills. Recognizing and accommodating these distinct learning styles can facilitate more effective and comprehensive education and training.

In view of the learning styles and delivery considerations, the table below provides a summary of commonly used training modalities, ideal applications, and pros and cons of each. While not exhaustive, the goal is to provide an overview to help guide selection decisions in accordance with user characteristics and the organization's training objectives (Table 5.1).

Table 5.1   Summary of Training Modalities

Method	Application	Pros	Cons
Workshops:	Facilitate group conversations and participatory learning. Ideal for challenging subjects that need hands-on practice. Learning is enhanced by immediate feedback and peer engagement.	Interactive, collaborative, builds relationships, and provides immediate feedback.	Resource-intensive, requires facilitator expertise, offers reduced reach due to inability to scale for larger organizations.
E-Learning:	• Offers flexibility and geographically dispersed learners that are located abroad.	Provides convenient, personalized learning pace, while being cost-effective and scalable.	Reduced engagement due to lack of face-to-face interaction.

(Continued)

Table 5.1 (Continued)

Method	Application	Pros	Cons
	• Economical for training programs on a wide scale. • Various learning styles may be accommodated through self-paced learning.		Requires self-motivation, discipline, and the ability to troubleshoot issues.
Microlearning:	• Offers targeted content in small, bite-sized, and highly focused learning units. • Focused on developing specific skills or knowledge and aims to close gaps through easily digestible content.	Efficient, targeted, and concise delivery of content. Just-in-time approach facilitates content delivery when needed most.	Offers limited depth due to focus content area. May lead to content fragmentation; as topic may be disconnected from large body of knowledge.
On-the-Job Training:	Offers immersive and experiential real-world application of knowledge and skills.	Offers immediate feedback, mentor guidance, and direct relevance to job duties.	Time-consuming for mentors. May offer inconsistent experience. Relies on mentor competency.

Develop Customized Content

It goes without saying that content is the heart of the training initiative. It focuses attention on the acquisition of skills and knowledge needed to develop the requisite competencies necessary for assuming new roles, performing new tasks, and ultimately achieving the strategic objectives of the organization. In developing customized content, one of first and essential steps includes creating an outline that maps the learning objectives with existing skill gaps. This allows for customization of the curriculum that includes topics to be covered, starting with the most important learning objectives first. This prioritization focuses attention on the immediate skills and knowledge areas that require mastery and allows for repeated reinforcement throughout the training program. This process is repeated recursively where the curriculum is refined, revised, and enhanced to ensure that the learning objectives are clearly established, prioritized, and supported using relevant training modalities for the target audience. In developing content, steps should be taken to ensure that relevant, up to date, engaging, and interactive materials are utilized to capture and maintain the target audience's attention. Strategies may include the use of presentations, short videos, interactive games, and professionally produced handouts. Content delivery is often enhanced using e-learning tools that facilitate electronic storage, retrieval, presentation, and archival of training materials. Advanced learning management systems (LMS) may also provide online content delivery for wider accessibility, enabling microlearning strategies through short videos, or provide access to entire training modules for just-in-time refresher training.

In developing effective content, it's imperative to incorporate interactive elements to enhance engagement and knowledge retention. Strategies may include the use of quizzes to test on material covered, simulations that illustrate real-life scenarios and responses, or other forms of interaction and engagement that focus on knowledge retention and skills mastery. In addition to using quizzes, the use of tests, practical assignments, and projects also are effective in assessing comprehension and the degree of skill acquisition gained during and following the training initiative. This process further allows for continuous improvement of the instructional strategy, collection of valuable feedback from participants, the ability to evaluate program effectiveness, and ultimately, glean valuable insight on areas for improvement.

Finalize Training Logistics

The final stage in the program design phase requires the finalization of logistics and completing implementation readiness assessments to ensure that the training program meets target goals. In this regard, several key factors must be taken into account to ensure the effectiveness of the training program. The first is determining the frequency of training sessions. Training frequency will be affected by the complexity of the material being covered and the amount of time required for participants to assimilate the concepts, all of which are moderated by the availability of participants. Striking the right balance in terms of frequency is crucial to prevent information overload while ensuring that participants have ample opportunity to absorb and apply what they've learned.

Secondly, the duration of each training session is a critical consideration. It's essential to provide enough time for meaningful learning, since long sessions will invariably overwhelm participants. This will result in learning fatigue and ultimately the loss of interest in completing the training program. For this reason, incorporating microlearning modules which deliver information in shorter, more digestible bursts, often provides a strategic advantage. Spacing is another key element in effective training program design. Implementing repetitive instructional cadences, where key concepts are revisited at pre-determined intervals, can significantly enhance learning retention, and reinforce understanding. This approach helps participants retain information over the long term rather than forgetting key concepts shortly after training delivery. Lastly, and as described in the earlier section, content prioritization that focuses on teaching critical skills and important concepts early in the training program is essential to maximizing the delivery, impact, and effectiveness. By addressing the most crucial aspects first, participants will quickly gain the foundational expertise they need, which can then be built upon as the program progresses.

Now that the foundational elements for the training program have been defined, the next crucial step is to smoothly transition into the actual training implementation. This phase operationalizes planning, content development, delivery refinement, and supporting logistics needed to ensure that the program unfolds successfully. The transition from program design to training implementation requires a seamless coordination of efforts. A focus on effective communication and monitoring ensures that training objectives are met, and that participants have the support they need to develop the skills and knowledge necessary to assume new roles within the new organizational paradigm.

Step 4: Training Implementation

Thus far, we established the need to set clear objectives and identify and prioritize training needs. All of these are essential inputs for effective training program design. Each of these critical steps relied on subject matter experts to guide the articulation of learning objectives, the selection of training modalities, and the development of engaging content and effective curriculum design. In this next and important phase, the critical role of expert facilitators and trainers comes into focus. Their role is central to the delivery of the curriculum which ultimately influences the overall training implementation.

Expert facilitators and trainers are often the most influential variable in the training delivery equation, bridging the gap between theoretical knowledge and practical application. They are the catalysts for a successful learning experience, turning a routine training program into an impactful and enduring educational journey. Their subject matter expertise and depth of experiential command equip them to effectively deliver accurate and relevant content, and provide alignment with best practices, current industry standards, and organizational-specific processes and procedures. While their subject matter expertise is pivotal for effective training delivery, equally important is their facilitation skills which encompass a range of competencies including the ability to actively engage participants, fostering an interactive and inclusive learning environment, and stimulating meaningful group discussions. This range of skills is vital for making the training relevant and engaging and operationalizes critical information needed for lasting change adoption.

The selection of expert facilitators who are also adept at using various pedagogical techniques to cater to different learning styles, is therefore critical in the early planning stages of the training initiative. Invariably, the most effective facilitators are the ones who can enable the transference of knowledge by ensuring each participant absorbs and applies the instructional material effectively. Skilled facilitators also possess the uncanny ability to translate complex concepts in a clear and understandable manner while decomposing difficult topics into relevant, digestible, and easily comprehensible segments. This clarity of communication is crucial in ensuring that training activities are not only informative, but also transformative, enabling participants to grasp and implement skills needed in the new organizational paradigm.

Now that much of the groundwork has been laid, and the training initiative is ready to get underway with the aid of expert facilitators and trainers, it is imperative to focus on several key strategies needed for effective training delivery. The first, which focuses on building core skills and knowledge, requires prioritizing the training initiative on developing the essential job competencies at the beginning stages of the training initiative. In addition to building essential competencies, facilitating the development of transferrable skills, such as critical thinking, problem-solving, effective communication, and team collaboration are also important enablers for lasting organizational success. These skills form the foundation for successful change adoption by facilitating individual skill mastery and enabling teams to adapt and thrive in evolving organizational environments.

Secondly, while it is important to focus on core job competencies, investing in leadership development programs is also essential. Building leadership efficacy and capacity aid to equip leaders with the requisite skills, awareness, and sensibilities needed to guide their teams and departments toward the attainment of the organization's strategic objectives. Concurrently, helping leaders develop initiative, strategic thinking, and sound decision-making skills are essential in developing critical leadership skillsets. These skills are instrumental in guiding teams through periods of organizational transformation. Further, cultivating a culture of continuous learning by encouraging self-directed learning and building self-awareness as a leader further aids in instilling a sense of lifelong learning. This also promotes a culture aimed at continuous improvement, agility, and adaptability.

As leaders employ the requisite skills needed to bring their organizations along the change continuum, creating a supportive environment during the training program is also pivotal for content assimilation, knowledge retention, and long-term change adoption. Creating a supportive learning environment is also a critical enabler for fostering individual growth and effective group learning. Supportive environments not only include up-to-date and relevant training materials, eLearning tools, and a comfortable learning space, but also includes providing one-on-one support and personalized coaching capabilities.

During the training implementation, time allocation is another important determinant for training success. Participants should be given sufficient time to participate, assimilate, and activate the training received without feeling pressured to resume their regular work responsibilities. This training prioritization signals to participants that the organization values their personal development and is willing to invest in them. This sends a clear message about its importance to the attainment of the organization's goals and objectives. Additionally, when leaders actively participate in training activities themselves, it visually reinforces the importance of acquiring core job competencies. Additionally, rewarding participants who apply new skills effectively, and consistently communicating the benefits and successes of the training program are also essential leadership activities. These activities go a long way in instilling trust and confidence, and ultimately foster a positive attitude toward learning and development across the organization. That's why creating supportive environments not only enhances the effectiveness of the training, but also contributes to a culture of continuous improvement and innovation. In so doing, it encourages participants to take ownership of their personal development, engage deeply with the training content, and apply their new skills confidently in new roles, further enabling organizational growth and success.

Supportive environments are often enhanced using technology. In today's digital age, technology offers myriad ways to make training more accessible, engaging, and effective. One essential technological tool is the LMS, which acts as a central hub for all training activities. An LMS simplifies access to training materials, allowing learners to engage with content at their own pace and convenience. This flexibility is particularly beneficial in accommodating diverse schedules and learning preferences. Frequently, LMS platforms include analytics, monitoring, and reporting capabilities that allow instructors and participants to monitor progress of the training program. As discussed earlier, relative to adopting engaging methods, LMS platforms may also offer interactive components such as virtual reality and simulation modules that significantly enhance the training experience by providing an immersive experience to help hone their new skills in a realistic yet controlled environment. Access to these advanced features and capabilities are particularly advantageous for training programs that require instruction on intricate and complex procedures, or high-risk performance scenarios. These simulating environments, therefore, provide a safe space for participants to practice without fear of failure, or the threat of dire real-world consequences. More specifically, simulations further offer the benefit of duplicate real-world business scenarios or job duties, providing participants with practical experience and the opportunity to evaluate various methodologies while deriving lessons from their results. Leveraging the use of technology not only enhances participant engagement but also improves knowledge transfer to the workplace by providing valuable experiential learning opportunities. These opportunities ultimately lead to higher effectiveness of the training program.

As discussed thus far, effective training and development programs have a significant influence on organizational culture, helping to promote ongoing learning and development. When organizations commit to implementing effective training and development programs, it promotes a mindset of continuous learning, improvement, development, and growth. Thus, a commitment to learning, signals a deep commitment and prioritization to personal and professional growth. This is a predicate for ongoing employee engagement, motivation, commitment, and loyalty. This heightened level of involvement often leads to a culture of increased innovation and productivity. Employees will invariably feel more connected and commit to providing their best work.

A culture that emphasizes continuous learning naturally cultivates an environment where feedback and constructive criticism are valued, and where mistakes are viewed as opportunities for learning and growth. This perspective encourages experimentation and the freedom to take calculated risks, recognizing that the organization will provide a degree of safety as its investment to creating a culture of learning. As a result, the organization becomes more dynamic, adaptable, and resilient, while being able to respond more swiftly to market changes, emerging technologies, and the ever-shifting web of customer expectations.

Effective training and development programs therefore do more than just enhance skills; they fundamentally transform the organizational culture. They build a workforce that is not only skilled and knowledgeable, but that is also deeply engaged and committed to continuous improvement. Through effective training and development programs, organizations are able to transform themselves into becoming more innovative, adaptable, and better positioned for long-term organizational success.

Step 5: Adaptation, Feedback, and Follow-Up

The transition from the training implementation to the final stages of adaptation, feedback, and follow-up signals an important shift from training delivery to organizational change adoption. This shift is important; as it supports the practical application of training received and the operationalizing of new competencies needed for the continuous evolution of the organization. This is where the real test of the training implementation begins. It is in the adaptation phase where new skills and knowledge are integrated into the daily operational processes for the organization.

Adaptation involves tailoring the newly acquired skills to fit the unique challenges and contexts of the workplace. It's a phase where theoretical learning is transformed into practical, actionable strategies. As the organization meanders through this adaptation phase, it is concurrently gathering feedback to aid in the refining of instructional material and how it is operationalized within the organizational context. This feedback, sourced from both the training participants and the instructional team, provides invaluable insights into the effectiveness of the training program. It shines a spotlight on areas requiring attention as part of the continuous improvement strategy. While gathering and analyzing feedback is an important component for process improvement, providing follow-up is even more important. It serves as the bridge that connects training delivery with individual competency and ultimately organizational growth. Furthermore, facilitating feedback ensures that the learning momentum is maintained, creating an eagerness to apply new information that aids in preventing the decay of newly acquired skills over time. Another strategy to mitigate knowledge drain is to provide regular follow-up sessions, refresher courses, and opportunities for ongoing development. These strategies will further solidify information received while fostering a culture of continuous improvement.

Ongoing development and follow-up are crucial components of effective training programs, emphasizing the fact that effective training and development programs are not one-time events but rather an integral part of organizational growth and continuous development. Given the rapid evolution of technology, organizational processes, and the competitive landscape, it's imperative for organizations to embrace continuous learning as an essential requirement for maintaining its competitive edge. That's why providing follow-up training sessions to help reinforce and build upon the knowledge and skills acquired, is critical for the adoption of new processes, systems, and technologies for which training has been provided. These sessions provide an opportunity for learners to revisit and solidify their understanding, discuss challenges they have encountered in applying new skills, and receive additional guidance. Moreover, refresher courses play a key role in keeping the workforce up-to-date with the latest industry trends, technologies, and best practices. This further allows the organization to correct flawed processes, clarify misunderstandings, offer course corrective measures, and introduce new concepts that may have emerged since the original training program was executed. Finally, consistent with continuous learning strategies, providing follow-up training helps to instill a culture of lifelong learning within the organization, encouraging employees to take ownership of their personal and professional development. Organizations that make ongoing professional development a priority communicate the importance of developing a workforce that is skilled, adaptable, and aligned with the organization's evolving needs.

Finally, while continuous growth and development is a hallmark for effective training and development programs, there is one final ingredient—scalability—that is focused on meeting the organization's future needs. The need for scalability is paramount in today's fast-paced organizations. Organizations must ensure that their training initiatives are designed to easily scale up or down, depending on the changing size, scope, and needs of the business. Thus, scalability ensures that training remains effective and relevant, whether it's being delivered to a small team or offered across a global enterprise.

> Organizations that make ongoing professional development a priority communicate the importance of developing a workforce that is skilled, adaptable, and aligned with the organization's evolving needs.

A close relative of scalability is flexibility, and this too is important for adapting the training content and methods to respond swiftly to new organizational challenges, market conditions, or technological advancements. Flexibility, therefore, allows the organization to keep their workforce skills aligned with industry trends and demands, enabling the organization to remain competitive in the delivery of its products and services. Flexibility in aiding organizational competitiveness requires frequent updates to training modules, instructional materials, and supportive aids. These updates should reflect new organizational realities, software advancements, and enhancements in processes and workflows to meet the rapidly emerging needs of the market.

When scalable and flexible approaches are employed, organizations are equipped to provide long-term sustainability of its training programs. Sustainability refers to the organization's ability to efficiently utilize resources while ensuring long-term effectiveness and viability of its training initiatives. When organizations design training and development programs that can be easily adjusted and scaled, they avoid the pitfalls of obsolescence. This ensures that their investment in employee development continues to yield positive returns over time. Ultimately, the organization's intentionality of using scalability and flexibility as critical success factors in the implementation of their training programs is not just a strategic choice. This is a necessity for fostering a resilient and future-ready workforce that is positioned to contribute to the sustainable growth and competitiveness of the organization.

Conclusion

In "The 5-Ps of Change," readers are taken on a comprehensive journey through the intricacies of organizational change, and the critical elements of effective change management are underscored. Each chapter delves deeper into the critical components of the 5-Ps framework, offering a rich tapestry of insights and strategies for navigating change, starting with—*purpose.* Chapter 1 highlights the significance of defining a clear and compelling purpose statement, which serves as the guiding light for all stakeholders involved in the change initiative. It demonstrates how a well-articulated purpose can galvanize an organization toward a common goal, ensuring clarity and alignment at every level.

In Chapter 2, the emphasis is placed on the strategic importance of planning as a continuous, dynamic process. Readers are provided with a roadmap for building a robust planning framework, which is crucial for setting objectives, defining strategies, and outlining the resources and actions required for effective change.

Chapter 3 explores the mechanics of process optimization, offering insights into creating efficient and adaptable business processes. It lays out a blueprint for establishing a structured approach to business process management, highlighting the

DOI: 10.4324/9781003544883-7

characteristics of effective processes and the transformative role of technology.

Chapter 4 delves into the intersecting realms of Critical Success Factors (CSFs), Key Performance Indicators (KPIs), and Assessment Metrics, collectively referred to as the "Big-Three" of performance measurement and management. It unpacks how these elements work in concert to provide a comprehensive view of organizational performance, emphasizing their alignment and interdependence.

Finally, Chapter 5 reinforces the centrality of the human element in change initiatives. It emphasizes the importance of aligning competencies, managing resistance, and fostering a culture of continuous learning and development. The chapter provides a step-by-step guide on addressing the human factors in organizational change, underscoring the value of empathetic understanding and effective communication.

In conclusion, "The 5-Ps of Change" presents a compelling call to action for executives, leaders, and decision-makers to embrace the principles of Purpose, Planning, Process, Performance, and People with unwavering commitment. By adopting this holistic framework, organizations are poised to navigate the challenges of change with confidence, driving innovation, growth, and sustainable success. This book serves as a clarion call to master the art and science of change management, urging leaders to unlock the full potential of their organizations in an ever-evolving business landscape. Embrace the 5-Ps, and lead your organization to new heights of excellence and resilience in the face of change.

References

Armenakis, A. A., & Harris, S. G. (2002). *Taking the Measure of Change: A Quantitative Approach to Understanding Organizational Transformation*. Oxford University Press.

Armenakis, A. A., & Harris, S. G. (2009). Reflections: Our journey in organizational change research and practice. *Journal of Change Management, 9*(2), 127–142.

Armenakis, A. A., Harris, S. G., & Mossholder, K. W. (1993). Creating readiness for organizational change. *Human Resource Management Review*, 125–147.

Buchanan, D. A., & Huczynski, A. (2010). *Organizational Behaviour: An Introductory Text* (7th ed.). Pearson Education.

Burke, W. W., & Litwin, G. H. (1991). A causal model of organizational performance and change. *Journal of Management, 17*(3), 523–545.

Burnes, B. (2004). *Managing Change* (4th ed.). Pearson Education.

Cameron, E., & Green, M. (2015). *Making Sense of Change Management*, 4th Edition. Pennsylvania: Kogan Page Limited.

Davenport, T. H. (1993). *Process Innovation: Reengineering Work Through Information Technology*. MA: Harvard Business Press.

Doran, G. T. (1981). There's a S.M.A.R.T. way to write management's goals and objectives. *Management Review*.

Dumas, M., La Rosa, M., Mendling, J., & Reijers, H. (2013). *Fundamentals of Business Process Management*. Berlin: Springer-Verlag.

Enochson, H. (2023, November 8). *27 Examples of Key Performance Indicators*. Retrieved from OnStrategy: https://onstrategyhq. com/resources/27-examples-of-key-performance-indicators/

Ford, J. D., & Ford, L. W. (2009). Resisting innovation: An examination of the antecedents and consequences of cultural resistance to change. *Journal of Applied Psychology, 94*(6), 1541.

Ford, J. D., Ford, L. W., & D'Amelio, A. (2008). *Managing Human Resources* (6th ed.). Wiley.

Garvin, D. A. (1998). The processes of organization and management. *MIT Sloan Management Review.*

Group, O. M. (2023, October 18). *BUSINESS PROCESS MANAGEMENT (BPM) CERTIFICATIONS.* Retrieved from https://www.omg.org/oceb-2/

Hammer, M., & Champy, J. (1993). *Reengineering the Corporation: A Manifesto for Business Revolution.* New York: HarperCollins Publishers, Inc.

Harmon, P. (2014). *Business Process Change: A Guide for Business Managers and BPM and Six Sigma Professionals.* MK/OMG Press.

Herzberg, F. (1968). One more time: How do you motivate employees? *Harvard Business Review, 46*(1), 53–62.

Kotter, J. P. (1996). *Leading Change.* Harvard Business School Press.

Kotter, J. P. (2007). *Leading Change* (Rev ed.). Harvard Business Press.

Kotter, J. P. (2012). *Leading Change.* Harvard Business Review Press.

Kotter, J. P., & Schlesinger, L. A. (1979). Choosing strategies for change. *Harvard Business Review, 57*(2), 106–114.

Kübler-Ross, E. (1969). *On Death and Dying.* Macmillan.

Lewin, K. (1947). Frontiers in group dynamics. *Human Relations, 1*(1), 5–41.

Lewin, K. (1947). Frontiers in group dynamics: Concept, method and reality in social science; social equilibria and social change. *Human Relations,* 5–41.

Linker, E. (2023, September 28). *Qualitative Metrics: The Narrative Behind Every Figure.* Retrieved from improvado.io: https://improvado.io/blog/what-are-qualitative-metrics#:~:text= Qualitative%20metrics%20are%20descriptive%20data, product%20reviews%2C%20and%20interview%20responses.

Mayer, R. C., Davis, J. H., & Schoorman, F. D. (1995). An integrative model of organizational trust. *Academy of Management Review, 20*(3), 709–734.

Meyer, M. H. (2005). *Organizational change for enterprise growth. Research Technology Management, 48*(6), 9.

Nadler, D. A., & Tushman, M. L. (1999). The organization of the future: Strategic imperatives and core competencies for the 21st century. *Organizational Dynamics, 28,* 45–60.

Neely, A., Adams, C., & Kennerley, M. (2002). *The Performance Prism: The Scorecard for Measuring and Managing Business Success.* Prentice Hall.

Olsson, J. A., Ovretveit, J., & Kammerlind, P. (2003). *Organizational change for enterprise growth. Research Technology Management, 48*(6), 9.

Oreg, S. (2003). Resistance to change: Developing an individual differences measure. *Journal of Applied Psychology, 88*(4), 680–693.

Ould, M. A. (2005). *Business Process Management: A Rigorous Approach.* British Computer Society, The Chartered Institute.

Parry, S. B. (1996). *Just what is a competency? And why should you care?* Retrieved from http://eric.ed.gov/.

Schein, E. (1969). *Process Consultation: Its Role in Organization Development.* MA: Addison-Wesley Publications.

Schein, E. (2004). *Organizational Culture and Leadership* (3rd ed.). CA: Jossey-Bass.

Sirkin, H. L., Keenan, P., & Jackson, A. (2005). *The hard side of change management. Harvard Business Review, 83*(10), 11.

Skinner, B. F. (1953). *Science and Human Behavior.* Macmillan.

Smith, M. A., & Lewis, K. (2011). The dark side of organizational change: A critical perspective on the role of culture. *Journal of Management Inquiry, 20*(1), 4–14.

van der Aalst, W. (2013). Business process management: A comprehensive survey. *ISRN Software Engineering.*

Weick, K. E., & Quinn, R. E. (1999). Organizational change and development. *Annual Review of Psychology,* 361–387.

Weske, M. (2012). *Business Process Management Concepts, Languages, Architectures.* Springer Berlin, Heidelberg.

Yukl, G. (2013). *Leadership in Organizations* (8th ed.). Pearson.

Index

Note: Page numbers in **bold** and *italics* refer to tables and figures, respectively.

Printed in the United States
by Baker & Taylor Publisher Services